NORMAN K ROBERTSON

UNDERSTANDING

END TIME PROPHECY

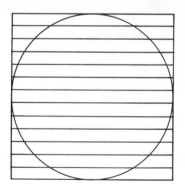

Sovereign World

Sovereign World Ltd.
P.O. Box 17
Chichester PO20 6YB
England

Conquest Publishers
P.O. Box 574
Randburg 2125
South Africa

ISBN 1 85240 038 2

FOREWORD.

Norman Robertson has been an Assistant Pastor to me at Rhema Bible Church and a close friend for the past 5 years.

The teaching gift that God has given him and the understanding and the revelation that he has of the Scripture, has been a great blessing, not only to our congregation and Bible School but also to many in the Body of Christ around the world.

I highly recommend this book to be read and studied and believe that it is important for people to have an understanding of just what the Church is going into and what will take place in the final hour.

RAY MC CAULEY

CONTENTS.

PREFACE.

The term "Eschatology" comes from two Greek words 'ESCHATOS' meaning LAST and "LOGOS' which means subject matter; therefore ESCHATOLOGY is the doctrinal study of last day events and the future destiny of mankind. God's Word abounds with references concerning the last days ...

"God has in these LAST DAYS spoken to us by His Son"...[Heb 1:2] "And it shall come to pass in the LAST DAYS".........[Acts 2:17] "In the LAST DAYS perilous times will come"..........[2 Tim 3:1] "In the LAST DAYS some will depart from the faith"...[1 Tim 4:1] "Little children, it is the LAST HOUR"............ [1 John 2:18] "Mockers and scoffers will come in the LAST DAYS"..[2 Peter 3:3]

The purpose of this book is not to supply an exhaustive study of ESCHATOLOGY or give an in-depth theological treatise on End Time Prophecy. This, Bible based, book is a simplified teaching guide on END TIME BIBLE PROPHECY, to give every Christian an understanding of where we are today in prophecy, what will take place in the LAST DAYS and God's plan for the future. In this book you will understand the following from God's Word...

* WHAT IS GOD'S PROPHETIC TIMETABLE FOR PLANET EARTH?
* WHAT IS THE RAPTURE?

* WHAT DOES GOD'S WORD SAY ABOUT THE ANTICHRIST?
* WILL THE CHURCH GO THROUGH THE 7 YEAR TRIBULATION PERIOD?
* WHEN WILL THE ANTICHRIST MAKE HIS APPEARANCE?
* WHAT YOU MUST KNOW ABOUT THE PROPHETIC SIGNS OF THE END TIMES.
* ARE THE JEWS GOING UP IN THE RAPTURE?
* IS THERE GOING TO BE A ONE WORLD GOVERNMENT?
* WHAT THE BIBLE SAYS ABOUT THE COMING RAPTURE AND THE DESTINY OF MAN.
* ARE ALL BORN AGAIN CHRISTIANS GOING IN THE RAPTURE?
* IS THE WORLD GOING TO BE DESTROYED BY A NUCLEAR HOLOCAUST?
* WHAT IS GOING TO HAPPEN ON EARTH TO THOSE WHO MISS THE RAPTURE?
* WHAT IS THE MARK OF THE BEAST AND THE MEANING OF 666?
* IS THERE A DIFFERENCE BETWEEN THE RAPTURE AND THE SECOND COMING OF CHRIST?
* HOW SOON CAN WE EXPECT THE RAPTURE TO TAKE PLACE?
* HOW DOES THE BIBLE DESCRIBE OUR RESURRECTION BODIES?
* IS THERE GOING TO BE A ONE WORLD DICTATOR AND IS HE OPERATING IN POLITICS NOW?
* WHO ARE THE FOUR HORSEMEN IN THE BOOK OF REVELATION?
* WILL COMMUNISM AND RUSSIA CONQUER THE WORLD?

* WHAT IS THE FUTURE OF ISRAEL?
* WHEN WILL ARMAGEDDON TAKE PLACE AND
  WHAT WILL THE OUTCOME BE?
* WHAT WILL HAPPEN WHEN JESUS RETURNS
  TO EARTH AS KING OF KINGS?

Rev 1:3
Blessed is he who reads and those who hear the words of this prophecy, and keep those things which are written in it; for the time is near.

As you read through this book please get your Bible together with your notebook and your pen, and ask the Holy Spirit who is the Great Teacher of the Church to give you understanding of this vital subject. My prayer for you is that through this teaching you will be informed, edified, inspired and motivated as never before to serve the Lord Jesus Christ and be a soul winner in these last days.

In His love and mine,

Norman. K. Robertson.

CHAPTER 1:
GOD'S WORD, OUR FIRM FOUNDATION.

2 Tim 3:16 "All Scripture is given by inspiration of God, and is profitable for doctrine, for reproof, for correction, for instruction in righteousness,"

What are we to understand by "INSPIRATION" of the Scriptures?

We are to understand that God directed men, chosen by Himself, to put into writing such messages, laws, doctrines, historical facts, and revelations, as He wished men to know. All Scripture is God-breathed. That is, God Himself, or through the Holy Spirit, told holy men of old just what to write. The Bible, then, IS the Word of God, and does not simply contain inspiration here and there. All Scripture is profitable for us, including the Prophetic Scriptures... and not just our favourite passages.

How do we know that the Bible is the word of God? Let us look at 5 key witnesses.

5 Key Witnesses Why the Bible is the Word of God.

1. Fulfilled Prophecy.
2. The Amazing Unity of the Bible.
3. Historical and Archaeological evidence.
4. Scientific accuracy.
5. The Supernatural Influence in people's lives.

1. Fulfilled Prophecy.

The acid test of the Bible is its ability to precisely predict the future. The Word of God is packed with accurate prophecies:

i]   dealing with the nation of Israel;
ii] dealing with the Gentile nations such as Egypt,
       Persia, Babylonia, Greece etc;
iii] dealing with specific cities such as Tyre, Jericho,
       Ninevah, Jerusalem, etc:
iv] dealing with our Lord Jesus Christ. For example on
       the day that He was crucified at Calvary, 33 Old
       Testament prophecies were fulfilled in exact detail.

The Prophetical accuracy of the Bible predictions, made centuries before they took place, reveals that it is the infallible and inspired Word of God and not just a religious book!

2. The Amazing Unity of the Word of God.

The 66 books of the Bible, 39 Old Testament and 27 New Testament books, were written over a period of 1600 years by 40 different authors with different backgrounds and occupations.

Moses was an Egyptian prince.
Joshua was a soldier.
Samuel was a priest.
David was a shepherd boy who became king.
Esther was a queen.
Ruth was a housewife.
Ezra was a scribe.
Isaiah was a prophet.

Daniel was a prime minister.
Matthew was a tax collector.
Luke was a physician.
Paul was a brilliant scholar and tentmaker.
Peter was a fisherman.

Despite the Bible being written over a period of more than 16 centuries by 40 different authors, most of whom never met each other, the theme of the Bible from Gen 1:1 to Rev 22:21 carries a continuous thread which is the declaration of God's love for mankind and His plan for man's salvation.

3. Historical Accuracy and Archaeological Evidence.

Halley's Bible Handbook lists 112 examples of historical accuracy.
Unger's Bible Handbook lists 96 examples of historical accuracy. These include evidence of:
The Garden of Eden;
The Tower of Babel;
The Destruction of Sodom and Gomorrah;
The Fall of Jericho;
Solomon's Gold;
Solomon's Stables;
Solomon's Copper Furnaces;
The tunnel of Hezekiah...etc.

Both historical and archaeological discoveries have proven time and again the reliability of the Bible and that it is indeed the Word of God. Every time the archaeological spade is turned in the Middle East more and more testimony is added to the absolute reliability of the Bible.

4.   Scientific Accuracy.

The Bible is not a book of Science but it contains many absolute statements of science given in Scripture hundreds of years before scientists made these discoveries

*   The scientific fact that the earth is SPHERICAL. [Isa 40:22] The earth was believed to be flat until the sea voyages of Columbus and Magellan in the 15th century.

*   The scientific fact that the earth is suspended in space. [Job 26:7] This was not discovered until the writings of Sir Isaac Newton in A.D.1687.

*   The fact that the stars are innumerable. [Gen 15:5]

*   The fact that all living things are reproduced after their own kind. [Gen 1:21] In 1862 Louis Pasteur discovered the Law of Heredity.

*   The facts of the human bloodstream. [Lev 17:11]

5.   The supernatural influence of the Scriptures.

Rom 1:16 For I am not ashamed of the gospel of Christ, for it is the power of God to salvation...

The Bible is the inspired Word of God because multiplied millions can testify to its transforming power in their lives. Cancer cases have been cured, alcoholics set free, homosexuals delivered, broken families restored, drug addicts transformed and for each one of us that is born again, we have been "delivered from the power of darkness

and translated into the kingdom of the Son of His Love."
[Col 1:13]

4 Reasons Why God's Word is Profitable.

2 Tim 3:16,17 tells us that God's Word is profitable, this is
referring to the WHOLE Word of God and not just favourite
chapters! The Word is profitable for:

1.   Doctrine - Sound Teaching.

2.   Reproof and Conviction of sin.

3.   Correction and Discipline.

4.   Instruction and Training. [Schooling in righteousness -
     living right.]

The net result will be;

> **2 Tim 3:17 that the man of God may be complete, thoroughly
> equipped for every good work.**

We must read, study and meditate upon the ENTIRE Word
of God to have a solid foundation upon which to build our
lives. Faith comes by hearing the WHOLE Word of God. All
Scripture is God breathed from Gen 1:1 to Rev 22:21. Thus
it is vital that we study the total Word of God including
prophetic Scripture.

CHAPTER 2:
THE IMPORTANCE OF THE
PROPHETIC WORD.

Approximately 27% of the Bible was written as prophecy, an amount equal in size to the entire New Testament! This makes Bible prophecy an enormously vital subject for those who desire to understand God's Word.

> 2 Pet 1:21 [Amp] "For no prophecy ever originated because some man willed it [to do so] - it never came by human impulse - but as men spoke from God who were borne along [moved and impelled] by the Holy Spirit".

* 17 out of 39 Old Testament books are prophetic.

* All the books of the Bible from ISAIAH to MALACHI are prophetic.

* Many of the PSALMS are PROPHETIC and there are many Bible prophecies in the writings of Moses.

* In the New Testament there are prophecies in the 4 gospels given by Jesus Christ e.g. Matt Ch 24,25, Mark Ch 13, Luke Ch 21 etc.

* Peter and Paul's prophecies concerning the Rapture and the Second Coming of Christ in their epistles.

* **PLUS** the entire Book of Revelation!!

As you can see Bible prophecy is **NOT** unimportant, insignificant or a message of BAD NEWS for these last days - it is not a doom and gloom message. The prophetic Word has been given to edify us and promote faith.

> **1 Cor 14:3** But he who prophesies speaks edification and exhortation and comfort to men.

> **Rom 10:17** So then faith comes by hearing, and hearing by the Word of God.

Don't be scared of prophecy or End Time teachings - Don't say, "It's too difficult!" or "It's too complex!" Don't cry, "I can't understand it!" or say, "None of the prophetic teachers agree". You have nothing to fear from studying End Time Bible Prophecy or reading the book of Revelation, in fact Rev 1:3 tells us that there is a special blessing in store for those who study the prophetic Word of God.

> **Rev 1:3** Blessed is he who reads and those who hear the words of this prophecy, and keep those things which are written in it; for the time is near.

God's message is NEVER one of doom or gloom to instil fear or condemnation upon the people.

> **Rom 2:4** Or do you despise the riches of His goodness, forbearance, and long-suffering, not knowing that the goodness of God leads you to repentance?

> **1 Cor 14:26** ... Let all things be done for EDIFICATION.

> **1 Cor 14:33** For God is not the author of confusion but of peace...

2 Tim 1:7 For God has not given us a spirit of fear, but of power and of love and of a sound mind.

1 John 4:18 There is no fear in love; but perfect love casts out fear, because fear is involved in torment. But he who fears has not been made perfect in love.

Fear proceeds from the devil - fear brings bondage and torment. BUT God's prophetic word is to bring edification, NOT magnify Satan's agent - the ANTICHRIST or lift up the mark of the Beast. For too long Satan has been deceiving the saints of God.

* Preachers, books, so-called Christian films magnify the Anti- Christ and his system promoting fear, doom and gloom!

* They are built on guesswork - speculation - sensational- ism BUT not the true word of God.

* Some of God's people are buying tribulation packs - in America one years supply will cost you $1,000!!!

Forget about the doomsters and gloomsters, fear is not from God. As you study this teaching you will gain a true understanding of the Prophetic Word which will dispel all fear, will eliminate confusion and will edify, bless, uplift and inform you!

PROPHETIC FAITH FOR THESE LAST DAYS

Rom 10:17 So then faith comes by hearing, and hearing by the word of God.

Faith comes by hearing the whole Word of God including the Prophetic word which makes up 27% of the Bible. The Prophetic Scriptures will build, strengthen, stimulate and excite your faith for living in these last days. God places a high priority on Bible Prophecy - some churches don't but God does!

It makes up $^2/_6$ ths or $^1/_3$ rd of the Foundational Christian Doctrines [Heb 6:1,2].

Now if prophecy wasn't that important then why has God taken up 27% of His Textbook to prepare us and instruct us in these end times?

Recognise that we in this generation have a distinct advantage over all previous generations because the seal of Daniel 12:4 has been opened to us and so we can understand END TIME PROPHECY and where we fit in today in God's Prophetic program. This should cause our faith to move into high gear!!

Bible prophecy is important because this generation is a PROPHETIC GENERATION - we are living eye-witnesses of the prophetic scriptures coming into rapid fulfillment in exact detail in our time AND the unsaved people around you are asking questions about what is happening in the world?... In the Middle East? They are asking, "Is Russia going to conquer the world?"..."Will the earth destroy itself in a nuclear holocaust?" etc.

The Bible has **ALL** the answers. Knowing the truth about END TIME PROPHECY in the Bible is a great SOUL WINNING KEY!!

CHAPTER 3:
END TIME BIBLE PROPHECY -
DEFINITION OF TERMS.

This chapter is informational and will give you a scriptural definition of the key words and events connected with End Times.

1. THE LAST DAYS : [1 Tim 4:1]

We are living in the last days - a period which extends from the ministry of Jesus until the time when He returns to the earth.

2. THE RAPTURE : [1 Thess 4:16-18]

This future event is when Christ is going to come in the air and take every member of the church, both living and dead, to heaven to be with Him. He will give every member of the church a resurrection body. This will be before the 7 year tribulation period begins on the earth.
When we use the word "Rapture" we do not mean the Second Coming of Christ, or any part, stage or phase of it, for the Rapture is a distinct and separate coming of the Lord with 7 years between these two events.

3. THE TRIBULATION : [Revelation Chapters 6-19]

This will be a period of 7 years on earth following the Rapture of the Church - a time of unparalleled satanic activity, wickedness and war, destruction and disturbance. It will be an especially difficult time for Israel. During the first three and a half years, the Antichrist will be rising to power over the 10 kingdoms inside the Old Roman Empire boundary lines, and during the last three and a half years, he will rule all 10 kingdoms. We call these last three and a half years the GREAT TRIBULATION because of it being the worst time of trouble on earth that has ever been, or will be. [Dan 9:27, Matt 24:15-31, Isa 66:7-8, Rev 7:14,12:1,19:21.]

4.   THE SECOND COMING OF CHRIST : [Revelation 19]

At the end of the 7 year Tribulation period, Jesus Christ will return to the earth with His angels and those believers who were previously raptured. [Matt 24, Rev 19.] Jesus comes back to the earth to destroy the Antichrist and his armies at the battle of Armageddon and to establish His rule on the earth for 1,000 years. He will judge those men on the earth that are still alive.

5.   DANIEL'S 70TH WEEK : [Dan 9:27]

This is the same as the 7 years of future tribulation, during which time the Antichrist will make a 7 year covenant with Israel.

6.   THE ANTICHRIST : [Revelation 13]

This refers to the man who will rise to great power following the Rapture. He is called the Antichrist because he will be controlled by Satan to attempt world conquest and strongly oppose Jesus Christ and God's programme for the human race in the last days.

His rise to power will only be in the 7 year tribulation period and he will be a dictator over 10 kingdoms inside the boundary lines of the Old Roman Empire. He will **NOT** be a worldwide dictator and not President of a ONE WORLD GOVERNMENT!

7.   THE FALSE PROPHET : [Revelation 13]

The Antichrist will be the political ruler who will work the works of Satan. The False Prophet will be the religious ruler who will undergird the work of the Antichrist. Both get their power from Satan. The False Prophet never will attempt to promote himself. He will never become an object of worship. He will do the work of a prophet in that he directs attention away from himself to the one who says he has the right to be worshipped [the Antichrist].

The False Prophet will imitate many miracles of God. He will cause fire to come down from heaven counterfeiting the miracles of Elijah in order to convince the nation of Israel that he [The False Prophet] is the Elijah whom Malachi promised was yet to come! Having achieved this deception the False Prophet will declare that since this miracle [bringing fire from heaven] shows that he is Elijah then the Antichrist is truly Christ and should be worshipped.

He will also build a statue, and through some satanic ability cause this statue [image] to talk and somehow come to life. When the people see this miracle they will fall down and worship the Antichrist believing him to be Christ.

8.   THE MARK OF THE BEAST : [Rev 13:16,17]

At the beginning of the second half of the seven year

Tribulation period, the Antichrist [who previously was setting himself up as a man of peace] will suddenly move against the Jews and those who accepted Christ as Saviour during the first three and a half years of this period.

> Rev 13:16,17 ...he [False Prophet] causes all, both small and great, rich and poor, free and slave, to receive a mark on their right hand or on their foreheads,
> 17 and that no one may buy or sell except one who has the mark or the name of the beast or the number of his name.

Therefore those living in the Antichrist's kingdom who refuse to submit to the authority of this system by having the mark [the mark of the Beast], either starve to death slowly, or else are slain by the representatives of the government, who will treat as traitors all who refuse to accept this identifying mark.

9. THE 144,000 : [Revelation 7]

This special company of Born Again Jews [NOT Jehovah Witnesses] are those in the restored nation of Israel who will miss the Rapture of the church but will get saved after it, in the first three and half years of Daniel's 70th week.

10. THE TRIBULATION SAINTS : [Revelation 7]

This company of believers are the people who will miss the Rapture and who will get saved after the Rapture of the church during the Tribulation period. Many will be martyred for Christ in the 7 year Tribulation period which is between the Rapture and the Second Coming of Christ. [Rev 6:9-11, 7:9-17, 13:1-18, 14:9-11, 15:2-4, 20:4-6.]

11. BATTLE OF ARMAGEDDON : [Revelation 19, Rev 14:14-20]

This will occur at the end of the 7 year Tribulation Period when the Lord Jesus Christ comes down from heaven and wipes out the combined armies of the Antichrist plus the 200 million strong Oriental army. The blood bath flows for over 200 miles in the valley of Megiddo in Israel. [Rev 14:20, 19:11-21]

12. THE MILLENNIUM : [Revelation 20]

This is a period when all the believers of all the ages reign with Christ on earth for 1,000 years. Those previously resurrected and translated in the Rapture of the Church and those saints who died in the Tribulation and were resurrected, will reign with Christ in the Millennial Age as resurrected believers. They will be given positions of responsibility in the Millennial Kingdom.

The 1,000 year reign of Christ on earth will be a time of universal peace, prosperity, righteousness, unity, health and blessing.

Gentiles and Jews alike who are still living at the close of the Battle of Armageddon, and who are permitted to enter the Millennial Kingdom, are known as Tribulation survivors. These were not raptured [they were not believers at the time of the Rapture], nor did they die in the Tribulation period [they survived]. They are still in their human unresurrected bodies. During the Millennium these Tribulation survivors will still be able to reproduce children.

13. THE BATTLE OF GOG AND MAGOG : [Revelation 20]

At the end of the 1,000 year Millennium period, Satan will have a brief and last opportunity to deceive people. You must remember that many will be born during the millennial period. Millions will follow Satan. This vast number of people will completely encircle the living believers within Jerusalem in a state of siege.

When this final rebellion occurs, God's judgment releases fire from heaven destroying the millions of Satan's army. [Rev 20:7- 10.]

A BIBLICAL ANALYSIS OF MATTHEW CHAPTERS 24 & 25

MATT 24:1-3 The 3 key questions Jesus was asked by His disciples.

MATT 24:4-8 These are signs that point to the Second Coming of Christ even though they describe present day conditions...and sound like the 6 o'clock news!

MATT 24:9-14 Describes events of the first $3\frac{1}{2}$ years of the tribulation period.
* First half of Daniel's 70th week.

MATT 24:15-26 Describes events of the GREAT Tribulation - the final $3\frac{1}{2}$ years of the Tribulation period.
* Second half of Daniel's 70th week.

MATT 24:27-51 Describes the second coming of Christ and not the Rapture.

PARABLES OF THE SECOND COMING OF CHRIST.

1. Matt 24:32,33 - Parable of the fig tree.
2. Matt 24:43,44 - Parable of the good man of the house.
3. Matt 24:45-51 - Parable of the faithful servant.
4. Matt 25:1-13   - Parable of the 10 virgins.
5. Matt 25:14-30 - Parable of the talents.

MATT 25:31-46 Describes the judgment of the living Gentile nations at the return of our Lord Jesus Christ.

A BIBLICAL ANALYSIS OF THE BOOK OF REVELATION.

REVELATION CHAPTERS 1-3 Deals primarily with the church on earth.

REVELATION CHAPTERS 4,5 Pictures the Raptured Church and the Old Testament Saints in heaven.

REVELATION CHAPTERS 6-19 Describes the 7 year Tribulation period on earth - Daniel's 70th week.

REVELATION CHAPTERS 19-22 Describes the Second Coming of Christ, the Millenium and the future heaven and earth.

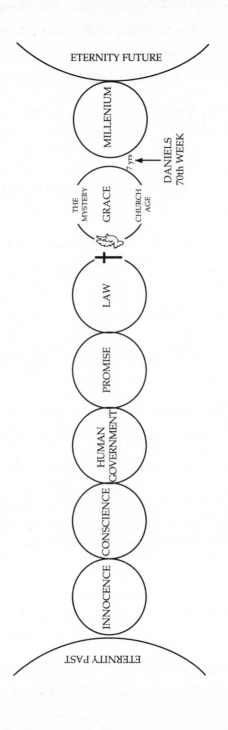

GOD'S PLAN OF THE AGES

ETERNITY PAST

INNOCENCE

CONSCIENCE

HUMAN GOVERNMENT

PROMISE

LAW

THE MYSTERY

GRACE

CHURCH AGE

7 yrs

DANIELS 70th WEEK

MILLENIUM

ETERNITY FUTURE

SEVEN MAJOR DISPENSATIONS IN GOD'S DEALINGS WITH MAN

(1)   <u>THE DISPENSATION OF INNOCENCE</u>

This extends from the CREATION of ADAM to his FALL
and EXPULSION from the Garden of Eden

(2)   <u>THE DISPENSATION OF CONSCIENCE</u>

This covers the period from the FALL OF ADAM to
the FLOOD OF NOAH

(3)   <u>THE DISPENSATION OF HUMAN GOVERNMENT</u>

This age was from the FLOOD OF NOAH to the
CALL OF ABRAHAM

(4)   <u>THE DISPENSATION OF PROMISE</u>

This dispensation covered a period of 430 years and extended
from THE CALL OF ABRAHAM to the EXODUS OF ISRAEL FROM
EGYPT

(5)   <u>THE DISPENSATION OF THE LAW</u>

This age covered the period from the EXODUS OF ISRAEL until
Jesus came to the earth and it ended at THE CROSS!! (Romans 10v4)

(6)   <u>THE DISPENSATION OF THE CHURCH, OR GRACE</u>

This is often referred to as THE CHURCH AGE or THE
DISPENSATION OF THE HOLY SPIRIT and began on the DAY OF
PENTECOST. This is the age that we are now living in and it will
end at the Rapture.

(7)   <u>THE DISPENSATION OF DIVINE GOVERNMENT — THE
MILLENIUM</u>

This age will cover the period from THE SECOND COMING OF
CHRIST and will extend for a period of 1,000 YEARS OF
UNIVERSAL RIGHTEOUSNESS AND PEACE

THE SEVEN THOUSAND YEARS OF HUMAN HISTORY

Psalm 90v4 speaks of a day with God as a thousand years

"For a thousand years in your sight are like yesterday when it is past, and like a watch in the night"

Peter in his second epistle declares the same thing
2 Peter 3v8

"But, beloved, be not ignorant of this one thing, that one day is with the Lord as a thousand years, and a thousand years as one day"

Bible chronology shows that a little less than 6 000 years have elapsed since Adam

The 1 000 years of the millennial rest will then complete the 7 000 years of the human week of God's plan for man

Thus we see that the 1 000 year reign of Christ with His saints, as revealed in the 20th chapter of Revelation, is coming to pass right on schedule

FromAdam **to** Abraham 2000 years (approx.) **Day 1 and 2**

From Abraham**to** Christ 2000 years (approx.) **Day 3 and 4**

From Christ **to** Present Day 2000 years (approx.) **Day 5 and 6**

**MILLENIUM – CHRIST'S 1,000 YEAR REIGN ON EARTH
DAY 7**

CHAPTER 4:
THE LAST DAYS.

QUOTATION FROM DR. BILLY GRAHAM.

"If you look in any direction, whether it is technological or physiological, the world as we know it is coming to an end. Scientists predict it, sociologists talk about it. Whether you go to the Soviet Union or anywhere else in the world, they are talking about it. The world today is in a state of shock."

HOW CAN WE KNOW FOR SURE THAT THIS GENERATION IS IN FACT LIVING IN THE LAST DAYS?

Reason no. 1 Because the ministry of Jesus and the Day of Pentecost marked the beginning of the Last Days.

> Heb 1:1,2 God, who at various times and in different ways spoke in time past to the fathers by the prophets,
> 2   has in these last days spoken to us by His Son...

> Acts 2:17-18 ... And it shall come to pass in the last days, says God, That I will pour out of My Spirit on all flesh; Your sons and your daughters shall prophesy, Your young men shall see visions, Your old men shall dream dreams.
> 18   And on My menservants and on My maidservants I will pour out of My spirit in those days; And they shall prophesy.

Reason no. 2 Because of the testimony of Peter, John and Jude.

> 2 Pet 3:3 ... that scoffers will come in the last days, walking according to their own lusts,

> 1 John 2:18 Little children, it is the last hour; and as you have heard that the Antichrist is coming, even now many Antichrists have come, by which we know that it is the last hour.

> Jude 17-19 But you, beloved, remember the words which were spoken before by the apostles of our Lord Jesus Christ:
> 18 how they told you that there would be mockers in the last time who would walk according to their own ungodly lusts.
> 19 These are sensual persons, who cause divisions, not having the Spirit.

Reason no. 3 Because Bible prophecy predicted living conditions in the last days.

> 1 Tim 4:1,2 Now the Spirit expressly says that in the last days some will depart from the faith, giving heed to deceiving spirits and doctrines of demons,
> 2 speaking lies in hypocrisy, having their own conscience seared with a hot iron,

> 2 Tim 3:1-5, 13 But know this that in the last days perilous times will come;
> 2 For men will be lovers of themselves, lovers of money, boasters, proud, blasphemers, disobedient to parents, unthankful, unholy,
> 3 unloving, unforgiving, slanderers, without self-control, brutal, despisers of good,
> 4 traitors, headstrong, haughty, lovers of pleasure rather than

lovers of God,

5 having a form of godliness but denying its power. And from such people turn away!

13 But evil men and impostors will grow worse and worse, deceiving and being deceived.

The Condition of Mankind in the LAST DAYS.

1. Selfish and self centred.
2. Money-lovers.
3. Boasters - they exaggerate their achievements to impress men.
4. Proud - haughty and arrogant.
5. Blasphemous - they speak abusively and slanderously.
6. Disobedient to parents.
7. Unthankful.
8. Unholy - living profane and wicked lives.
9. Unloving - without family affection, they lack love for their families.
10. Unforgiving.
11. Slanderers - They sow strife, discord and promote quarrels hoping to gain from them.
12. Without self-control.
13. Brutal [savage].
14. Despisers of good.
15. Traitors [betrayers] - whether to a country, an oath, a position of authority or someone in danger.
16. Headstrong - hasty, reckless.
17. Haughty [drunk with pride] - high minded, conceited, full of self importance.
18. Pleasure lovers.
19. Have a religion but no reality of Christ and the power of the Gospel.
20. Swindlers, cheats and exploiters.

21. Christians being deceived by false doctrines of demons
    e.g. Jehovah's Witnesses, Moonies, Mormons, Herbert
    Armstrong's Plain Truth, Christian Science etc.

Reason no. 4 Because of the two identifying END TIME
signs of DANIEL the Prophet.

> Dan 12:4 "But you, Daniel, shut up the words, and seal the book
> until the time of the end; many shall run to and fro, and knowledge
> shall increase."

Sign 1. Travel and Speed will Increase.

Until the nineteenth century, there was very little change in
the way that people travelled. Abraham could get from one
place to another about as rapidly as Shakespeare could.
Until the turn of the twentieth century, the average person
travelled in a vehicle drawn by animals. Today, travellers
span continents in jet planes in a matter of hours; and space
travel [already being booked] will offer speeds permitting
one to circle the globe faster than Abraham could get to the
next village.
Look at the rapid development in travel over the past 80
years...

1903 - Ford begins car production.
1903 - First powered flight by the Wright brothers.
1927 - Lindbergh flies the Atlantic.
1939 - Jet age begins with German gas turbine jet engine.
1957 - Sputnik 1 is launched by the Soviets.
1969 - American astronauts land on the moon.
1976 - Concord becomes first supersonic airliner.
1981 - France's Train Grande Vitesse becomes world's

fastest train, achieving a speed of 235 mph [386 km/
h] surpassing the previous record-holding Japanese
Bullet trains.

199? - Space colonies are being planned for the future.

Sign 2. The Knowledge Explosion.

Dan 12:4 ...and knowledge shall increase.

The increase of knowledge this century has been
unparalleled. Until the invention of the printing press, and
the discovery of the new world, the sum of human
knowledge was not appreciably greater than it was in the
Golden Age of Greece and Rome. The Renaissance was
really only the rediscovery of the cultures of ancient Greece,
Egypt, Arabia and China. Today's scientists have split the
atom, developed nuclear power, explored human genes,
travelled to the moon, photographed the planets at a close
range, and computerised all statistics and most industrial
production.

It has been estimated that three-quarters of present
knowledge has been acquired in the last fifty years, and that
70% of modern medicines and surgical procedures have
been developed since World War II. Three quarters of all the
scientists who have ever lived are alive today. With the use
of computers, in an hour a modern engineer can duplicate
the work of a lifetime of an engineer working before 1940.

Think about the explosion of mankind's knowledge in the
following statistics.

From 4th Century - 1900   ... Knowledge doubled in **1500 years**

From   1900 - 1950   ... Knowledge doubled again in **50 years**

From   1950 - 1965   ... Knowledge doubled again in **15 years**

From   1965 - 1975   ... Knowledge doubled again in **10 years**

Today in the 1980's knowledge is increasing and doubling every **three and a half years**.

By the 1990's it is expected that knowledge will **DOUBLE** every 5 **MONTHS**.

Many Hi-Tech manufacturers in the computer and electronic fields are worried because by the time their product gets to the retail outlets it is already OBSOLETE!

Notable Achievements this Century.

AVIATION AND SPACE.

1903 1st powered flight by Wright brothers.
1927 Lindbergh flies the Atlantic.
1933 Radio astronomy allows deep probe of space.
1939 Jet age begins with German gas turbine jet engine.
1957 Sputnik 1 is launched by Soviets.
1969 American astronaut lands on the moon.
1976 Concord becomes the 1st supersonic airliner.
1970's Space frontier exploration by rockets.
1980's Satellites, space stations, space probes etc.

MEDICINE AND HEALTH

1901 Pioneering work in serums intensifies.

1914 England uses 1st biological and safe treatment of public sewerage.

1941 Penicillin enters public use.

1950's Open heart surgery and human organ transplants begin.

1953 DNA molecule explains how genetic information is stored.

1970's Genetic engineering by fusion of genes.

1980's Characteristics of different living things promises human benefits and dangers.

COMMUNICATIONS AND INFORMATION.

1900 Radio in infancy.

1929 1st transmission of colour T.V.

1944 1st digital computer. [5 tons, 8' high, 51' long, 500 miles of wiring!] in operation, Harvard University.

1952 Japanese introduce pocket sized transistor radios.

1962 Era of trans-Atlantic TV begins as satellite Telstar is launched by US.

1971 The microprocessor [microchip] is introduced.

1980's New breakthroughs in computer technology.

TRANSPORT, TRADE AND TRAVEL.

1903 Ford begins car production.
1914 Opening of Panama Canal.
1916 Electronic beacons on coastlines allow ships to make all weather bearings.
1959 St. Lawrence Seaway allows vessels to sail to the heart of the US.
1965 Pre-packed truck-train containers for container ships. 1981 French train achieves speed record of 386km/h.

ENERGY, INDUSTRY AND CONSTRUCTION.

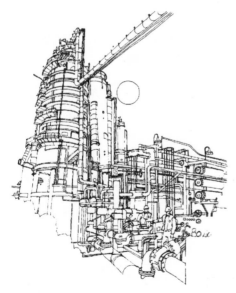

1903 1st fully automatic bottle making machine.

1904 Stainless and high speed steels developed.

1905 Albert Einstein proposes theory of relativity.

1907 Refiner for petrol production developed.

1909 Age of plastics begins.

1910 Air pollution from factory chimneys reduced by electrostatic precipitators.

1913 High quality sheet glass produced.

1920's High voltage electricity developed.

1930's Huge dams constructed or begun for Hydro-electric power.

1931 Empire State building completed.

1947 Off-shore oil drilling pioneered.

1970's Nuclear energy developed for electrical power.

1980's Superstrong plastics and ceramics introduced.

7 SIGNS OF THE LAST DAYS

(1) The rise of false cults and increase in deception
(Matthew 24v4,5,11 : 1 Timothy 4v1-3)

(2) Progress in travel and the explosion
of knowledge
(Daniel 12v4)

(3) An increase of wars and strife within nations
(Matthew 24v6,7)

(4) An acceleration of famines, plagues,
earthquakes and unusual weather conditions
(Matthew 24v7)

(5) The rebirth of Israel as a nation on
14th May 1948
(Matthew 24v32-34)

(6) An increase in the breakdown of marriages
and family life
(2 Timothy 3v1-4)

(7) Russia's military involvement in the
Middle East, setting the stage for
World War 3
(Ezekiel 38)

CHAPTER 5:
THREE IMPORTANT
QUESTIONS.

MATTHEW 24 : MARK 13 : LUKE 21 are three sister chapters which go together in answering the 3 key questions that the disciples asked Jesus on the Mount of Olives. Bible scholars refer to Jesus' End Time teaching from the Mount of Olives as the Olivet Discourse.

Matt 24:3 Now as He sat on the Mount of Olives, the disciples came to Him privately, saying, ...

1. "Tell us when will these things be?
2. And, what will be the sign of Your coming? [Second Coming, not Rapture.]
3. And of the end of the age?"

So in Matthew 24, Mark 13 and Luke 21, Jesus is answering these three questions -

1. When will the temple and its buildings be destroyed?
2. What will be the sign of Your Second Coming?
3. What signs will signal the end of the Age?

You will notice that in these three chapters there is no reference to the Church, this is because the Church Age was not in existence - the Church had not yet begun to function! So you will NOT find the Rapture of the Church in these chapters! The Olivet Discourse directly applies to Israel, NOT the Church.

Question 1

When will the temple and its buildings be destroyed?

This was answered in A.D.70 by the Roman destruction of Jerusalem under General Titus.

> **Luke 21:20-24** "But when you see Jerusalem surrounded by armies, then know that its desolation is near.
> **21** Then let those in Judea flee to the mountains, ...
> **22** For these are the days of vengeance, that all things which are written may be fulfilled.
> **23** ... For there will be great distress in the land [Israel] and wrath upon this people [the Jews].
> **24** And they will fall by the edge of the sword, and be led away captive into all nations. And Jerusalem will be trampled [controlled] by Gentiles until the times of the Gentiles are fulfilled.

Question 2

What will be the sign of Your Second Coming and return to earth?

This question does not concern the Rapture but the Second Coming of Christ to the earth with His saints. The disciples knew nothing of the Rapture for it was a MYSTERY reserved for the Apostle Paul to reveal in the CHURCH AGE. The answer for this second question is given in MATTHEW 24:27-51.

Don't connect the Rapture and the 2nd Coming together - they are two distinct and separate END TIME EVENTS!

Question 3

What signs will indicate the end of the Age?

We know that at that particular time Jesus, operating under the Old Testament was in the Jewish Age thus, when He answers the disciples questions, Jesus makes reference to the Jewish Age. And in this third question He tells them what will take place at the end of the Jewish Age - the last period of Jewish Time - DANIEL'S 70TH WEEK - THE 7 YEAR TRIBULATION. The answer is given in MATTHEW 24:9-26.

GUIDELINES FOR INTERPRETING BIBLE PROPHECY.

1.   **Study each prophecy as a whole** - not just isolated parts. For example, when studying the prophecy about the Antichrist in Daniel 11:36-45, be sure to start reading at 10:1.

2.   **Know the historical context of the times.** The prophets composed their books from about 850 B.C. till possibly as late as 400 B.C. Generally speaking, this was a time of great unrest, politically and economically as Egypt, Babylon, Assyria and Persia [to name the larger powers] grew in prominence and then waned in power and influence - with the inhabitants of Israel frequently caught in the middle! It was also a time of unfaithfulness on the part of God's chosen people - even after their return from exile.

3.   **Know what the book, that contains the prophecy, is about.** Know what the author is talking about; Why he is talking about it. This will put the prophecy that you are

studying into perspective.

4.   **Know the context of the prophecy you are studying.**

*   Who are the characters?
*   What do they do?
*   What is the result?
*   Where does it happen?

5.   **Check to see if the symbol or symbolism is explained or introduced in earlier Scripture.** Understanding the symbolism in Ezekiel and especially Daniel is crucial in order to understand the book of Revelation.

6.   **Check to see if there are other prophecies which parallel the one that you are studying.** For example, the subject matter of Daniel 2 parallels the subject matter of Daniel 7.

7.   **Distinguish between the symbolic and the literal, the prophecy and the interpretation.** The interpretation is not symbolic and is meant to be understood literally.

8.   **Interpret animals, colours and numbers literally unless the author reveals that they are approximations** by using words such as: like, as, or about. The prophets describe fantastic sights and there are times when they simply run out of earthly things with which to describe heavenly things.

> "And He who sat there was <u>like</u> a jasper and a sardius stone in appearance" [Rev 4:3].

> "The first living creature was <u>like</u> a lion" [Rev 4:7].

"And I saw something <u>like</u> a sea of glass mingled with fire" [Rev 15:2].

9.   If a prophecy has not been completely fulfilled in the past, you can assume that it will be completely fulfilled in the future.

10. Bible commentators and commentaries make mistakes - so don't assume that they are right and you're wrong if you differ.

At all times depend upon the Holy Spirit to guide you, teach you and give you revelation knowledge of the Scriptures.

DISPENSATIONAL ANALYSIS OF THE NEW TESTAMENT
FROM THE GOSPEL OF MATTHEW TO THE BOOK OF REVELATION

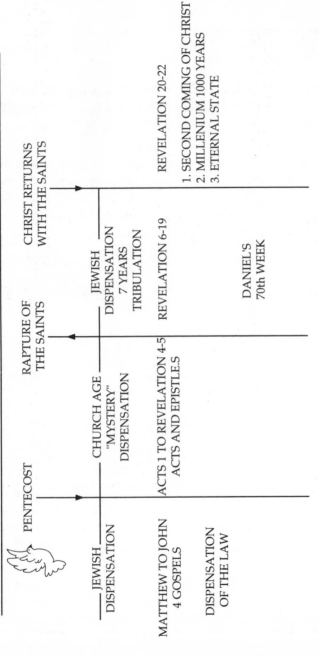

PENTECOST

CHRIST RETURNS
WITH THE SAINTS

RAPTURE OF
THE SAINTS

JEWISH DISPENSATION

CHURCH AGE
"MYSTERY"
DISPENSATION

JEWISH
DISPENSATION
7 YEARS
TRIBULATION

REVELATION 20-22

ACTS 1 TO REVELATION 4-5
ACTS AND EPISTLE.S

REVELATION 6-19

1. SECOND COMING OF CHRIST
2. MILLENIUM 1000 YEARS
3. ETERNAL STATE

MATTHEW TO JOHN
4 GOSPELS

DANIEL'S
70th WEEK

DISPENSATION
OF THE LAW

GOD'S ORDER OF END TIME EVENTS

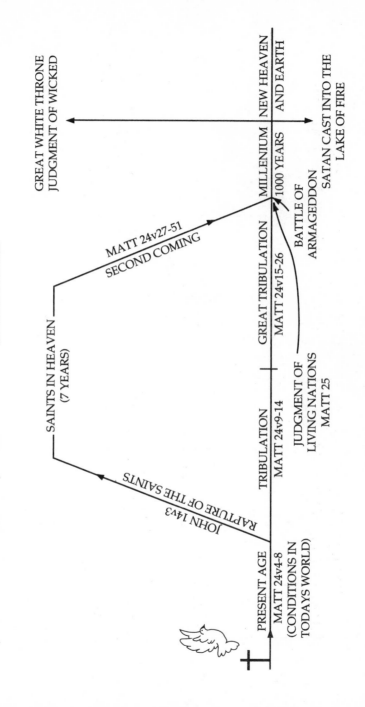

BELIEVER'S JUDGMENT   MARRIAGE FEAST

GREAT WHITE THRONE
JUDGMENT OF WICKED

SAINTS IN HEAVEN
(7 YEARS)

MATT 24v27-51
SECOND COMING

RAPTURE OF THE SAINTS
JOHN 14v3

PRESENT AGE
MATT 24v4-8
(CONDITIONS IN
TODAY'S WORLD)

TRIBULATION
MATT 24v9-14

JUDGMENT OF
LIVING NATIONS
MATT 25

GREAT TRIBULATION
MATT 24v15-26

BATTLE OF
ARMAGEDDON

MILLENIUM
1000 YEARS

NEW HEAVEN
AND EARTH

SATAN CAST INTO THE
LAKE OF FIRE

CHAPTER 6:
EXPLORING THE SIGNS OF THE END TIMES (PART I)

First of all we must realise that the Rapture of the Church and the Second Coming of Jesus Christ are two separate and distinct events which are separated by Daniel's 70th week, i.e. the 7 year Tribulation period.

Titus 2:13 identifies the Rapture of the Church where Jesus Christ appears in the atmosphere "FOR" His saints. Rev 19:11-16 identifies the Second Coming of Jesus Christ when He literally returns to the earth "WITH" His saints.

Now Jesus cannot come back to the earth to set up His Kingdom "WITH" His saints until He, first of all, comes back "FOR" His saints and raptures them all into His presence.

Child of God, if you take two Bibles and follow ALL of the signs of Matt.24, Mark 13, Luke 17 and Luke 21 and compare these signs with the events of Revelation chapters 6-19 you will see they are identical!

Matt 24, Mark 13 and Luke 21 are all "sister" chapters giving details of Christ's Olivet discourse. This teaching came as a direct result of the three questions that Jesus was asked by His Jewish disciples. So in Matt 24, Mark 13 and Luke 21 Jesus is answering these three questions.

You will notice that in these chapters there is no reference to the Church because the Church Age had not yet begun. It was still in the Jewish dispensation.

The Olivet discourse directly applies to Israel not the Church and so the signs of Matt 24, Mark 13 and Luke 21 point to the Second Coming of Christ and NOT the Rapture of the Church.

All the signs point to the Second Coming and since the Rapture of the Church will take place 7 years BEFORE the Second Coming, the signs that we are seeing fulfilled in this generation indicates that the Rapture is imminent!

Dr. M.R. DeHaan put it this way, "A sign along the way may not be for me at all, but certainly I can read it. I drive along the highway and I see a sign which reads, "Turn here for the boilermaker's picnic". I am not a boilermaker and I am not going to their picnic. I have no business there. This does not prevent me from reading the sign and knowing where and when the boilermakers are going to come together for their picnic. So, too, with the signs of the return of the Lord Jesus Christ to earth.

Although these signs are primarily for the Tribulation Period and Israel, and will come about only after the Church is raptured and point only to the Second Coming of the Lord Jesus Christ, I do thank God that I can still read the signs and know how near we are to that day."

Living in this final generation, the body of Christ must clearly recognise the SIGNS of the LAST DAYS and be motivated by these signs to do more for God than ever before.

Sign Number 1
The Increase in Knowledge and the Mobility of Mankind

Daniel 12:4 This prophecy spoken by an angel indicates that at the end-time there would be an unprecedented increase in human knowledge. Secondly, that there would be a startling increase in travel upon the earth. These developments, the angel would have us to understand, would be KEY SIGNS in discerning the approach of the end of the age.

> Dan 12:4 "But thou O Daniel, shut up the words, and seal the book, even to the time of the end for the people shall travel to and fro [at great speeds] and knowledge shall be increased."

Sign Number 2
The sign of Deception - the rise of False Cults and False Prophets.

> Matt 24:4,5 "And Jesus answered and said to them: "Take heed that no one deceives you.
> 5   For many will come in My name, saying, I am the Christ, and will deceive many".

> Matt 24:11 "Then many false prophets will rise up and deceive many".

> Matt 24:23,24 "Then if anyone says to you, 'Look, here is the Christ!' or 'There!' do not believe it.
> 24 "For false christs and false prophets will arise and show great signs and wonders, so as to deceive, if possible, even the elect".

> 1 Tim 4:1,2 Now the Spirit expressly says that in the last days

**some will depart from the faith, giving heed to deceiving spirits
and doctrines of demons,
2   speaking lies in hypocrisy, having their own conscience
seared with a hot iron.**

Every Child of God needs to understand that false prophets
and false teachers are agents of demons with devil inspired
doctrines.
The Apostle Paul in this statement [1 Tim 4:1,2], makes it
clear that the Spirit emphasised the fact that in the last days
or toward the end of the age, people would depart from the
simplicity of the faith and give heed to seducing spirits. To
mention but a few - The teaching of Evolution, the Jehovah's
Witnesses, the un-Christian "Christian Science", the Mor-
monism myth, Herbert Armstrong and the Plain "Truth",
the diabolical "Moonies" plus many others that have risen
in this 20th Century. Take for example "Christian Science"
which is neither Christian nor Science. Its founder Mrs.
Mary Baker propounded a religion that was a system of
denials. She said that there was no such thing as sickness,
sin, disease or death. It was all in the imagination.

DECEPTION IS ON THE INCREASE, CONSIDER
THESE STAGGERING STATISTICS...

*   Explosion of false religious cults... over 5000 in the
     U.S.A.
*   Brazil has over 60 million people involved in
     spiritualism.
*   More rise in false prophets and teachers in the last 50
     years than in the past 2,000 years.
*   Over 60 million occult followers in the U.S.A. -
     Astrology, Witchcraft, Satanism and Black Magic.

> **2 Tim 3:5** "Having a form of godliness but denying its power. And from such people turn away!"

> **2 Tim 4:3,4** For the time will come when they will not endure sound doctrine, but according to their own desires, because they have itching ears, they will heap up for themselves teachers;
> 4   and they will turn their ears away from the truth, and will be turned aside to fables.

These false teachers and modernistic churches with liberal theology **DENY** the cardinal doctrines of Christianity.

THEY DENY;

* The reality of heaven and hell.
* The power in the Blood of Jesus.
* The person of the Holy Spirit.
* The Virgin birth of Jesus.
* The Second Coming of Christ.
* Salvation by personal faith in Christ.
* The Bible is the divinely inspired Word of God.

> **1 John 4:1,3** Beloved, do not believe every spirit, but test the spirits, whether they are of God; because many false prophets have gone out into the world.
> 3   and every spirit that does not confess that Jesus Christ has come in the flesh is not of God.

Child of God, these are the days to protect yourself from deception by reading your Bible every day, staying full of the Holy Ghost and being a committed member of a local church that exalts Jesus Christ and teaches the uncompromising Word of God!

2 Peter 2:1,2 But there were also false prophets among the people, even as there will be false teachers among you, who will secretly bring in destructive heresies, even denying the Lord who bought them, and bring on themselves swift destruction.

2   And many will follow their destructive ways, because of whom the way of truth will be blasphemed.

Sign Number 3
The Sign of Warfare.

Matt 24:6,7 "And you will hear of wars and rumours of wars. See that you are not troubled; for all these things must come to pass, but the end is not yet.

7   "For nation will rise against nation, and kingdom against kingdom. And there will be famines, pestilences, and earthquakes in various places".

These verses outline the increase of WARS, TERRORISM and UNREST amongst the nations of the world e.g. Africa, Middle East and South America.

WARFARE IS ON THE INCREASE; CONSIDER THESE STAGGERING STATISTICS,

*   1914 -1918 World War I involved 28 countries and 6 continents: killed 10 million soldiers, 10 million civilians; 20 million more died due to war related famine, disease and political unrest.

*   1939 -1945 World War II - virtually every nation involved, 17 million military dead, 43 million civilians dead.

* 1945   Nuclear weapons age begins with Hiroshima and Nagasaki.

* 1952   First U.S. hydrogen bomb exploded.

* 1950's   Biological and chemical warfare agents developed, stockpiles begin.

* 1985   More than 50,000 nuclear weapons exist in the world, with an estimated yield of 13,000 million tons of TNT.

* 1980's   Over 35 countries are now producing nuclear weapons.

              Over 70 wars are now in progress worldwide.

              More than 1,000 U.S.A. Corporations are legally producing weapons of war. [Ford,IBM, General Motors etc.]

              115 countries now have nuclear capabilities.

              Over half of the world's scientific and technical manpower are employed in the manufacture of weapons of war.

Current stockpiles of nuclear weapons are so great - it is estimated that there are at least 60,000 hydrogen bombs - that the earth could be destroyed about 20 times over. If they were detonated all together, the fireball would achieve 130 million degrees Fahrenheit - a temperature so phenomenally high that it is unspeakable even to think about what it would do to planet earth.

Quotation from President Ronald Reagan;

"We see around us today the marks of a terrible dilemma, predictions of doomsday. Those predictions carry weight because of the existence of nuclear weapons, and the constant threat of global war... so much so that no president, no congress, no parliament can spend a day entirely free of this threat."

Sign Number 4
The Sign of Famine and Mass Hunger.

Matt 24:7 ...And there will be famines, pestilences, and earthquakes in various places.

Luke 21:11 "And there will be great earthquakes in various places, and famines and pestilences; and there will be fearful sights and great signs from heaven".

FAMINE AND FOOD SHORTAGE STATISTICS.

*   Until 1950, apart from periodic famines, developing nations were virtually self-sufficient in food supplies and were even food exporters. Between 1900 and 1985 world population tripled.

*   Today more than 100 of the world's nations are importers of sizeable, or major portions, of their food needs. 90% of the earth's annual population increase

are in developing nations with serious food shortages.

*   In the 1980's many African nations produce less food than they did a decade earlier. Millions are malnourished and starving, due not only to the bad weather, but also civil war, tribal conflict, political corruption and instability.

*   Over 30 million children, worldwide, die each year from malnutrition and starvation.

*   In recent times Ethiopia and other parts of Africa, India and Russia have suffered famine and food shortages.

*   Population explosion - by the year 2000 there will be over 7 billion people on earth and an estimated 5 billion will be starving to death.

THE POPULATION SNOWBALL.

*   It took 5,830 years from the time of Adam to the year 1830 for the first billion people to come forth on this planet.

*   It only took 100 years for the second billion to come forth. That was in 1930.

*   It only took 31 years for the third billion to come forth. That was in 1961.

*   It only took 15 years for the fourth billion to come forth. That was in 1976.

* It only took 11 years for the fifth billion to come forth. That was in June of 1987.

* In approximately 8 years and 3 months there will be 6 billion.

* By the year 2000 A.D. there will be over 7 billion.

India's population will achieve a billion before this century has finished its course. The population of the world will reach 7 billion by that time. It will have doubled to a staggering 14 billion by the year 2050!

Dr. Albert Sabin, the developer of the oral vaccine against polio, has said, "If changes are not made now, by the year 2000 there is doubt as to whether we will survive. By that time there will be 7 billion people in the world, and 5 billion of them will be starving, uneducated, and totally desperate."

Sign Number 5
The Sign of Deadly Pestilence.

> **Matt 24:7** ...And there will be famines, pestilences and earthquakes in various places.

> **Luke 21:11** "And there will be great earthquakes in various places, and famines and pestilences; ...

WHAT ARE THE PESTILENCES? Pestilences can refer to plagues and epidemics of deadly disease such as AIDS, as well as the thought provoking situations listed below.

POLLUTION, Today pollution has become global after

decades of dumping multiple thousands of dangerous chemicals into the air, water, land and ocean dumps.

> Isa 24:4-6 "The earth is drooping, withering...for the earth has been polluted by the dwellers on its face... mortals are dying off, till few are left" (Moffat Translation). The ancient prophet accurately foretold of this modern day.

ACID RAIN, caused by acidic pollutants in the air, is damaging everything it falls on. Particularly hard hit are farms, lakes and forests in the N.E. United States and nearby areas of Canada. For the first time in history, in July 1972, an entire town was declared unfit for human habitation because of air pollution. That was the village of Knapsack in the Rhineland of Germany. Scientists are saying that across Europe you will soon find that 85% of their forests are dead because of acid rain.

There are also deadly pollutants that are destroying the layer of the atmosphere that protects us from the sun, **the ozone layer**. It stops the ultra-violet rays from penetrating down and reaching us. This shield is being destroyed, letting in an increase in ultra-violet rays, changing the biological balance.

THE GREENHOUSE EFFECT, According to one scientist, carbon dioxide is causing a greenhouse effect. Sunlight cannot penetrate through but ultra-violet light can. This causes the earth to get hotter and hotter instead of cooling off each night. What we are seeing is a steady global increase in temperature.

INSECTS AND INSECTICIDES, There are 364 insecticide resistant insects in the world. They are devouring crops and bringing discomfort, disease and sometimes death to millions of people.

The World Health Organization reports that 84 species of insects that carry dreaded tropical diseases are now surviving and multiplying in the face of every imaginable insecticide.

THE OCEANS, Scandinavian scientists have made the alarming discovery that the Baltic Sea is dying. They have been unable to discover traces of oxygen at any point below 200 feet. Down at the bottom nothing lives.

OUR BODIES, Pollutants threaten our lives at every level because the food we eat is not as nutritionally rich as it was only 40 years ago. They contribute to all our health problems, but especially to the incidence of cancer. A baby born today has one chance in three of suffering some kind of cancer.

AIDS, According to **Time Magazine** October 28, 1985, the U.S.A. has the largest number of AIDS cases in the world.

"AIDS was the number 1 killer of New York City men between the ages of 30-39 last year and the 2nd leading cause of death among women aged 30-34, health officials said. Statistics gathered by the city Health Department show that more men in both the 30-35 and 35-39 age groups died last year from acquired immune deficiency syndrome than from homicide, suicide or cancer."

What are you going to do with all these startling facts? What are you going to do with this catalogue of bad news? Can you ignore it and hope it will go away? **It will not!** We must take the signs of the times we live in seriously!

Sign Number 6
The Sign of Earthquakes and Increase in Nature's Upheaval.

Jesus Christ, almost 2,000 years ago, accurately predicted these horrendous times of earthquakes, severe droughts, hurricanes, volcanic eruptions, unusual weather patterns and floods dramatically increasing.

> Matt 24:7 ... And there will be famines, pestilences and earthquakes in various places...

In the 14th century the Europeans recorded reports of 137 earthquakes. In this century, seismologists sometimes record that many a month. More than a million people have died as a result of earthquakes this century. The damages have been estimated at 10 billion dollars. The advent of the Richter Scale and scientific monitoring devices, together with a global communications system, have increased our awareness of nature's upheaval.

The predictions of Jesus are true. In addressing the subject of earthquakes, geophysicist, **Dr. Carl Von Hake of the National Geophysicist Data Center** in Colorado said, "We estimate that there are as many as a million earthquakes a year around the world. Of course, there is a plus or minus factor in there. But that represents all size 'quakes from the very largest ones down to the really small ones". Many people have died as a result of earthquakes. One earthquake in the past caused the death of 830,000 people in China. A quarter of a million people died on July 28,1976, when the strongest earthquake recorded since 1964 hit Tientsin-Tangshan, China. On November 23, 1980 an earthquake flattened 133 villages and left 300,000 people homeless in

Southern Italy. Funerals were conducted for the 2,735 victims of the 'quake.

In a two-month period between mid-April and mid-June in 1984, **the New York Times** reported a dozen notable earthquakes from around the world. They occurred in Austria, Wales, New Jersey, California, Italy, Colorado, the Chinese seaboard and the southwestern Indian Ocean. One in California hit in late April and registered 6.0 on the Richter Scale. It severely damaged the city of San Jose where a fire broke out from a broken fuel line.

Some of the largest earthquakes are many times greater than any bomb that has been set off. So, nature still seems able to create much larger energy releases than mankind.

HURRICANES, Hurricane Olivia claimed over 1,300 lives in Central America in 1982. In 1984, the fiercest typhoon in 15 years hit the Philippines and killed about the same number of people. During just 2 days in April 1974, 148 tornadoes descended on 13 states in the South and Midwest U.S.A. The injured numbered over 6,000 - 329 were dead. Property damage stood at $540 million.

FLOODS, One million people died in 1939 when floods hit northern China. Not as many drowned during the flood as starved to death afterwards because of the destruction of crops. In Tulsa, Oklahoma, more than a dozen motorists were swept to their deaths by floodwaters on May 27, 1984. In 1988 we are facing untold damages after the severe flooding in Bangladesh.

CHAPTER 7:
EXPLORING THE SIGNS OF THE
END TIMES (PART II).

The Bible is being fulfilled with amazing accuracy in this hour! This generation has been seeing more Bible literally fulfilled than any previous generation that has ever existed in the entire history of the Church.

> **Luke 21:28 "Now when these things begin to happen, look up and lift up your heads, because your redemption draws near."**

Jesus was telling us here to recognise certain key events that would begin to be fulfilled, signalling the day of His appearing to receive His disciples to Himself and there complete the work of salvation on our behalf!

SALVATION is an on-going magnificent work of God - at the New Birth **our spirits** were Born Again and REDEEMED - Daily, as we feed upon God's Word renewing our minds, **our soul** is being progressively saved. At the Rapture **our physical body** will be redeemed and we will receive a glorified body like Jesus Christ. According to 2 Cor 4:16 your outward body is aging daily and has yet to enjoy FULL salvation. None of us have glorified bodies yet - that aspect of God's great plan of REDEMPTION will take place at the Rapture [1 Cor 15:51-53, Phil 3:20,21, 1 Thes 4:16-18, 1 John 3:1-3].

At the Rapture our bodies will receive the last phase of salvation and we will be changed, in an atomic second, receiving our glorified bodies.

Jesus said in Luke 21:28 that when certain prophesied events begin to be fulfilled that is a Divine Indication to all believers that they should recognise these signs and move into a victorious attitude, looking for the appearing of Jesus!

> Mark 13:29 "So you also, when you see these things happening, know that it is near at the very doors."
>
> Luke 21:28 "Now when these things begin to happen, look up and lift up your heads, because your redemption draws near".

Jesus said to us ...

* When these things **begin** to happen -
* When the prophetic process gets underway -
* When the process of fulfillment of certain things begin to take place -

Then "Look" up because your redemption draws near.

The definition of this word, "**LOOK**" means to anticipate with joy a certain coming event. THE WORD "**UP**" describes the positive ongoing, joyous, victorious attitude of the Believer. The word "**REDEMPTION**" means to receive the fullness of your Salvation i.e. The **Glorification** of the physical body which is the final act of our Salvation [1 Cor 15:52,53].

Jesus told us when certain **PROPHETIC SIGNPOSTS**, Prophetic events, begin to be fulfilled the believer should look up, start rejoicing because the glorious appearing of Jesus is at hand.

Sign Number 7
The Sign of the Budding Fig Tree - Rebirth of Israel as a Nation.

> Matt 24:32-34 "Now learn this parable from the fig tree: When its branch has already become tender and puts forth leaves, you know that summer is near.
> 33 "So you also, when you see all these things, know that it is near, at the very doors.
> 34 "Assuredly, I say to you, this generation will by no means pass away till all these things are fulfilled."

Jesus told us to learn a lesson from the fig tree: "When its branch has already become tender and puts forth leaves, you know that summer is near. So you also, when you see all these things, know that it is near, at the very doors" Then He added a startling comment: "Assuredly I say to you, **this generation** will by no means pass away till all these things are fulfilled". "This generation" is the generation of people who see the fig tree putting forth leaves from tender branches.

WHAT IS MEANT BY THE FIG TREE?

That brings us to ask, "What is meant by the fig tree?" Here we need to resort to symbolism to help us unlock the mystery, but the symbolism is not difficult or obscure. **The fig tree stands for the restored nation of Israel**. The leaves of fig trees are common ornaments on government buildings in Israel. If you order breakfast anywhere in Israel it is always served with some figs.

In the Bible the majority of references to the fig tree are symbolic. It appears often as an illustration in stories and parables. Jothan used it about the trees [Judg 9:10-11], Jeremiah told a parable concerning the exiles [Jer 24 and Jer 29:17] which employed the fig tree. The fig tree is often symbolic of peace and prosperity [1 Kings 4:25, 2 Kings 18:31]. The fig tree has always been a symbol of the nation of Israel. If you were trying to find the 4 most important symbols of Israel, they would be the Star of David, the menorah, the olive branch and the fig tree.

From these things we must conclude that Jesus' use of the fig tree in talking about the end of the age was not casual. For those who had ears to hear, it meant that Israel itself would be the key sign of the imminence of Jesus coming back.

THE REBIRTH OF THE NATION OF ISRAEL

We are the first and only generation to witness the restoration of the nation of Israel on the 14th May 1948, symbolised by the fig tree [Jer 24:5-7].
Jesus is giving us a parable of the fig tree using nature to convey a spiritual truth - Just as in the natural we can recognise the coming of summer - the fig tree is a symbol, type of the nation of Israel.

THE BIBLE PROPHESIED THE RETURN OF THE JEWS TO THE LAND OF ISRAEL.

Isa 11:12   He will set up a banner for the nations, And will assemble the outcasts of Israel, And gather together the dispersed of Judah From the four corners of the earth.

Jer 29:14 "I will be found by you, says the Lord, and I will bring you back from your captivity; I will gather you from all the nations and from all the places where I have driven you, says the Lord, and I will bring you to the place from which I caused you to be carried away captive.

Jer 32:37,38 "Behold I will gather them [the Jews] out of all countries where I have driven them in My anger, in My fury and in great wrath; I will bring them back to this place [Israel], and I will cause them to dwell safely.
38 They shall be My people and I shall be their God;"

Ezek 11:17 "Therefore say, 'Thus says the Lord God: "I will gather you from the peoples, assemble you from the countries where you have been scattered, and I will give you the land of Israel."'

Ezek 20: 34,41,42 "I will bring you out from the peoples and gather you out of the countries where you are scattered, with a mighty hand, with an outstretched arm, and with fury poured out".
41 "I will accept you as a sweet aroma when I bring you out from the peoples and gather you out of the countries where you have been scattered; and I will be hallowed in you before the Gentiles.
42 "Then you shall know that I am the Lord, when I bring you out into the land of Israel, into the country for which I lifted My hand in an oath to give your fathers".

Ezek 36:24 "For I will take you from among the nations, gather you out of all countries, and bring you into your own land".

Read the details of the prophecy in Ezek 37:1-14,21,22.

In many Bible passages God prophesied that the Jews

would no longer be dispersed among the nations but that they would be supernaturally re-gathered to their ancient homeland in the last days! At the present time the Jews have returned to the land of Israel from over 120 Gentile nations and speaking 83 languages.

> Jer 23:3 "But I will gather the remnant of My flock out of all the countries where I have driven them, and bring them back to their folds; and they shall be fruitful and increase".

> Ezek 37:21 "Then say to them, thus says the Lord God: "Surely I will take the children of Israel from among the nations, wherever they have gone, and will gather them from every side and bring them into their own land;"

> Amos 9:14,15 "I will bring back the captives of My people Israel; They shall build the waste cities and inhabit them; They shall plant vineyards and drink wine from them; They shall also make gardens and eat fruit from them.
> 15 I will plant them in their land, And no longer shall they be pulled up From the land I have given them," Says the Lord your God.

PROPHECY TO THE LAND

Long ago Ezekiel [Ezek 36:1-15] prophesied that the land of Israel would become fruitful in the latter days after having been turned into a wasteland by its enemies. In Innocents Abroad Mark Twain described Palestine in the 19th Century as desolate and swampy, barren and mosquito-ridden. Today, Israel blossoms like a rose. The promise of the Bible is that once Zion has been rebuilt, then the Messiah will return in glory. Since 1948 over 140 million trees have been planted in Israel. Thousands of acres of swampland have been drained and many more thousands of acres, irrigated. The land could only support some few thousand people a century ago. Now Israel's population exceeds 4 million.

Ezekiel prophesied that, "I, the Sovereign Lord, am going to take all My people out of the nations where they have gone, gather them together, and bring them back to their own land. I will unite them into one nation in the land, on the mountains of Israel" [Ezek 37:21-22 TEV]. The fulfillment of this ancient prophecy in our day is a miracle and a sign of the nearness of Jésus coming back.

THE RAPTURE GENERATION.

Jesus said... When the fig tree BUDS - Look up! When Israel as a nation is restored - Look up! Remember that when Jesus gave the Olivet Discourse to His disciples in A.D 30 there was NO nation of Israel on the earth! Since 608 B.C. with the Babylonian Captivity, Israel ceased as a nation.
This was succeeded by the Persian captivity which was then succeeded by the Grecian captivity and then by the Roman captivity – ISRAEL AT THAT TIME WAS OUT OF EXISTENCE FOR OVER 600 YEARS.

On the 14th May 1948, Israel came back into national existence and the prophecies relating to the restoration of the nation of Israel began to be accurately fulfilled. In Ezek 36 and 37 God prophesies directly to the land of Israel in Babylonian captivity. We must realise that when Israel was taken into captivity the heathen invaders plundered, wasted and stripped the land of Israel **UNTIL** it became a barren desert and malaria infested swamps for centuries! A land unfit for human habitation. Israel today has supernatural fertility, productivity and fruitfulness e.g 80 tons of tomatoes per acre and an average of 4 bales of cotton per acre. The land of Israel is filled with abundant produce and is today, like a garden of Eden.

Look at Israel since 1948 - the fig tree has not only;

i]   budded
ii]   but has put on leaves
iii] and is producing fruit!

Jesus said that the generation that is alive to witness the restoration of Israel is the generation that will continue existing until all things are fulfilled -

-    The Remainder of the Church Age;
-    The glorious appearing of Jesus and the Rapture of the Church;
-    The 7 year Tribulation period;
-    The 2nd Coming of Christ back to the earth with all the saints;
-    The Millennium; 1000 year reign of Christ bringing universal peace, prosperity and righteousness to the earth.

This generation that has seen the Restoration of Israel on **MAY 14TH 1948** is the Rapture Generation!

Remember **you cannot** fix a time period to this generation because **if** a generation was 40 years then with the budding of the fig tree [Israel] 14th May 1948 **then** the second coming of Christ should have taken place on the 14th May 1988! **So don't set dates** - this is Biblically UNSOUND!

Sign Number 8
The Sign of Jerusalem coming back under Jewish Control in 1967.

ISRAEL REPOSSESSES JERUSALEM DURING THE 6 DAY WAR - JUNE 7TH, 1967

> **Luke 21:24** "And they [the Jews] will fall by the edge of the sword, and be led away captive into all nations. And Jerusalem will be trampled [under Gentile control] by Gentiles until the times of the Gentiles are fulfilled.**

In Luke 21:24 Jesus prophesies the tragic future of the city of Jerusalem - the siege upon the city itself and the destruction of the temple in A.D. 70. Jesus says that Jerusalem is to be conquered and controlled by Gentiles - foreign nations and unbelieving nations, **UNTIL** the times of the Gentiles be fulfilled. Here Jesus accurately predicts that Jerusalem is going to be dominated and governed by foreigners "UNTIL" their time should run its course.

In June, 1967 the new, re-established nation of Israel recaptured and repossessed the ancient, biblical city of Jerusalem. Since Babylonian captivity from 608 B.C. until 1967 the city of Jerusalem was held in the hands of the Gentiles.

Up until the 6 Day War of June 1967 Jerusalem, for over 2,500 years, was under Gentile dominion - governed and controlled by Gentiles. So Luke 21:24 was fulfilled in 1967 and the times of the Gentiles began to be fulfilled. Today we are living in the closing out period known as the "TIMES OF THE GENTILES."

Sign Number 9
The Sign of Russia's Military Involvement in the Middle East.

This is a prophetic forerunner of **Ezekiel 38 & 39.**

In 1956 the nation of Russia was drawn into the Middle East to back Egypt in the Suez Canal War. For the first time Russia became militarily involved in the Middle East fulfilling Ezek 38:4 ["military jaws"] and setting the stage for Russia's prophetic collision course of Revelation 6:3,4 & Ezekiel 38 & 39. From a study of Ezekiel 38 & 39 we see that it is stated, 17 times, that in the last days Russia and her allies will march against the tiny nation of Israel.

In 1956 Russia began its initial military involvement in the Middle East to help Egypt in the war against Israel. Since then Russian military hardware has heavily supplied the Arabs against Israel both in the 1967 Six Day War and the 1973 Yom Kippur War. This is a progressive build up to the Russian invasion of Israel which will be an action replay of David and Goliath!

* 1956 - Russia assisted Egypt in the war against Israel.

* 1967 - The 6 Day War: Russian military equipment given to the Arab States to fight Israel.

* 1973 - Russia backs Arabs in the Yom Kippur War.

* 1979 - Russia's rapid deployment forces invade Afghanistan.

* 1980's- Russia continues to be militarily involved in the Middle East.

All these events have set the stage for the fulfillment of Ezekiel 38 and Russia's coming invasion of Israel.

Sign Number 10
The Sign of the Kings of the East.

In 1948 China came into world prominence with the communistic take-over of China. China fits into the prophetic process in Revelation 9:13-21 and Revelation 16:12,16 when it begins its prophetic assignment, during the last 13 months of the Tribulation period, marching to attempt world conquest.

China which has been the most populous nation of the world, but weak because of backwardness, has had a tremendous military renaissance under Communism, and is now regarded as one of the four strongest nations on the globe. In 1971 the Communist government of China officially stated that, **"China now has the military capability of fielding an army of 200 million."** This has been confirmed in recent times!

Sign Number 11
The Sign of the Middle East Peace Agreement

PHASE 1 OF THE MIDDLE EAST PEACE AGREEMENT COMPLETED

In 1979, Egypt made peace with Israel to begin the fulfillment of the prophecies of Ezekiel 38:8,11,14 where the prophet Ezekiel clearly establishes that in the last days, Russia will invade Israel when Israel is at peace with its surrounding 5

Arab nations - Egypt, Syria, Lebanon, Jordan and Saudi Arabia. ON **MARCH 26TH, 1979** - Egypt and Israel signed peace treaties!

Child of God, Ezekiel 38:8,11,14 prophesies Israel will be at rest, dwelling in peace and safety in the last days with its 5 neighbours.
Keep your eyes on the Middle East and you will see the pieces of the End Time Prophetic Picture come together!

Sign Number 12
The Sign of the European Common Market.

TEN NATION LAUNCHING PAD FOR THE ANTI-CHRIST IS READY!

In January 1981, we saw Greece become the 10th member of the European Common Market, the geographical area which is a forerunner of the Antichrist kingdom. This is an alliance of 10 nations within the boundaries of the Ancient Roman Empire according to the prophecies of Daniel.

Sign Number 13
The Present Day Mighty Outpouring of the Spirit

It has always been recognised by Bible scholars, in times past, that the end of the Age would be marked by a manifestation of the miraculous. In the year 1866, Michael Baxter, founder of the Christian Herald, in his book **Baxter's Forty Wonders**, wrote these words : "Increased faith to work miracles... and unparalleled boldness in the preaching of the Gospel, will characterise the coming Pentecostal outpouring of the Spirit in the last days".

The Word of God is clear about this end-time Holy Ghost visitation and unprecedented revival! **Joel 2:28,29; Hosea 6:3; and Zech 10:1.**

James 5:7 indicates that the great harvest of the earth must await the "early and latter rain." Surely the time for this fulfillment is upon us now.

Daniel, speaking of the time of the end said, "the people that know their God shall be strong and do exploits." Dan 11:32.

The Church of these last days is not destined for Doom and Gloom or Apostasy, but is destined to graduate from glory to glory and win millions with the supernatural Gospel of Christ. The Church that Jesus is coming back for is not one that is being run over by the devil but a glorious church that is running over the devil!

Smith Wigglesworth prophesied, in the 1930's, before his death about the coming End Time revival and said, by the Spirit of God, 3 key things:

1.   "There will be a move and an outpouring of the Spirit." This was fulfilled in the 1960's and '70's with the Charismatic Renewal.

2.   "There will be a move and revival of the Word of God and the Teaching ministry." This was fulfilled in the '70's and '80's with the Word of Faith message and emphasis on teaching "THE WORD".

3.   "At the end of the Word of Faith Movement - at the end

of the 80's there will be the greatest move of God and the greatest anointing of the Holy Spirit ever in the history of the Church. It shall be a combination of;

THE MINISTRY OF THE WORD OF GOD and THE MINISTRY OF THE SPIRIT.

It will be an outpouring of miracles, the supernatural and the power of God.

This final wave of God will climax at the Rapture of the Church!"

Rejoice Child of God for the Glorious and Victorious Church things can only get better!

CHAPTER 8:
EXPLORING THE SIGNS OF THE END TIMES (PART III)

Luke 21:28 "Now when these things begin to happen, look up and lift up your heads, because you redemption draws near."

Jesus said to us ... When these things begin to happen - When the Prophetic process gets underway - When the process of fulfillment of certain things begin to take place - **THEN "LOOK" UP BECAUSE YOUR REDEMPTION DRAWS NEAR.**

Jesus told us that when certain PROPHETIC SIGNPOSTS - Prophetic events begin to be fulfilled the Believer should look up, start rejoicing because the glorious appearing of Jesus is at hand.

John 14:3 "And if I go and prepare a place for you, I will come again and receive you to Myself; that where I am, there you may be also."

DO NOT CONFUSE the receiving of the Glorious Church at the Rapture, when Jesus appears in the atmosphere, with the Return of the Church back to the earth from Heaven 7 years later.

We are the most important generation that has ever lived in the history of the Church because we are living eye witnesses of the restoration of Israel - the fig tree has budded and Jesus said that this generation would not pass away until all things would be fulfilled. The early Church began in a wave of glory - the Church of today will climax and go out in an even greater wave of glory!

This generation is a prophetic generation.
From 1948 this generation will be alive to see:

* The Rapture of the Church,
* The Revelation of the Antichrist,
* The 7 year Tribulation Period,
* The fulfillment of Revelation Chapters 4-20,
* The Second Coming of Christ and the establishing of the 1,000 year reign of Christ on earth.
* All the rest of the prophecies of Matt.24 & 25 coming to pass.

Since the rebirth of the nation of Israel in May 1948 God's End-Time Prophetic Timetable has really got underway and we have, literally, witnessed a series of major Bible prophecies fulfilled with great accuracy.

Sign Number 14
The Sign of Space Activities - Signs in the Sun, Moon and Stars

> Luke 21:25 "And there will be signs in the sun, in the moon, and in the stars; and on the earth distress of nations, with perplexity, the sea and the waves roaring".

DEVELOPMENT OF THE SPACE PROGRAMME AND SPACE CONQUEST

In 1957, our generation witnessed the beginning of space

exploration prophesied by Jesus in Luke 21:25.
Jesus **was not** giving His disciples a study in Astronomy -
which is the pure science of studying the planets and
heavenly bodies. Neither was Jesus talking about
"Astrology" which is an occult practice - **Astrology is
witchcraft and sorcery** - according to God's Word it is the
work of demons. If you are a person who reads the "DAILY
HORRIBLESCOPE" it means that you are flirting with
death.

> **Luke 21:25** **"Signs in the sun, moon and stars"** refers to the
> activities of men in space with the space programme.

This generation is the first and only generation to see man
propel himself into space. From the Sputnik in 1957 to the
space shuttle in the late 1970's and now to space cities and
space stations in 1980's and 1990's. [See also Gen 11:4-6]

Today we are watching the forerunners of space activities
that are the preliminaries of Buck Rogers and Flash Gordon!

Sign Number 15
The Sign of Distress among the Nations

> **Luke 21:25** ...and on the earth distress of nations, with perplexity,
> **the sea and the waves roaring.**

As we look at current world affairs the nations of the world
are standing helpless, confused and not knowing which
way to turn to find answers to economic difficulties, political
turmoil, civil war and strife, terrorism, population explosion
and great social problems.
We are living, today, in a generation that witnesses great

turmoil amongst the governments of the world as they face unsolved problems socially, economically and politically.

"**PERPLEXITY**" in this context means to be greatly embarrassed over internal problems which you lack natural resources to solve.

Perplexity also means problems which defy human solutions.

Sign Number 16
The Sign of Men's Hearts Failing them for Fear

> Luke 21:26   "men's hearts failing them from fear and the expectation of those things which are coming to the earth..."

No doubt this verse may be interpreted to refer to the apprehension caused by the catastrophic judgments which will come upon the earth during the final events of the Tribulation.

One thing is certain, the above prophecy is having literal fulfillment at this present time. In these days when the science of preventative medicine has developed to its highest level in history, heart disease has reached its highest incidence on record. The strain of this intense age is, literally, causing the hearts of people to fail. In the United States more than a million people die from heart disease each year. In fact, it has become the number one killer!

In other countries, especially in Europe and Asia, the condition is even more aggravated. War and rumours of war, pestilence and famine, have bred such fear in the minds of people as to cause many to age and to die prematurely.

In South Africa heart failure is today's number 1 killer because of incorrect diet, tension, stress, strain, anxiety, fear and the extreme pressure of the 20th Century lifestyle.

Sign Number 17
The Sign of High Increase in Crime

Matt 24:12 "And because <u>lawlessness</u> will abound, the love of many will grow cold".

2 Tim 3:13 [Greek New Testament] "But wicked men and deceivers will go from bad to worse using deceit and being cheated on themselves".

These Bible verses reveal the high increase in crime, corruption and lawlessness in the last days.

CONSIDER THE FOLLOWING CRIME STATISTICS,

*   The past ten years has seen a widespread increase of rape, violent crime, mugging, shoplifting, drug trafficking and acts of terrorism.

*   Teenage crime on the increase - in the U.S.A. today, 1 out of 4 serious crimes are committed by youths under the age of 18.

*   Over 100,000 businessmen and executives in the U.S.A. have their own personal bodyguard.

*   Illegal drug explosion - opium, heroin and cocaine is a $25 billion a year racket.

*   In many countries corruption is rife amongst police forces and government officials.

*   Building jails is a booming industry in the U.S.A. - over a 10 year period from 1970 to 1980, 524 prisons were built.

Sign Number 18
The Sign of Family Breakdown

> **2 Tim 3:1-4 But know this, that in the last days, perilous times will come:**
> **2   For men will be lovers of themselves, lovers of money, boasters, proud, blasphemers, disobedient to parents, unthankful, unholy,**
> **3   unloving, unforgiving, slanderers, without self-control, brutal, despisers of good,**
> **4   traitors, headstrong, haughty, lovers of pleasure rather than lovers of God,**

BREAKDOWN OF THE FAMILY AND SEXUAL IMMORALITY INFORMATION

Divorce has spiralled in many nations. Between 1900 and 1985 in the U.S. the divorce rate [per 1,000 population] increased 700%. Single-parent families by the scores of millions are struggling to cope.

Many children are being neglected. Runaways are a big problem and sexual abuse of children, a scandal.

* In the U.S.A. over 65% of all marriages end in divorce.

* Child abuse is now a major problem in today's society.

* Over 1,25 million abortions [50% of these are teenagers] in the U.S.A.each year.

* 70% of High School teenagers in U.S.A. drink alcohol or are involved with drugs. There is a marked increase in teenage suicides.

* Sharp rise in sex crimes such as rape, incest and sexual abuse.

* 15 million pornographic magazines are sold each month in U.S.A.

* 20% of U.S.A. population suffers some form of V.D.

* 25 million homosexuals in U.S.A.

   Lev 20:13 "If a man lies with a male as he lies with a woman, both of them have committed an abomination. They shall surely be put to death. Their blood shall be upon them".

   2 Tim 3:3 "Unloving, unforgiving, slanderers, without self-control, brutal, despisers of good."

Without self-control means given over to the lust of the flesh.
* In 1979 the viral disease AIDS [ACQUIRED IMMUNE DEFICIENCY SYNDROME] - began to bring about an epidemic of deaths.

*   More than 70% of all cases of AIDS have been linked to sexually active homosexuals. So far AIDS is incurable and untreatable.

Extramarital and homosexual sex are widely tolerated and accepted. Pornography, X-rated movies, video tapes and books abound in public places.

Matt 24:37	Genesis 6:5
"But as the **days of Noah** were, so also will the coming of the Son of Man be".	"Then the Lord saw that the wickedness of man was great in the earth, and that every intent of the thoughts of his heart was only evil continually".

Luke 17:28,29 "Likewise as it was also in the days of Lot: They ate, they drank, they bought, they sold, they planted, they built; 29 "but on the day that Lot went out of Sodom it rained fire and brimstone from heaven and destroyed them all".

In describing the days just before His coming, Jesus likened them to the moral conditions that existed in the days of Lot just before the destruction of Sodom.

As conditions were in the days of Sodom, so are they prevalent today. Murder, lust, immorality and depraved practices exist today just as they did in the cities of Sodom and Gomorrah.

The prophet Ezekiel, in Chapter 16:49,50, describes the conditions that existed in the city of Sodom. He declares that there was,

1. pride,
2. fullness of bread - materialistic society,
3. abundance of idleness,
4. neither did she strengthen the hand of the poor and needy,
5. they were arrogant and committed abomination before the Lord.

It is not difficult to see a similarity between conditions of that day and this.

THE DRUG EPIDEMIC.

Drug abuse has become so widespread in the United States that the sales of cocaine have placed it among the top 5 money-making forms of business in the country!
The drug choice among Americans and people throughout the world is still alcohol. The consumption of alcohol is the 4th largest cause of death, after heart disease, cancer and strokes.

Most of the drugs that people take are some kind of narcotic. The purpose of narcotics is to dull pain and induce sleep. Alcohol and heroin are the prominent narcotics.
An increasing number of people are using cocaine. Cocaine is not a narcotic, but a stimulant, just as are amphetamines. They produce talkativeness, hyperactivity, dilated pupils, restlessness, loss of appetite and the like. According to official estimates 5 million Americans use cocaine and 25 million have tried it! Whether people use narcotics or stimulants, they have this in common: They are running away from life.

In 1983 more than 29,000 people succeeded in committing suicide. Experts estimate that nearly half a million youngsters attempt suicide every year. Mental illness in some form affects about 20 million Americans, of whom about 679,000 require hospitalization each year!

Sign Number 19
The Sign of People being Lovers of Pleasure rather than Lovers of God

> 2 Tim 3:4 [Greek New Testament] "They will betray their friends, they will be reckless and puffed up with pride, pleasure loving [vain amusements] rather than worshipping God. They will put entertainment and pleasure in the place of God."

ENTERTAINMENT AND PLEASURE INFORMATION.

* The movie JAWS cost 8 million dollars to produce and 2 million dollars to promote and advertise.
  Within 90 days of its release, it netted 100 million dollars and until now has netted over 200 million dollars for the movie makers, showing the kind of priority people put on entertainment.

* Billions are spent each month at the casinos and racetracks.

* Average mothers in the U.S.A. spend 31 hours a week watching T.V.! Average fathers spend 25 hours each week in front of the T.V.! The children spend 26 hours each week in front of the T.V.

* Censors release permissive films without age restriction.

* T.V. Networks spend over a billion dollars a year covering major sporting events e.g. Wimbledon tennis, Boxing, Olympic Games etc.

Sign Number 20
The Sign of the Living Conditions in the Last Days

2 TIM 3:1-5,13 [Greek New Testament]

Verse 1   But understand this that in the Last Days there is going to be difficult and troubled times.

Verse 2   For people will be selfish and self-centered, they will be greedy for money, arrogant, boastful, and blasphemous. They will be disobedient to parents with no respect for authority, unthankful, and unrighteous.

Verse 3   Hard-hearted, unforgiving, slanderers, without self-control they will think nothing of immorality, troublemakers, hating that which is good.

Verse 4   They will betray their friends, they will be reckless and puffed up with pride, pleasure loving, rather than worshipping God. They will put entertainment, vain amusements and pleasure in the place of God.

Verse 5   They will have an outward form of religion but turn their backs on the reality of the Gospel and the power of God.

Verse 13 But wicked men and deceivers will go from bad to worse using deceit and being cheated themselves.

ROMANS 1:26-30 [Greek New Testament]

Verse 26 So God handed them over to follow the lustful passions of their hearts and even the women perverted natural for unnatural intercourse and indulged in sex sin with each other. [LESBIANS].

Verse 27 And the men instead of having normal sex relationship with women burned with lust for each other - men practicing shameful things with men [homosexuals] and receiving in themselves the penalty [AIDS] for such perversions.

Verse 28 So it was that when they gave God up and would not even acknowledge Him, God gave them up to doing everything their evil minds could think of.

Verse 29 Their lives became full of every kind of wickedness and sin, of greed and hate, envy, murder, fighting, lying, bitterness and gossip.

Verse 30 They were backbiters, haters of God, insolent, proud braggarts, always thinking of new ways of sinning and continually being disobedient to their parents.

A SUMMARY OF THE SIGNS OF THE END TIMES (NOT COINCIDENCES!!)

* PROGRESS AND INCREASE IN TRAVEL - [DAN 12:4]

* THE EXPLOSION OF KNOWLEDGE - [DANIEL 12:4]

* RISE OF FALSE CULTS, FALSE PROPHETS AND DECEPTION - [MATT 24:11]

* WARS AND RUMOURS OF WARS - [MATT 24:6,7]

* FAMINE AND MASS HUNGER - [MATT 24:7]

* EARTHQUAKES AND NATURE'S UPHEAVAL - [MATT 24:7]

* PESTILENCE AND EPIDEMICS - [MATT 24:7]

* BREAKDOWN OF THE FAMILY UNIT - [2 TIM 3:1-4]

* HIGH INCREASE IN CRIME AND CORRUPTION - [MATT 24:12]

* PEOPLE LOVING PLEASURE MORE THAN GOD - [2 TIM 3:4]

* SIGN OF SPACE ACTIVITIES - [LUKE 21:25]

* DISTRESS AMONG THE NATIONS WITH NO SOLUTION - [LUKE 21:25]

* MEN'S HEARTS FAILING BECAUSE OF FEAR - [LUKE 21:26]

* SIGN OF RUSSIA'S INVOLVEMENT IN THE MIDDLE EAST - [EZEK 38]

* THE RISE OF COMMUNIST CHINA - [REV 16:12]

* MIDDLE EAST PEACE AGREEMENT BEGUN - [EZEK 38:14]

* SIGN OF THE EUROPEAN COMMON MARKET

PREPARING ANTICHRIST'S LAUNCHING PAD -
[PROPHECIES OF DANIEL]

* RETURN OF JEWS BACK TO THEIR ANCIENT
  HOMELAND - [AMOS 9:14,15]

* REBIRTH OF ISRAEL AS A NATION IN 1948 - [MATT
  24:32-34, EZEK 37:21]

* SIGN OF JERUSALEM COMING BACK UNDER
  JEWISH CONTROL, JUNE 1967 - [LUKE 21:24]

GOD'S PROPHETIC CALENDAR

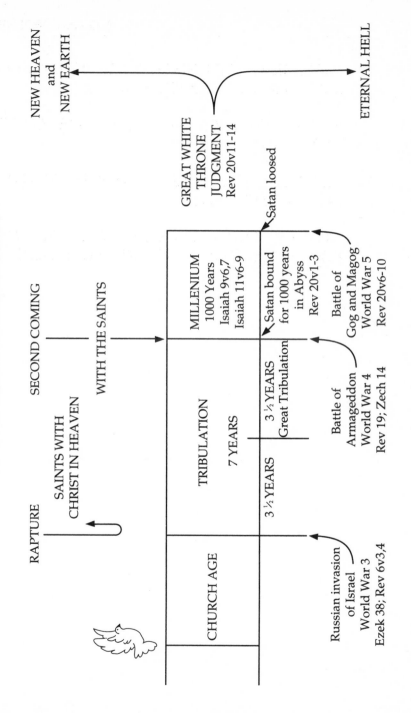

CHAPTER 9:
GOD'S UNFOLDING PLAN FOR THE FUTURE - (Putting the pieces together)

What is the future of Planet Earth?

Where **are we** today in God's prophetic timetable?
What is God's plan for the future of planet earth?
Will Russia, or China, achieve world conquest?
Will the earth survive the next 50 years?
What is going to happen in the Middle East?
Will we be destroyed in a mushroom cloud of atomic warfare?
Wouldn't it be wonderful to KNOW what is going to happen?

THE BIBLE, GOD'S PLAN FOR MAN, TELLS US EXACTLY WHAT LIES AHEAD.

The Bible says that God made the earth. It tells us,

> **Jeremiah 51:15 He has made the earth by His power; He has established the world by His wisdom, And stretched out the heaven by His understanding.**

In the first chapter of Genesis it tells us, "In the beginning, God created the heaven and the earth."
So He is the builder, developer and, ultimately the OWNER of this planet. David said, in the first verse of the 24th Psalm, "The earth is the Lord's and all its fullness; the world, and those who dwell therein."

Thus we know that the earth belongs to the Lord, and that He did not make the earth only to allow it to be destroyed by Satan. John 10:10 tells us of the destructive motives of Satan and the blessed purpose of our Lord Jesus Christ. Therefore all of the human tragedy, suffering and problems we see in the world today are caused, directly or indirectly, by Satan, while none are caused by God. And God still has plans for this planet. He has clearly outlined it within His Word and this is what we have to look forward to!

SEEING THE OVERALL PICTURE

End Time Bible Prophecy can be likened to a giant picture puzzle with different pieces of information found all over the Bible in the books of Daniel, Ezekiel, Jude, Matthew, Luke, Jeremiah, Revelation etc. etc.
Our purpose in this Chapter is to, scripturally, give the Born Again Believer a simplified step by step order of End Time Events and with the aid of charts to put the prophetic pieces together. Although this is a large chapter it is extremely informative and by the time that you have read it you will have clear knowledge concerning what the future holds in store.

WHAT DOES THE FUTURE HOLD?

*   THE RAPTURE OF THE CHURCH

*   THE CHURCH IN HEAVEN FOR 7 YEARS
     - Judgment Seat of Christ
     - Marriage Supper of the Lamb.

*   THE TRIBULATION FOR 7 YEARS ON EARTH
     - Release of the 4 horsemen of the Apocalypse

- Antichrist begins his 7 year satanic assignment
- 144,000 Born-Again Jewish evangelists selected, sealed and sent forth
- At Mid-Tribulation Antichrist breaks his peace treaty with Israel and introduces the mark of the Beast
- Ministry of the 2 Witnesses

* THE SECOND COMING OF CHRIST

* THE BATTLE OF ARMAGEDDON

* THE JUDGMENT OF THE LIVING GENTILE NATIONS

* SATAN IS BOUND FOR 1,000 YEARS IN THE BOTTOMLESS PIT

* THE 1,000 YEAR MILLENNIAL REIGN OF JESUS ON EARTH

* SATAN IS LOOSED

* BATTLE OF GOG AND MAGOG AT THE END OF THE MILLENNIUM

* THE PRESENT EARTH RENOVATED BY FIRE

* THE GREAT WHITE THRONE JUDGMENT

* THE NEW HEAVEN AND THE NEW EARTH

God's Prophetic Timetable –
The Scriptural Sequence of End Time Events!

1.   The Pre-Tribulation Rapture of the Church.

John 14:3 "And if I go and prepare a place for you, I will come again and receive you to Myself; that where I am, there you may be also."

1 Cor 15:51-53 Behold I tell you a mystery: We shall not all sleep, but we shall all be changed -
52 in a moment, in a twinkling of an eye, at the last trumpet. For the trumpet will sound, and the dead will be raised incorruptible, and we shall be changed.
53 For this corruptible must put on incorruption, and this mortal must put on immortality.

1 Thess 4:16-18 For the Lord Himself will descend from heaven with a shout, with the voice of an archangel, and with the trumpet of God. And the dead in Christ will rise first.
17 Then we who are alive shall be caught up together with them in the clouds to meet the Lord in the air. And thus we shall always be with the Lord.
18 Therefore comfort one another with these words.

2 Thess 2:1 Now, brethren concerning the coming of our Lord Jesus Christ and our gathering together to Him, ...

The Rapture is the next great event on God's Prophetic calendar and can occur any day now. It involves a two-fold supernatural operation which takes place simultaneously in an "atomic" second -

i]   The **RESURRECTION** of all the SAVED DEAD.

ii] The **TRANSLATION** of all BORN AGAIN BELIEVERS alive on the earth at the time of the Rapture.

It is commonly believed that at the end of the world there will be a general resurrection in which all of the dead, both good and bad, will have to stand at the judgment bar of God. This is not the teaching in the Holy Scriptures [Dan 12:2, John 5:28,29].
Jesus said that there would be a resurrection of life and a resurrection of damnation. In Rev 20:4,5 the Apostle John makes it plain that these two resurrections will be separated by a period of a thousand years. The Apostle Paul describes the first resurrection in 1 Cor 15:51-58. In 1 Thess 4:16,17 he says, "The dead in Christ shall rise first."

So the next great event on the horizon of end time prophecy is the Rapture. Of course, the specific word "rapture" is not found in the Bible, but basically it means: "ecstatic joy" and also a "catching away". There is going to be [because it is described in Scripture], a "snatching away", and I think we can be assured that this will be - for the Church - a time of unparalleled joy.

This is the "first resurrection", the resurrection of life. This is the time when every child of God who has ever lived - all the way from Adam until the trump of God sounds - will be "instantly changed" in the "twinkling of an eye."

The Bible assures us that corruption shall put on incorruption, and mortality shall put on immortality. The soul and the spirit of every Believer who has ever lived will then be reunited with their deceased bodies. Their bodies will be resurrected and simultaneously changed as they reunite with their souls and spirits in the air, when they meet Jesus.

We call this the "Rapture", it is going to be the most powerful event ever to take place in all of human history. What better way to get the attention of mankind than to instantly withdraw millions of people from the face of the earth in a split second?

QUALIFICATIONS TO PARTICIPATE: The **only** requirement for participating in the Rapture is to be saved by the blood of the Lord Jesus Christ. Joining a particular church will not qualify you. Accepting the doctrines of a specific denomination will not do. Trusting in any church to save you will prove hopeless, as the only condition for inclusion is salvation through the blood of the Lamb of God.

WHEN? The Word of God is clear that the Rapture **must** occur **before** any part of the 7 year tribulation period commences and **before** the Antichrist is revealed on the world's political scene. [2 Thess 2:1-8]. The Raptured saints are clearly seen in heaven at the throne of God in Revelation chapters 4 & 5, before any part of the 7 year Tribulation begins in Revelation 6. The Scriptures are clear and specific that, **THE CHURCH HAS NO PART, OF THE 7 YEAR TRIBULATION ON EARTH.**

WHO ARE THE 24 ELDERS IN REVELATION 4 & 5 ?

The 24 Elders are described as sitting on thrones, wearing white raiment [robes of righteousness], and wearing crowns. (See Rev. 4:4 AMP). They sing the new song of the redeemed in which they confess, "We represent all races and nations of people and all languages on the earth. We have been redeemed by the blood of the Lamb, and we shall reign as kings and priests on the earth" [Rev 5:9]. This description is that of every Born Again follower of Jesus Christ according to the New Testament.

By the number 24, we know that they are representatives. This is the double of God's Word : 12 representing the 12 tribes of Israel and 12 representing the 12 apostles of the Lamb from the Church Age.

Throughout the New Testament, the word ELDER identifies one who is called to represent the Church of the Lord Jesus Christ on earth. Because all the single representatives of the Church are in heaven and because all the angels are present around the throne, we know that the entire Church is in heaven. If it weren't, the angels wouldn't be there. Angels are on divine assignment on behalf of the Church [Heb 1:13,14]. The 24 elders are selected representatives of the Church company in heaven. The Rapture of the Church terminates the Church Age and ushers in the 7 year Tribulation period. [N.B. We know that the Tribulation period is 7 years in length because of Scriptures such as Dan 9:27 & Ezek 39:9.]

2. Following the Rapture :
Future Events in Heaven for the 7 year Period.

i] BELIEVERS IN HEAVEN STAND BEFORE THE JUDGMENT SEAT OF CHRIST

The 3 key Scriptures for a study of this subject are :

Rom 14:10 ... For we shall all stand before the judgment seat of Christ.

2 Cor 5:10   For we must all appear before the judgment seat of Christ, that each one may receive the things done in the body, according to what he has done, whether good or bad.

See also 1 Cor 3:9-15.
This is not a judgment to determine whether or not people are saved or lost. In this judgment, Born Again Believers will be judged and rewarded according to their works. All Christian service is described as being: wood, hay, stubble, or silver, gold and precious stones. Our works will be tried by the fire of God and only those works which are the gold, silver and precious stones will stand the test of fire. The works that will stand the test of fire are NOT what are commonly referred to as good deeds or "living right", but they are works which God has ordained for each individual believer to walk in. All else will be burned up.

ii]   THE WEDDING OF THE LAMB, FOLLOWED BY THE MARRIAGE SUPPER OF THE LAMB [Rev 19:1-10].

3.   Future events on Earth for 7 year Tribulation Period. Study Revelation Chapters 6-19

This future 7 year Tribulation period on earth is known as DANIEL'S 70TH WEEK and is Biblically divided into 2 halves:

a]   First $3\frac{1}{2}$ years Tribulation - Matt 24:9-14
b]   Second $3\frac{1}{2}$ years Great Tribulation - Matt 24:15-26.

Christ's teaching in Matt 24, Mark 13, and Luke 21 contains details of end time signs in the Last Days, the 7 year Tribulation period and His Glorious Second Coming!

MATT 24:4-8 DESCRIBES PRESENT DAY CONDITIONS

MATT 24:9-14 DESCRIBES EVENTS OF THE TRIBULATION (FIRST $3\frac{1}{2}$ YRS)

MATT 24:15-26 DESCRIBES EVENTS OF THE GREAT TRIBULATION (LAST $3\frac{1}{2}$ YRS)

MATT 24 :27-51 DESCRIBES THE SECOND COMING OF JESUS.

This 7 year Tribulation period is also called; **the day of the Lord** [Zeph 1:7], **the day of calamity** [Jer 46:21], **the day of vengeance** [Isa 63:4], **the day of wrath** [Rev 6:17], **a time of trouble** [Dan 12:1], **the time of Jacob's trouble** [Jer 30:7], **the indignation** [Isa 26:20] and **the hour of temptation** [Rev 3:10].

The very names that are given to this period give us an inkling of what it will be like. Chapters 6 through 19 of the book of Revelation show that the judgment of God is visited on the earth in three series of judgments :

i] the opening of the 7 seals,

ii] the blowing of 7 trumpets,

iii] the pouring out of the 7 bowls of God's wrath.

The book of Revelation informs us that the sun will become black as sack cloth of hair and the moon will become as blood. The rivers and the fountains of water will be turned to blood. In those days men will desire to die, and death will flee from them. Men will gnaw their tongues for pain and will curse and blaspheme the God of Heaven but will not repent of their murders, nor of their sorceries, nor of their fornication, nor of their thefts.

THE LENGTH OF THE TRIBULATION - Daniel's 70th week [Dan 9:27] is yet to be fulfilled. The Tribulation will be that week of 7 years. Twice in the book of Revelation we read of 1,260 days [3$\frac{1}{2}$ years] (Rev 11:3, Rev 12:6) and twice we read of 42 months (Rev 11:2, Rev 13:5) which is 3$\frac{1}{2}$ years. When the weeks of years, the 1,260 days and the 42 months are all considered together it is quite obvious that the tribulation period will last 7 years. [See also Ezek 38 & 39].

4. The 7 year Tribulation begins with the Opening of the Seals of Revelation 6.

The release the of the 4 horsemen of the Apocalypse [destroy a quarter of earth's population!]

Seal 1; WHITE HORSE - Revelation of Antichrist to begin his 7 years of Satanic assignment on earth. [Dan 9:27]

Seal 2; RED HORSE - World War III, Russian Invasion of Israel. [Ezek 38 & 39]

Seal 3; BLACK HORSE - Famine.

Seal 4; PALE HORSE - Death and Hell [its companion rider].

From Rev 6:1 we see that Jesus alone is worthy to open the 7 seals.

THE FIRST SEAL = THE WHITE HORSE [Rev 6:1,2].

When the first seal is opened, a white horse comes into view [Rev 6:1,2]. Its rider is carrying a bow in his hand, is wearing a crown, and goes forth, "conquering and to conquer." Bible students have long asked, "Who is this rider on the white horse?" Several clues are given in the passage which help us make a positive identification.

i] He is on a white horse. This speaks of success, for white horses were ridden by conquering war heroes when they returned from battle for a grand triumphal parade.

ii] The bow suggests military power and the lack of arrows very likely refers to the rider's pose as a peace-loving diplomat.

iii] The crown he is wearing is the kind that might be given to a victor, such as one who wins an athletic contest. [Jesus, the Conqueror, has many crowns and needs for no-one to give Him a crown.]

iv] The statement that he went forth "conquering and to conquer" is a further indication that the rider will at least temporarily succeed in his ambitions.

Yes, this rider on the white horse will be successful for a time. As a result, he'll be looked upon as the great hope for mankind and will usher in a brief period of peace and safety. Many will bow to him in worship. With this information we can positively identify this rider as the Antichrist, the false messiah of Revelation 13.

This interpretation is in keeping with the prophetic script-ures, which often describe the Antichrist as one who first appears to be a man of peace. In Daniel 9, for example, he is called, "the prince that shall come," and the same passage speaks of a covenant he will make, "with many for one week" [v27]. This refers to the peace pact to be made with Daniel's people, the Jews, involving the city of Jerusalem.

Three times in 2 Thess 2:1-9 we see that the Antichrist cannot be revealed until the Church has first departed from earth to heaven for the Judgment Seat of Christ.

THE SECOND SEAL = THE RED HORSE
[Rev 6:3,4].

This rider is given POWER! We can see that he is certainly no idle threat. He is given the ability to take peace from the earth. A great sword is given to him...nuclear warfare? The second seal of war is, in reality, WORLD WAR III. This is the war that takes place almost immediately after the Rapture. [Ezek 39:9, Dan 9:27] Up to this point, Israel is at peace [Ezek 38:8,11,14] and so developed that Russia moves in and hopes that Israel will be an easy prey. Russia needs this conquest to take over the Middle East with all of its riches and wealth, position of military strategy and Israel's food. The battle is quick and decisive. It lasts one day and Israel is the victor with Divine Intervention - A miracle of God destroys Russia and the enemies of Israel!
The Antichrist now takes a step forward and moves into the role of world Super-Man, attempting world conquest **but failing miserably** as he is confined to the European and Middle East areas! However, the zenith of his rule does not take place until around mid-Tribulation. We know that the first seal has already been opened, so he is rising to power as a man of peace and a great diplomat.

THE THIRD SEAL = THE BLACK HORSE
[Rev 6:5,6].

The colour of this horse depicts death through hunger. Famine always follows war. The scales and the measures of grain suggest the meting out of daily rations. Famine will be upon the earth, bringing starvation to millions. Food prices will be so high that purchasing power will be diminished to one-eighth of what it was in times of plenty. Everyone but the very rich will suffer hunger, and many will die for lack of food.

What a colossal failure the Antichrist proves to be! He promises peace but brings war. He promises plenty but brings famine.

THE FOURTH SEAL = THE PALE HORSE [Rev 6:7,8].

John, in his vision of future judgments, now sees a horrible pale horse. The Greek word translated "pale" is chloros, which denotes a ghastly, yellowish-green colour, like one who is deathly ill. It's rider is named "Death", and he is followed by "Hades", the realm of departed spirits. The apostle tells us that this fourth horseman will be given authority to kill one-quarter of the earth's population through the sword, famine, pestilence and wild beasts. By today's figures this means that over one billion people will die. Think of it - one billion people! Never has the world known such destruction!

The four horsemen continue their ride throughout the entirety of the 7 years of the Tribulation and their activity increases as the 7 years progress.

5. The Selection and Sealing of the 144,000 Jewish Evangelists. [Rev 7:1-8, Rev 14:1-5].

At the beginning of the 7 year Tribulation period when

Russia and all her allies invade Israel and God supernaturally destroys them, it will have a dramatic impact upon the Jews. Multitudes of Jews witnessing this miracle of DIVINE INTERVENTION will accept Jesus Christ as Messiah and Lord and be born again. From this vast number of Born Again Jews, God will sovereignly select and seal 12,000 Born Again Jewish men from each of the 12 tribes of Israel (N.B. 10 tribes are not lost!)

This company of 12 x 12,000 making 144,000 Born Again Jews [NOT Jehovah's Witnesses] are divinely sealed and protected by God and cannot be killed [Rev 9:4]. They are sent forth on Global Evangelism to carry the Good News to Jews and Gentiles worldwide.

As a result of their anointed ministry in all nations:

i]   millions of Jews are Born Again - almost all of Israel is saved [Rom 11:25,26];

ii]   not only are millions of Jews saved at this time but there will be a minimum of 10 times as many Gentiles Born Again [Zech 8:23, Rev 7:9-17].

> **Zech 8:23**   Thus says the Lord of hosts: In those days ten men from every language of the nations shall grasp the sleeve of a Jewish man, saying, "Let us go with you, for we have heard that God is with you."

6.   Mid-Tribulation Events.

i]   The Antichrist breaks his agreement with Israel and sets himself up as god in the Jewish Temple in Jerusalem [Dan 9:27, 2 Thess 2:4, Matt 24:15, Rev 13:11-18].

According to Dan 9:27, the Antichrist makes a peace covenant with the Israeli government at the beginning of Daniel's 70th week which is the 7 year Tribulation period. The Antichrist cannot be a communist for at mid-Tribulation he sets himself up as god!

Antichrist means **"false pretender"** and this is an apt description for he is indeed a wolf in sheep's clothing!! At mid-Tribulation the Antichrist with his armies invades Israel and sets up his headquarters in Jerusalem, declaring himself to be god. At this point in time he introduces his second in command - the False Prophet.

ii] The False Prophet, by satanic power, gives life to the statue or image of the Beast in the Temple and demands that all people worship the image of the Beast. [Rev 13:14,15]

iii] The False Prophet announces the mark of the Beast and the number of the Beast, 666, to be branded on all people as an identifying mark for those who will serve the Antichrist and be a part of his system. Those who refuse will be unable to buy or sell [Rev 13:16,17].

iv] The ministry of the 2 Witnesses begins for the last $3\frac{1}{2}$ years of the Tribulation [Rev 11:1-13].

These 2 witnesses will be God's supernatural agents on earth preaching the Gospel and opposing the Antichrist. They will be divinely protected by God and supernaturally empowered by the Holy Spirit to perform great miracles. At the conclusion of their ministry they will be permitted to be martyred and then they will be resurrected to heaven during the final week of the Tribulation!

v]   The beginning of the Trumpet Judgments releasing the
      upheaval of nature and horrific plagues on earth [Rev
      Ch 8 & 9].

vi] The Rapture of the 144,000 Jewish Evangelists [Rev
      14:1-5].

vii] The angel's special end-time assignment begins [Rev
      14:6-11]. The angels are seen preaching the Gospel and
      warning the people on earth not to worship the image
      of the Beast nor receive his mark.

7.   The Antichrist's Days are Numbered.

During the final three years of the Great Tribulation we see
the downfall of the Antichrist. At Mid-Tribulation he has
announced himself to be "god" but he is completely power-
less and helpless against ...

a]   The ministry of God's 2 supernatural agents,
b]   The plagues caused by nature's upheaval,
c]   The angel's end-time ministry,
d]   People in his empire rebelling against him and refusing
      his mark.

How can he be "god" if he can't control nature? ...two men?
... and angels? The Antichrist's attempt at world conquest
has totally failed and he meets his crushing defeat at the
Battle of Armageddon!

8.   The Rapture of all the Tribulation Saints.
     [Rev 6:9-11, 7:9-17, 13:7, 14:9-13, 15:1-4, 17:6,

GOD'S PLAN FOR THE FUTURE NO 1

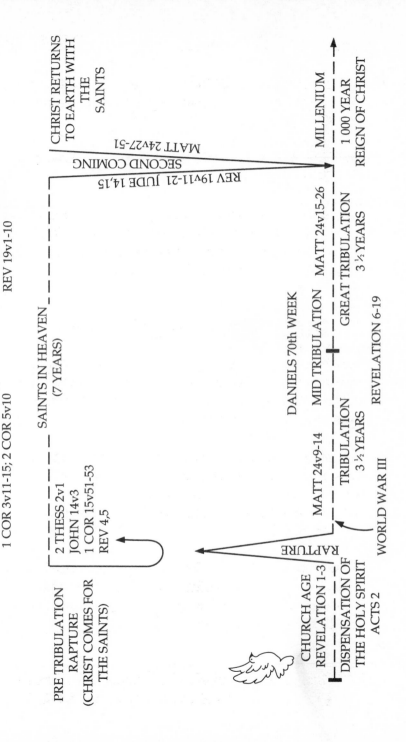

BELIEVERS JUDGMENT
1 COR 3v11-15; 2 COR 5v10

MARRIAGE SUPPER
REV 19v1-10

SAINTS IN HEAVEN
(7 YEARS)

2 THESS 2v1
JOHN 14v3
1 COR 15v51-53
REV 4,5

PRE TRIBULATION
RAPTURE
(CHRIST COMES FOR
THE SAINTS)

CHRIST RETURNS
TO EARTH WITH
THE
SAINTS

SECOND COMING
REV 19v11-21 JUDE 14,15
MATT 24v27-51

MILLENIUM

1 000 YEAR
REIGN OF CHRIST

DANIELS 70th WEEK

MID TRIBULATION   MATT 24v15-26

MATT 24v9-14

GREAT TRIBULATION
3 ½ YEARS

TRIBULATION
3 ½ YEARS

REVELATION 6-19

WORLD WAR III

RAPTURE

CHURCH AGE
REVELATION 1-3

DISPENSATION OF
THE HOLY SPIRIT
ACTS 2

GOD'S PLAN FOR THE FUTURE NO 2

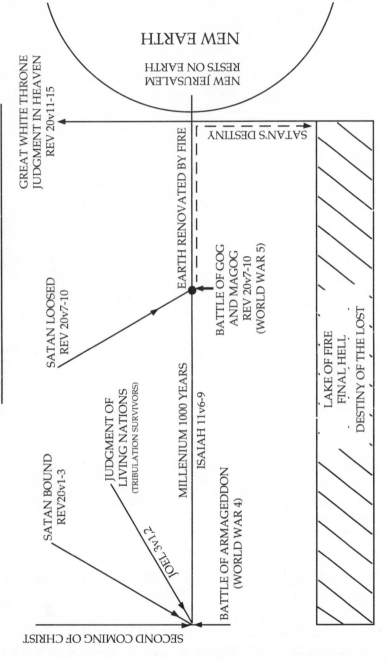

GREAT WHITE THRONE
JUDGMENT IN HEAVEN
REV 20v11-15

NEW EARTH

NEW JERUSALEM
RESTS ON EARTH

EARTH RENOVATED BY FIRE

SATAN'S DESTINY

SATAN LOOSED
REV 20v7-10

BATTLE OF GOG
AND MAGOG
REV 20v7-10
(WORLD WAR 5)

JUDGMENT OF
LIVING NATIONS
(TRIBULATION SURVIVORS)

JOEL 3v12

MILLENIUM 1000 YEARS
ISAIAH 11v6-9

SATAN BOUND
REV20v1-3

LAKE OF FIRE
FINAL HELL.
DESTINY OF THE LOST

BATTLE OF ARMAGEDDON
(WORLD WAR 4)

SECOND COMING OF CHRIST

19:1-10, 20:4-6].

This includes all persons who were Born Again and those who were martyred in the time between the Rapture of the Church and before the close of the Tribulation. This takes place in the closing stages of the Great Tribulation.

i] The first ones of this Tribulation company of saints were told to wait until all who were to be martyred in the Tribulation would be killed and then their death would be avenged [Rev 6:9-11].

ii] The Word says they will all be raptured as a separate and distinct company of saints and martyrs of the Tribulation period as seen from Rev 15:1-4.

iii] A great many are spoken of as being beheaded by the Beast for their commitment to Christ [Rev 20:4-6].

9. The Rapture of the 2 Witnesses [possibly Elijah and Enoch] Rev 11:7-12.

This will take place during the final week of the 7 year Tribulation, after they are martyred and lie dead in the streets of Jerusalem for $3\frac{1}{2}$ days, God will supernaturally rapture them to heaven.

10. Armageddon and the Last Day of the Great Tribulation.

i] On the final day of the 7 year Tribulation there will occur a tremendous earthquake and upheaval of nature

[Rev 6:12-17, 11:13-19, 16:16-21].

Can you visualise the terror and destruction with the combination of a massive cyclone, hurricane, typhoon, tornado and a great earthquake plus hailstones, weighing 120lbs., raining on the earth, [Rev 16:21], ALL happening at one time?

ii]   The Antichrist and the combined armies of his 10 nations kingdom [Rev 17:10-14], plus his allies and the 200 million demon-controlled oriental army [Rev 9:13-19, 16:12,16], are gathered for the Battle of Armageddon.

iii] The Second Coming [Rev 19:11-21, Jude 14,15]. Jesus Christ returns to the earth as King of kings and Lord of lords with the angels and millions of His saints to defeat the Antichrist and his forces at the Battle of Armageddon.

Matt 24:30   "Then the sign of the Son of Man will appear in heaven, and then all the tribes of the earth will mourn, and they will see the Son of Man coming on the clouds of heaven with power and great glory.

This is called the **"Second Coming of the Lord"** which is totally different from the Rapture. At the time of the Rapture, the Lord will come for His saints. At the Second Coming, He will come with them.

At the Rapture, the Lord will not touch this earth; He will come only part-way between heaven and earth. At the Second Coming He will actually set His feet upon the Mount of Olives [Zech 14:4].

Zech 14:4   And in that day His feet will stand on the Mount of

Olives, Which faces Jerusalem on the east. And the Mount of Olives shall be split in two, from east to west, Making a very large valley; Half of the mountain shall move towards the north And half of it toward the south.

His Coming will start a new era, an era of greatness and glory for 1,000 years.

iv] The Battle of Armageddon [Isa 34:1-8, 63:1-6, Rev 19:15]. This is pictured as the "Winepress of God's wrath" Rev 14:14-20. [The destruction of these massive armies will cause a river of blood to flow almost 200 miles long and 5 feet deep.] As Jesus speaks, "The Word of God", from His position on the Mount of Olives [Zech 14:1-5] it releases the plague that absolutely destroys the vast military armada gathered at Armageddon in one hour [Rev 19:15,21, Zech 14:12, Rev 14:20].

Jesus speaks the Word which releases a plague to smite the vast armies of the Antichrist and the 200 million strong Oriental army. They are immediately blinded; their eyes are consumed away in their sockets. They are immediately dumb; their tongues are consumed away in their mouths. In fright, they reach out and grab one another for security. That only frightens them more, so they turn to fight among themselves. Their flesh begins to consume away from their bones. Their blood gushes to the earth, creating the pool of blood described in Revelation 14. It stretches over an area of about 185 miles in the valley of Megiddo and the Plains of Jezreel. In Zechariah 14 we have seen the events that take place at the Lord's return to earth and so we can readily see the distinct difference between His return and the Rapture!

v]   The Antichrist and the False Prophet are cast alive into the Lake of Fire becoming the first occupants of "Gehenna", the future final hell [Rev 19:20].

11. Satan is captured by an angel of God, chained and then cast into the Bottomless Pit for 1,000 years [Rev 20:1-3].

During the Millennium on earth, Satan is imprisoned in solitary confinement in the Abyss - where he can deceive and tempt no-one.

12. The Judgment of the Living Gentile Nations (Tribulation Survivors)

This will be the gathering of the living nations at the Second Coming [Matt 25:31,32] of Christ to determine who is worthy in each nation to go into the Millennial Kingdom of Christ on earth. Those who have oppressed Israel during the future Tribulation will be sent to Hell, and those who have not, nor have taken the mark of the Beast will continue to live on earth as earthly natural subjects of Christ in the 1,000 year Kingdom [Matt 25:31-46, Zech 14:16-21, Joel 3:1,2 Jude 14,15].

13. The Millennium - The 1,000 year reign of Jesus Christ on Earth [Ps 2:6, Ps 72:7-11, Jer 23:5,6, Rev 20:1-6].

14. Satan Loosed for a Short Season resulting in the Battle of Gog and Magog - The Final World War [Rev 20:7-10].

Satan will be loosed from the pit at the end of the 1,000 years and then goes forth and deceives many people who have lived with Christ but decide to give Satan a try. Satan does not limit his activity to just the area of Russia and her coasts, but also the whole world. **REMEMBER**: this is not the same group as described in Ezekiel 38 & 39, for those armies consist only of Russia and her allies, plus Ethiopia, Persia, Libya and others. They will do battle primarily against Israel and those nations we know as Great Britain and her offspring. Don't confuse these verses with those verses in Ezekiel. This is World War V and the final battle of the ages.

With Satan as their leader, they number as the sand of the sea and surround the world capital, Jerusalem, where Jesus is King of kings, attempting to destroy His Kingdom. God rains down fire on them and devours them.

Then He casts Satan into the Lake of Fire where the Antichrist and the False Prophet have been for the last 1,000 years. His reward is torment forever, day and night.

15. The Present Earth Renovated by Fire [2 Pet 3:7-13, Rev 20:11].

16. The Great White Throne Judgment in Heaven [Rev 20:11-15].

This last Judgment or the Great White Throne Judgment takes place after Satan is cast into the Lake of Fire at the end of the 1,000 years. God sits on this throne in heaven to judge and sentence the unrighteous of all ages!

17. The Eternal State - The New Heaven and The New Earth [Isa 66:22, Rev 21:1-5].

CHAPTER 10:
THE RAPTURE

This is the most exciting time to be living in the earth, if you are born again, because the next event in God's prophetic timetable is the Rapture of the Church.

In the next several chapters you will learn the following from God's Word and be able to answer these questions,

* **What is the Rapture?**

* **How** do the New Testament Scriptures describe the Rapture?

* **When** will the Rapture take place?

* **What** will happen at the Rapture?

* **Who** will be left behind on earth after the Rapture?

* **What** are the Spiritual qualifications for being included in the Rapture?

* **How** should Christians be living in view of the nearness of the Rapture?

* **The Bible** speaks of at least seven raptures!

* **The difference** between the Rapture and the Second Coming of Christ.

FOUNDATION SCRIPTURES
FOR THE RAPTURE.

John 14:3 "And if I go and prepare a place for you, I will come again and receive you to Myself; that where I am, you may be also".

1 Cor 15:51,52 "Behold, I tell you a mystery: We shall not all sleep, but we shall all be changed -
52 in a moment, in the twinkling of an eye, at the last trumpet. For the trumpet will sound, and the dead will be raised incorruptible, and we shall be changed.

Phil 3:20,21 "For our citizenship is in heaven, from which we also eagerly wait for the Saviour, the Lord Jesus Christ,
21 who will transform our lowly body that it may be conformed to His glorious body, according to the working by which He is able even to subdue all things to Himself.

1 Thess 4:16,17 "For the Lord Himself will descend from heaven with a shout, with the voice of an archangel, and with the trumpet of God. And the dead in Christ will rise first.
17 Then we who are alive and remain shall be caught up together with them in the clouds to meet the Lord in the air. And thus we shall always be with the Lord".

1 Thess 5:23 "Now may the God of peace Himself sanctify you completely; and may your whole spirit, soul, and body be preserved blameless at the coming of our Lord Jesus Christ.

2 Thess 2:1 "Now, we ask you brethren, concerning the coming of our Lord Jesus Christ and our gathering together to Him".

Titus 2:13 "Looking for the blessed hope and glorious appearing of our great God and Saviour Jesus Christ".

Heb 9:28 "So Christ was offered once to bear the sins of many. To those who eagerly wait for Him He will appear a second time, apart from sin, for salvation".

1 Peter 5:4 "And when the chief Shepherd appears, you will receive a crown of glory that does not fade away".

1 John 3:2 "Beloved, now we are children of God; and it has not yet been revealed what we shall be, but we know that when He is revealed, we shall be like Him, for we shall see Him as He is".

So the New Testament describes the Rapture using the following key phrases ...

The believers are, "**received by the Lord**" [John 14:3].

The saints are, "**raised incorruptible**" [1 Cor 15:51,52].

The believers are, "**transformed by the Lord**" [Phil 3:20,21].

Those IN CHRIST are, "**caught up to meet the Lord**" [1 Thess 4:16,17]

The saints of God will experience a, "**gathering together unto Him**" [2 Thess 2:1].

The Rapture is called, "**The glorious appearing of Jesus**" [Titus 2:13, Heb 9:28, 1 Peter 5:4]

WHAT IS THE RAPTURE?

Biblically defined **THE RAPTURE** is the Appearing of Jesus and the supernatural catching up of the Church.
Somebody might say ...
The word "rapture" is not found in the Bible and of course they are right.
However, we use other terms that are not found in the Bible but we know what they mean. For example: Prodigal Son is a term used to describe the wayward son in Luke 15 and yet the word "prodigal" is not found in the Bible, even so we know what the word prodigal means.

WEBSTER'S DICTIONARY defines **RAPTURE** as a state or experience of being carried away by overwhelming emotion!

The word "RAPTURE" as applied to the resurrection of the saved dead and the translation of the living saints comes from the Latin verb, "RAPIO" and also the Greek word "HARPAZO" ["CAUGHT UP" - 1 Thess 4:17].

These words together mean the following:

1. To seize by force - to be forcibly removed from the earth.
2. The act of transporting from one location to another.
3. To be transplanted from earth to heaven.
4. To snatch up suddenly.
5. To be carried away by a sudden energy.
6. To be pulled up by an irresistible force greater than gravity.

The RAPTURE or CATCHING UP of God's people from the

earth to heaven is a proven ability of God with solid scriptural basis as the Bible records 3 raptures that have already taken place.

THREE RAPTURES HAVE ALREADY TAKEN PLACE.

RAPTURE NO. 1
The rapture of **Enoch** almost 5,160 years ago [Gen 5:21-24].

> **Hebrews 11:5** {Original Greek} By faith Enoch was translated from the earth into heaven so that he never died - He disappeared from this world because God promoted him For before he was taken from the earth evidence was given him That he had become well-pleasing to God.

RAPTURE NO. 2
The rapture of **Elijah** about 3,500 years ago. God "raptured" Elijah and he was taken up bodily into heaven and the Bible reveals that angels were involved with this [2 Kings 2:1,8-12].

RAPTURE NO. 3
The Rapture of **Jesus Christ** when He went to heaven - physically and bodily at His ascension [Acts 1:9-11].

THERE ARE AT LEAST FOUR FUTURE RAPTURES IN SCRIPTURE.

1.   The Rapture of **the Church** before the Tribulation [1 Thess 4:16-18].

2.   The rapture of the **144,000** Jewish evangelists just after

Mid-Tribulation [Rev 14:1-5].

3. The rapture of the **Tribulation Converts** [Rev 7:9-17, Rev 20:4-6].

4. The rapture of **the 2 Witnesses** [Enoch/Elijah] during the final week of the Great Tribulation [Rev 11:3-12].

You will never understand the Bible concerning God's end-time truth unless you realise certain basic facts ... There are **TWO** future comings of Jesus:

1. The **Rapture** - Jesus is coming FOR His Church.

2. The **Return** of Christ - Jesus is coming back WITH His saints to the earth 7 years later.

> 1 Cor 15:51-54 Behold, I tell you a mystery: We shall not all sleep, but we shall all be changed-
> 52 in a moment, in the twinkling of an eye, at the last trumpet. For the trumpet will sound, and the dead will be raised incorruptible, and we shall be changed.
> 53 For this corruptible must put on incorruption, and this mortal must put on immortality.
> 54 So when this corruptible has put on incorruption, and this mortal has put on immortality, then shall be brought to pass the saying that is written: "Death is swallowed up in victory."

Here the Apostle Paul is referring to the BODY OF CHRIST - "The Ecclesia" - THE CALLED OUT ONES described in Heb 12:23 as the General Assembly and Church of the Firstborn.

> 1 Cor 15:51 Behold, I tell you a mystery: We shall not all sleep,

but we shall all be changed -

This word, "MYSTERY", is important. Take your Bible and underline this vital word. It means in the scriptural sense -

i]   A Divine truth which is now revealed after being hidden from men in Old Testament times.

ii]   A Divine truth concealed from previous ages and generations but now made known to the New Testament Church.

The unveiling of the mystery is known as Paul's Revelation and it covers about two-thirds of the New Testament. The Church Age and the teachings of the MYSTERY were kept secret until the ministry of Paul - The Apostle to the Gentiles. You cannot go to the Old Testament and find any references to the Church Age.
You cannot find the Church in the 4 Gospels.
MATTHEW'S Gospel is NOT part of the mystery. Matthew Chapters 24 and 25 really concern Israel, the Tribulation and the Second Coming of Christ and not the Church Age.

Most preachers try to put the Rapture of the Church in Matthew 24 & 25 and they try to make the ten virgins apply to the Body of Christ which is unscriptural.

Child of God, I challenge you to take two Bibles and compare all the New Testament verses on the Rapture and compare them with **MATTHEW 24 & 25 : MARK 13 : LUKE 21**, and you will see that the events that take place at the Rapture do not correspond to those in **MATTHEW 24 & 25 : MARK 13 : LUKE 21.**

> 1 Thess 5:9 "for God has not appointed us to incur His wrath -
> He did not select us to condemn us - but that we might obtain His
> salvation and deliverance through our Lord Jesus Christ."

Nahum 1:2 declares that God reserves His wrath and judgment for His enemies. Those who teach that the Church is going through the Tribulation draw their scriptures from Matt 24, Mark 13 or Luke 21 and the Book of Revelation.

You **cannot** find the Church in any of the Gospels.

Rev 3:22 is the last scripture in the Book of Revelation where the words, "Church" **or** "Churches" are mentioned. All prophetic teachers agree that Chapters 6 through 19 of Revelation describe the horror of the Tribulation and the Great Tribulation period. Now if the Church were to be present on earth during the Tribulation Period as some teach, [Mid-Tribulation, Post- Tribulation] then why isn't the Church mentioned after **Revelation Chapter 3**?

The answer, of course, is that the Church will not be on earth but in heaven with the Lord Jesus Christ!

> 1 Cor 15:52   in a moment, in the twinkling of an eye, at the last
> trumpet. For the trumpet will sound, and the dead will be raised
> incorruptible, and we shall be changed.

It is interesting to note that the Greek word "Moment" is "Atomos" and it is from this Greek word that we get our English word "Atom". The New International Version says IN A FLASH. The Bible is talking about an atomic moment, the smallest particle of time, a space of time too small to be divided! THE RAPTURE OF THE CHURCH WILL TAKE PLACE IN AN ATOMIC SECOND!

OUTLINE OF SEVEN BIBLE RAPTURES

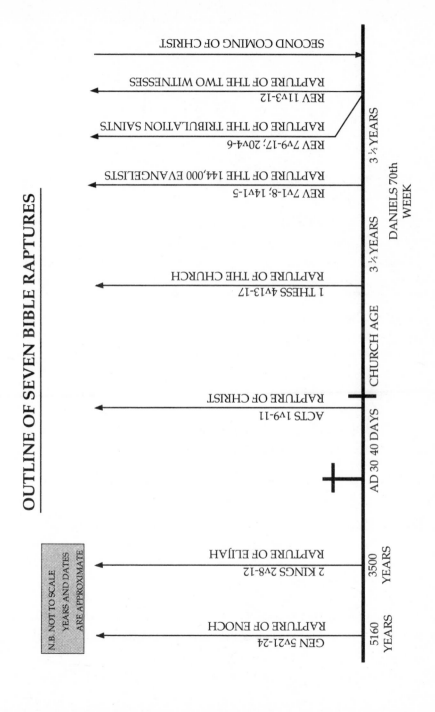

SECOND COMING OF CHRIST

RAPTURE OF THE TWO WITNESSES
REV 11v3-12

RAPTURE OF THE TRIBULATION SAINTS
REV 7v9-17; 20v4-6

3 ½ YEARS

RAPTURE OF THE 144,000 EVANGELISTS
REV 7v1-8; 14v1-5

DANIELS 70th WEEK

3 ½ YEARS

RAPTURE OF THE CHURCH
1 THESS 4v13-17

CHURCH AGE

RAPTURE OF CHRIST
ACTS 1v9-11

AD 30 40 DAYS

RAPTURE OF ELIJAH
2 KINGS 2v8-12

3500 YEARS

RAPTURE OF ENOCH
GEN 5v21-24

5160 YEARS

N.B. NOT TO SCALE
YEARS AND DATES
ARE APPROXIMATE

SEVEN BIBLE RAPTURES

(1)   The rapture of Enoch
(Genesis 5v21-24)

(2)   The rapture of Elijah
(2 Kings 2v8-12)

(3)   The rapture of our Lord Jesus Christ
(Acts 1v9-11)

Past

---

(4)   The rapture of the Church before the
Tribulation
(1 Thessalonians 4v16-18)

(5)   The rapture of the 144,000 just after the
middle of the Tribulation
(Revelation 14v1-5)

(6)   The rapture of the Tribulation saints at the
close of the Tribulation
(Revelation 7v9-17)

(7)   The rapture of the two witnesses in the
final week of the Tribulation
(Revelation 11v3-12)

Future

Read **1 THESS 4:13-18**

v.13 - God does not want His children to be ignorant! - **"Them which are asleep"**. Here Paul is referring to the Christians who had died and went on to heaven, THE SAVED DEAD, THE SAINTS IN "HEAVEN".

2 Cor 5:8   We are confident, yes, well pleased rather to be absent from the body and to be present with the Lord.

v.14 - At the Rapture, Jesus will personally bring with Him from heaven [Paradise] the spirits and souls of every departed believer so that they can be joined to their respective resurrection bodies and be a total person - SPIRIT - SOUL - BODY.

V.15 - "by the word of the Lord" This was given to Paul by special, direct revelation. God reserved the mystery of the Church Age and the Rapture as a special revelation for Paul.
"The coming of the Lord"
This does not refer to the Second Coming when Jesus returns to the earth. NO!! Here Paul is referring to the Rapture - the Coming of the Lord Jesus in the air to receive the saints to Himself.

Again let me say that you will never understand END TIME PROPHECY in the Bible unless you distinguish between the TWO FUTURE COMINGS OF JESUS:

FIRST OF ALL - Jesus is coming FOR His Church, this is called the Rapture.

SECONDLY -   Jesus is coming back to earth WITH His Church, this is called the Second Coming.

At the Rapture Jesus does not return to the earth - He appears personally in the "AIR" [ATMOSPHERE] to meet the SAINTS closing the Church Age before the Tribulation begins on earth!

The Second Coming takes place 7 years later at the end of the Tribulation period when King Jesus comes back to earth with His saints to set up His 1,000 year Kingdom on earth.

> 1 Thess 4:16,17 For the Lord Himself will descend from heaven with a shout, with the voice of an archangel, and with the trumpet of God. And the dead in Christ will rise first.
> 17 Then we who are alive and remain shall be caught up [raptured] together with them in the clouds to meet the Lord in the air. And thus we shall always be with the Lord.

At the Atomic-second Rapture - **first** of all there will take place the **resurrection of the saved dead** and **then** the **translation of the living saints**.

At the sound of the trumpet the graves will burst open and the dead saints will be raised and will receive GLORIFIED, RESURRECTION BODIES and will be RE-UNITED with their respective spirits and souls as they meet the Lord in the air.

All living believers in Christ will be instantly transformed and receive a glorified body in the likeness of Jesus' resurrection body - we will shed our earth-suit and put on a brand new glorified suit! Then we will be caught up together with the resurrected saints to be with Jesus Christ in Heaven.

"SO SHALL WE EVER BE WITH THE LORD" - WHAT COMFORT! WHAT HOPE IN THESE WORDS!

Can you imagine the global impact of this event? Suddenly,

millions of people, will disappear from this planet. These will be people from all walks of life. Pilots will instantly disappear from the cockpits in their 'planes; millions of people will suddenly disappear from behind the wheels or from the passenger seats in their cars - as they are changed, in the twinkling of an eye.

I further believe that every single child, below the age of accountability, will go in the Rapture. Oh yes even babies of unsaved parents. I believe that all children alive at the time of the Rapture will be removed with God's Church. Newscasters will remain on the air 24 hours a day as a liberal world tries to explain away that which cannot be explained - the sudden disappearance of millions and millions of people without so much a trace of where they went!

> 1 Thess 4:18   Therefore comfort one another with these words.

Notice "Comfort" - NOT confusion, NOT fear, doom or gloom! Paul under the Holy Spirit's inspiration instructs us to **comfort** each other concerning the Endtimes and the GOOD NEWS about the Rapture!

> 1 Thess 4:16-18   For the Lord Himself will descend from heaven with a shout, with the voice of an archangel, and with the trumpet of God. And the dead in Christ will rise first.
> 17   Then we who are alive and remain shall be caught up together with them in the clouds to meet the Lord in the air. And thus we shall always be with the Lord.
> 18   Therefore comfort one another with these words.

By the inspiration of the Holy Spirit, Paul is confirming here what Jesus Christ told us in John 14:1-3.

1. The Lord Jesus Christ Himself will descend from heaven to the earth's atmosphere to receive us.

2. God will resurrect the dead saints - this includes all the Old Testament saints from Adam until Calvary **PLUS** all the believers in Christ who died during the Church Age.

3. In the next instant God will supernaturally catch up **"The Living Church"** to be with the resurrected saints to meet Jesus in the air.

4. We will change our location from planet earth to heaven!

5. We are to comfort each other - encourage and edify one another with this GOOD NEWS!

There are many voices today in the Church world declaring that JUDGMENT and DOOM are coming on the Church. They tell us that the Church must be purged and purified by passing through the Tribulation. Some Christians have been so misled by this "NEGATIVE THEOLOGY" that they have headed for the hills - hidden themselves away in caves with a 7 year supply of dehydrated food and guns to protect themselves! The Tribulation is 7 years of judgment in which God's wrath is poured out upon the earth.

According to Scripture Christians will never be included in God's judgments upon the wicked.

When the wrath of God is poured out - He is not going to pour His wrath out on His Church. God will not pour out His punishment on His own children! [This would be contrary to God's Character and God's ways]. The judgment and wrath of God will be held back until we are super-naturally lifted out of the earth at the appearing of Jesus for His saints!

THE BELIEVER'S GLORIFIED BODY.

PLEASE READ 1 Cor 15:42-54 and Phil 3:20,21.

5 Characteristics of the Believer's Glorified Body.

1. A body that is identical to the resurrected body of the Lord Jesus Christ.

2. A body that is a material flesh and bone body without blood! A tangible body NOT a ghost!

3. A body that is INCORRUPTIBLE and IMMORTAL.

4. A body that is GLORIOUS and SUITABLE FOR LIVING CONDITIONS IN HEAVEN.

5. A body where our personal identity will be preserved - when Jesus rose from the dead He did not lose any of His identity.

> 1 John 3:2,3 Beloved, now we are children of God; and it has not yet been revealed what we shall be, but we know that when He is revealed, we shall be like Him, for we shall see Him as He is. 3 And everyone who has this hope in Him purifies himself, just as He is pure.

The nearness of the Rapture is the Blessed Hope of the Church and is a "Purifying" Hope for the Christian. Every Child of God, in these last days, should desire to live in holiness and be active in doing the MASTER'S work.

UNDERSTANDING 2 THESSALONIANS CHAPTER 2

TEN TRUTHS OF 2 THESS 2:1-12 THAT PAUL TAUGHT THE THESSALONIANS.

1. That it was possible to be deceived about the Rapture and the Second Coming [2 Thess 2:1-3].
2. That the Day of the Lord, or the Second Coming of Christ, was not at hand therefore, it was not the time for the Lord to be here reigning on earth [2 Thess 2:3]
3. That they were not to permit themselves to be deceived [2 Thess 2:3].
4. That this day of the Lord, or Second Coming, could not have already come because the Rapture and the revelation of the man of sin had not yet come [2 Thess 2:3].
5. That the man of sin will take over the Jewish temple at Mid -Tribulation in Jerusalem and declare himself to be "god" [2 Thess 2:4, see Rev 13].
6. That the man of sin, [the wicked one or the Antichrist], has a definite time to be revealed [2 Thess 2:6-8].
7. That "he" who hinders lawlessness and holds back the man of sin must be removed before the Antichrist will be revealed [2 Thess 2:5-8].
8. That Paul's doctrines had not changed regarding the Rapture and the day of the Lord, as false teachers had reported, even forging a letter in his name [2 Thess 2:2,5].
9. That the man of sin [Antichrist] would be destroyed by Christ at the Second Coming when the day of the Lord

begins [2 Thess 2:7,8].
10. That the Antichrist will come after the working of Satan with counterfeit power and great deceptions. [2 Thess 2:8-12, Rev 13:1-8, Dan 8:24-25, 11:37-45].

A WORD STUDY IN 2 THESSALONIANS 2:3

Paul said in this third verse that this man of sin cannot be revealed except there come **a falling away first**.

Dr. Roy Hicks states that there are two ways to interpret the Greek word APOSTASIA [translated in this third verse as "falling away"]. This word APOSTASIA is interpreted by some scholars to mean "falling away" or "rebellion". However, the other interpretation of the word by excellent Greek scholars is "departure". Tyndale, for example, translated it in this way in his first translation from Greek to English.

Dr. Hicks says that Greek scholars agree that to pinpoint the true meaning of the Greek noun, it is necessary to look at the verb from which that noun is derived. The Greek noun APOSTASIA comes from the root verb APHISTEMI, meaning "to go away, depart, remove". This root verb is used 15 times in the Bible, and in only 3 of those times does it speak of falling away. It is most often translated "depart", and usually refers to "one person departing from another person or place".

The results of consulting several Bibles **from the 15th Century** present 2 Thess 2:3 as follows:

> **"Let no man deceive you by any meanes for [that day shall not come], except there come a departing first, and that man of sinne be disclosed, [even the sonne of perdition..."] {Geneva Bible}.**

"Let no man deceave you by eny meanes, for the Lorde shall not come excepte there come a departynge fyrst, and that synful man be opened, the sonne of perdicyon ..."{Great Bible}.

"Let no man deceave you by eny meanes, for the Lorde cometh not, excepte ther come a departinge fyrst, and that that synfull man be opened, the sonne of perdicion ..."{Tyndale}.

Then we come to the translation of an excellent, widely recognised commentator, Kenneth S. Wuest who in the New Testament - an Expanded Translation - translates 2 Thess 2:3 as follows:

"Do not begin to allow anyone to lead you astray in any way, because that day shall not come except the aforementioned departure [of the Church to heaven] comes first and the man of lawlessness is disclosed [in his true identity], the man of perdition..."

John Lineberry, B.A. translates 2 Thess 2:3; "Do not let anyone beguile you in any way, because the day will not come [day of the Lord] except there comes the departure [Rapture of the Church first] and the man of lawlessness be revealed [unveiled, uncovered] the son of perdition [eternal misery, doom and destruction]."

Our final word about the concept of using the word DEPARTURE instead of FALLING AWAY - Peter's sermon on the day of the outpouring of the Holy Spirit refers to Joel 2:28,29, where he said, "It shall come to pass in the last days ..." [Acts 2:17]. What shall come to pass in these last days? A great falling away? Never- no, never! What will come to pass, even beginning then, is A MIGHTY OUTPOURING OF THE HOLY SPIRIT on all flesh. A person who insists on the use of "falling away" in 2 Thess 2:3 and who sees the Church in rebellion, apostasy and backslidden has contradicted Peter's sermon and the Old Testament prophecy from Joel.

WHO OR WHAT IS THE RESTRAINER OF LAWLESSNESS?

2 Thess 2:7,8 For the mystery of lawlessness is already at work; only he who now restrains will do so until he is taken out of the way.
8   And then the lawless one will be revealed, whom the Lord will consume with the breath of His mouth and destroy with the brightness of His coming.

Paul definitely said that the restrainer of lawlessness would continue to restrain lawlessness UNTIL HE BE TAKEN OUT OF THE WAY **and then** shall the wicked be revealed whom the Lord shall destroy at His Second Coming.

3 Things that Restrain Lawlessness in the World Today ;

1.   Human Governments [Gen 9:1-8, Rom 13].

2.   The Holy Spirit [John 14:16, 15:26, 16:7-11].

3.   The Church [Matt 5:13-16, 1 Peter 4:10-19].

In no scripture in the two letters to the Thessalonians did Paul mention governments or the Holy Spirit as being taken out of the world, but he repeatedly referred to the Church as being raptured out of the world and from the earth. [1 Thess 1:10, 2:19-20, 5:1-11, 2 Thess 2:1,7-8]. We must therefore conclude that the Church is the restrainer of lawlessness, and for the following reasons.

1. HUMAN GOVERNMENTS will never be taken out of
    the world to permit the revelation of the Antichrist. He,
    himself, will even reign over 10 kingdoms when he
    comes [Rev 17:8-17], and many other governments will
    be here in other parts of the world throughout all the
    days that the man of sin [Antichrist] will be here.

2. THE HOLY SPIRIT **will never be taken from the
    world,** for Jesus promised "that He may abide with you
    forever" [John 14:16]. As the agent of salvation [Titus
    3:5], the Holy Spirit will still be here actively working
    throughout the Tribulation and the reign of the Anti-
    christ. He therefore could not be the restrainer of law-
    lessness referred to, that will be taken out of the way.

3. THE CHURCH will be taken out of the world by the
    Rapture. It is the only one of the above mentioned 3
    restrainers of lawlessness that is to be taken out of the
    world, so it must be the restrainer of 2 Thess 2:7,8. That
    this restrainer of lawlessness will literally be taken out
    of the world is clear from the statement, "ek mesou
    genetai," which means "out of the midst be gone" [2
    Thess 2:7-8]. The Greek phrase "ek mesou" literally
    means "from among".

So rejoice child of God because when the 7 years Tribulation
starts you will not be here on earth. You will already be in
Heaven with God the Father, Jesus and the multiplied
millions of other Raptured saints! Glory to God!

> **Rev 19:6 And I heard, as it were, the voice of a great multitude,
> as the sound of many waters and as the sound of mighty
> thunderings, saying, "Alleluia! For the Lord God Omnipotent
> reigns!"**

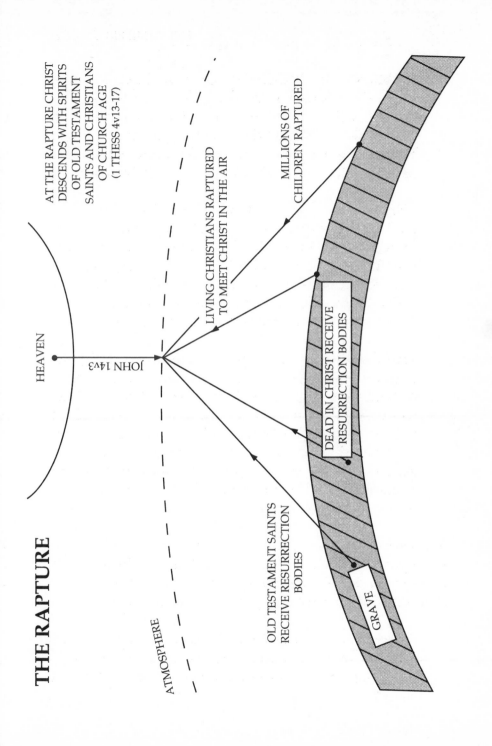

THE RAPTURE

HEAVEN

JOHN 14v3

ATMOSPHERE

AT THE RAPTURE CHRIST DESCENDS WITH SPIRITS OF OLD TESTAMENT SAINTS AND CHRISTIANS OF CHURCH AGE (1 THESS 4v13-17)

MILLIONS OF CHILDREN RAPTURED

LIVING CHRISTIANS RAPTURED TO MEET CHRIST IN THE AIR

DEAD IN CHRIST RECEIVE RESURRECTION BODIES

OLD TESTAMENT SAINTS RECEIVE RESURRECTION BODIES

GRAVE

7 FACTS ABOUT THE BELIEVER'S GLORIFIED BODY

(1)   It will be a recognizable body - our personal identity will be preserved. When Jesus rose from the dead He did not lose any of His identity
1 Corinthians 13v12

(2)   It will be a body like the resurrection body of our Lord Jesus Christ
1 John 3v2

(3)   It will be a glorious body and suitable for living conditions in heaven
1 Corinthians 15v43

(4)   It will be an incorruptible, immortal and eternal body
1 Corinthians 15v42

(5)   It will be a body of material flesh and bone and a body that will permit eating
Luke 24v41-43

(6)   It will be a body in which the Spirit controls and governs
1 Corinthians 15v49

(7)   It will be a body unlimited by time, gravity or space
John 20v19,26

CHAPTER 11:
END TIME CONFUSION???

Right at this present time, and for a number of years in the Church, there has been false teaching and false "theories" about the Rapture. [Brother Kenneth Hagin says **a theory** is a supposition established upon ignorance of the subject under discussion!]

There has been much confusion about when the Born Again believers will be raptured - is it going to be before, in the middle or at the end of the Tribulation period? There has also been confusion about the Rapture and the Second Coming of Christ because many pastors have preached to their congregations as if the Rapture and the Second Coming were the same event.

So it is our intention in this chapter with the Word of God and with the help of the Holy Spirit, to clear all confusion from your mind.

FALSE TEACHINGS ABOUT THE RAPTURE.

1. **That the Rapture is the same as the Second Coming of Christ.**

This is unscriptural because at the Rapture Jesus **comes for His saints** in the air, while at the Second Coming He literally and physically comes back to the earth, **with His saints**. [See Jude 14,15, Rev 19:11-16].

2. **That the Rapture will include only "Spiritual" Christians -**

that carnal Christians will miss the Rapture and be left behind on earth to endure the 7 year Tribulation.
This teaching is inconsistent with God's Word which clearly informs us that, at the Rapture, Jesus will "catch away" the **entire** body of Christ, both spiritual and carnal Christians.

> 1 Cor 15:51 Behold, I tell you a mystery: We shall not all sleep, but we shall all be changed
> N.B "WE shall ALL be changed"

> 2 Cor 5:10   For we must all appear before the Judgment Seat of Christ, that each one may receive the things done in the body, according to what he has done, whether good or bad.
> N.B. "WE must ALL stand at the Judgment Seat of Christ."

This "partial" Rapture or "overcomers" Rapture teaches that not all believers will be taken at the translation of the Church, but rather only those who are "watching" and "waiting" for that event, who have reached some degree of spiritual attainment that makes them worthy to be included. This "limited" or "selective" Rapture is based on Heb 9:28 and Luke 21:36 and teaches that only a prepared and expectant section of believers will be translated and that only those overcoming Christians will be taken who "wait", "look for", and "have loved His appearing."
Do you possibly think that when Jesus, the **Head** of the Church, appears for His Body that He will leave behind on earth His left leg or His right hand? The parable of the ten virgins in Matt 25 has got nothing to do with the Church or the Rapture - although some have preached great sermons on this!

Surely if **ALL** the "DEAD IN CHRIST" [1 Thess 4:16-18] will be resurrected at the Rapture then certainly ALL who are "ALIVE IN CHRIST" will be raptured. If only the OVERCOMING SAINTS are worthy to be raptured then millions of the "DEAD IN CHRIST" who lived carnal Christian lives will not be resurrected on that day but be left in the grave.

Supporters of the **Partial Rapture theory**, as well as those who believe that the Church must go through some or all of the Tribulation, contend that Tribulation is necessary to purify the Church and make her ready for the Bridegroom. This belief contends for a kind of "Protestant purgatory". If the saints, alive at the end of the age, need purging by tribulation, it would seem that the Lord would need to resurrect the dead saints for a period of tribulation previous to **their** rapture. An absurd thought of course!

The main purpose of the believers standing before Jesus at the Judgment Seat in heaven is to receive CROWNS and REWARDS for living as overcoming saints on earth. According to 1 Cor chapter 3 the "spiritual" believers have produced quality works of GOLD, SILVER AND PRECIOUS STONES and will be in line for "Heavenly Awards".
Carnal believers have nothing but works of **wood, hay and stubble** and ,yes, they are definitely in heaven, but they will have no crowns and no rewards.

3. The Non-Rapture Theory.

Many "modern" denominations have completely rejected any concept of the Rapture. These denominations, in their repudiation of **literal** interpretation of the Scripture, have completely suppressed any consideration of our Lord Jesus

Christ's returning physically to reign as King of kings and Lord of lords. It is not surprising, therefore, that they also reject the idea that His Body will rise to meet Him in the clouds at the **time** of His appearing for the Church.

4.   The Mid-Tribulation Rapture Theory.

The Mid-Tribulation Rapture theory teaches that all born again believers will go through the first $3\frac{1}{2}$ years of the Tribulation on earth and be caught up at the MID-POINT. The reason is given that the CHURCH must first be purged, purified and perfected **before** being raptured.

The Mid-Tribulation position is erroneous because God's ordained method of perfecting the saints is by the double agency of the Holy Spirit and the Word of God.
The purpose of the 5 fold ministry God set in the Church is to "PERFECT" and "EQUIP" the Body of Christ. [Eph 4:11,12].

Those who teach a Mid-Tribulation Rapture say that the last trumpet, mentioned in connection with the Rapture in 1 Cor 15:52, is identified with the seventh trumpet sounded in Rev 11:15 which occurs in the middle of the Tribulation [Rev 11:2,3]. If the two trumpets are identical, then the Rapture occurs in the middle of the Tribulation.
However the trumpets in 1 Cor 15 and Rev 11 are NOT the same. Paul's "trump of God" is a trumpet call of victory over death; John's seventh trumpet is the seventh in a series of announcements of judgments upon the wicked. DO NOT CONFUSE THESE TRUMPETS!

5. The Post-Tribulation Rapture Theory.

This teaches that all the saints of God will continue on the earth through all of the 7 year Tribulation period and be caught up on the final day of the Tribulation at the same time Jesus is returning to the earth at the Second Coming. It is impossible that the character and nature of God, our Heavenly Father, would cause His own children to suffer His wrath and the horrendous effects of the 7 year Tribulation period when the Bible states that God reserves His wrath for His enemies.

> **Nahum 1:2 God is jealous, and the Lord avenges; The Lord avenges and is furious. The Lord will take vengeance on His adversaries, And He reserves His wrath for <u>His enemies;</u>**

If the Church is going to be raptured only at the end of the Tribulation then there is no time for the Believer's Judgment seat or the Marriage Supper of the Lamb - there is not even time for a "coffee break"!
We could safely call this the great "U" turn theory.

THE TRUTH OF SCRIPTURE is PRE-TRIBULATION RAPTURE. For the Church will be raptured before the 7 year Tribulation begins and **will not** go through any part of the Tribulation. The Rapture of the Church is a valid, documented scriptural fact - a fact that cannot be denied.

We believe that the Rapture could take place at any moment. We do not believe there is any Scripture that must be fulfilled before the Rapture can take place. [There are many Scriptures that must be fulfilled before the Second Coming but not before the Rapture.]

We believe that the Church will be taken out of this earth before the Tribulation bursts upon the world scene and that, as stated, the Rapture could take place at any moment.

We believe this is a purifying hope that serves two necessary purposes for the Christian: first, as a source of motivation and, secondly, as a source of consecration.

It is all too common today to hear preachers denounce the doctrine of the Rapture. These individuals influence many people, and, depending upon which one a person listens to, he is told to expect many different events to occur in the near future. Some teachers state that the Antichrist will appear very soon. Others tell us that the Church must go through the Tribulation period in order to be purified.

BUT WHAT DOES THE BIBLE SAY?

Nowhere do we find within the Word of God that the Church is to look for the appearing of the Antichrist. Neither does the Bible tell us that the Church will have to be purified during the Tribulation. What it **DOES** tell us is to look for the blessed hope of **"the glorious appearing of the great God and our Saviour Jesus Christ"** [Titus 2:13].

THE DIFFERENCE BETWEEN THE RAPTURE AND THE SECOND COMING.

We should **not confuse** these two end time events because they are two entirely individual and distinct events separated by seven years.

THE RAPTURE takes place first and occurs before the

IS THE RAPTURE .....

PRE TRIBULATION ?	<u>YES</u>
MID TRIBULATION ?	NO
POST TRIBULATION ?	NO

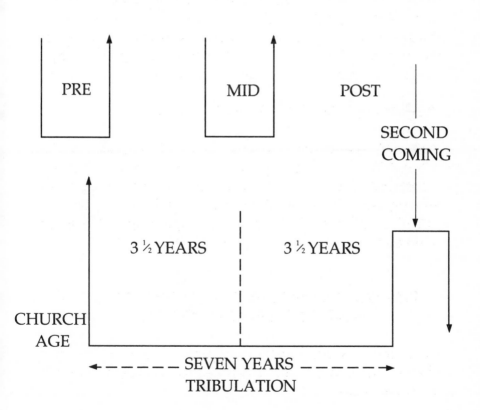

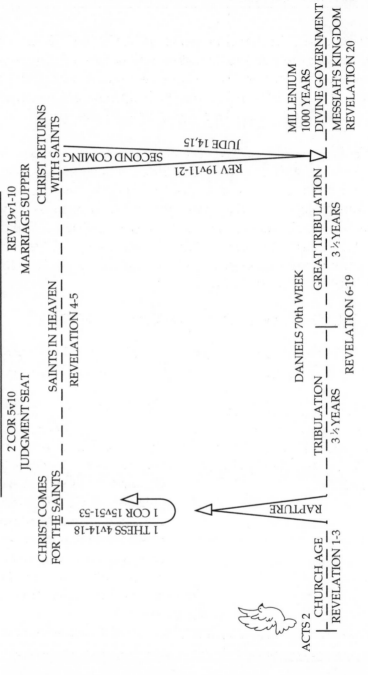

GOD'S UNFOLDING PLAN FOR MAN

REV 19v1-10
MARRIAGE SUPPER

2 COR 5v10
JUDGMENT SEAT

CHRIST RETURNS
WITH SAINTS

SAINTS IN HEAVEN

REVELATION 4-5

CHRIST COMES
FOR THE SAINTS

1 THESS 4v14-18

1 COR 15v51-53

SECOND COMING

JUDE 14,15

REV 19v11-21

MILLENIUM
1000 YEARS
DIVINE GOVERNMENT
MESSIAH'S KINGDOM
REVELATION 20

GREAT TRIBULATION
3½ YEARS

DANIELS 70th WEEK

REVELATION 6-19

TRIBULATION
3½ YEARS

RAPTURE

CHURCH AGE
REVELATION 1-3

ACTS 2

Tribulation. At that time Jesus will **COME FOR** the saints and meet them in the air, take them to heaven and present them to the Father. For 7 years they will remain in heaven where they will stand before the Judgment of Rewards and then partake in the Marriage Supper of the Lamb.

THE SECOND COMING OF CHRIST takes place 7 years after the Rapture and at that time Jesus comes back to the earth bringing all the saints WITH HIM. At the Second Coming Jesus, as King of kings and Lord of lords, defeats the Antichrist and his armies at Armageddon and then will establish the Millennial Kingdom on earth. The Second Coming cannot take place until after the events of Revelation Chapters 4-19 are fulfilled.

SCRIPTURAL COMPARISON BETWEEN:

THE RAPTURE OF THE CHURCH	THE SECOND COMING OF CHRIST.
John 14:3 "And if I go and prepare a place for you, I will come again and receive you to Myself; that where I am, there you may be also."	Jude 14,15 Now Enoch, the seventh from Adam, prophesied about these men also, saying, "Behold, the Lord comes with ten thousands of His saints, to execute judgment on all, to convict them of all their ungodly deeds which they have committed in an ungodly way, and of all the harsh things which ungodly sinners have spoken against Him."
1 Cor 15:51,52 Behold, I tell you a mystery: We shall not all sleep,	Zech 14:4,5 And in that day His feet will stand on the Mount of

but we shall all be changed - in a moment, in the twinkling of an eye, at the last trumpet. For the trumpet will sound, and the dead will be raised incorruptible, and we shall be changed.

Olives, Which faces Jerusalem in the east. And the Mount of Olives shall be split in two, from east to west, Making a very large valley; Half of the mountain shall move toward the north and half of it toward the south. Then you shall flee through My mountain valley, For the mountain valley shall reach to Azal. Yes, you shall flee as you fled from the earthquake. In the days of Uzziah king of Judah. Thus the Lord my God will come, and all the saints with You.

1 Thess 4:16,17 For the Lord Himself will descend from heaven with a shout, with the voice of an archangel, and with the trumpet of God. And the dead in Christ will rise first.
Then we who are alive and remain shall be caught up together with them in the clouds to meet the Lord in the air. And thus we shall always be with the Lord.

Matt 24:29,30 "Immediately after the Tribulation of those days the sun will be darkened, and the moon will not give its light; the stars will fall from heaven, and the powers of the heavens will be shaken. Then the sign of the Son of Man will appear in heaven, and then all the tribes of the earth will mourn, and they will see the Son of Man coming on the clouds of heaven with power and great glory."

Phil 3:20,21 For our citizenship is in heaven, from which we also eagerly wait for the Saviour, the Lord Jesus Christ, who will

Matt 25:31 "When the Son of Man comes in His glory, and all the holy angels with Him, then He will sit on the throne of His glory.

transform our lowly body that it may be conformed to His glorious body, according to the working by which He is able to subdue all things to Himself.

2 Thess 2:1 Now brethren, concerning the coming of our Lord Jesus Christ and our gathering together to Him...

2 Thess 2:8 And then the lawless one will be revealed, whom the Lord will consume with the breath of His mouth and destroy with the brightness of His coming.

Col 3:4 When Christ who is our life appears, then you also will appear with Him in glory.

Micah 1:3,4 For behold the Lord is coming out of His place; He will come down and tread on the high places of the earth. The mountains will melt under Him, and the valleys will split like wax before the fire, like waters poured down a steep place.

1 John 2:28 And now, little children, abide in Him, that when He appears, we may have confidence and not be ashamed before Him at His coming.

Rev 1:7 Behold, He is coming with the clouds, and every eye will see Him, and they also who pierced Him. And all the tribes of the earth will mourn because of Him.

1 Peter 5:4 And when the Chief Shepherd appears, you will receive the crown of glory that does not fade away.

Rev 19:11,14 Then I saw heaven opened, and behold, a white horse. And He who sat on him was called Faithful and True, and in His righteousness He judges and makes war. And the armies in heaven, clothed in fine linen, white and clean, followed Him on white horses.

Titus 2:12,13 teaching us that, denying ungodliness and worldly lusts, we should live soberly, righteously, and godly in the present age, looking for the blessed hope and glorious appearing of our great God and Saviour Jesus Christ.

2 Thess 1:7-9 And to give you who are troubled rest with us when the Lord Jesus is revealed from heaven with His mighty angels, in flaming fire taking vengeance on those who do not know God, and on those who do not obey the gospel of our Lord Jesus Christ. These shall be punished with everlasting destruction from the presence of the Lord and from the glory of His power.

1 John 3:2 Beloved, now we are children of God; and it has not yet been revealed what we shall be, but we know that when He is revealed, we shall be like Him, for we shall see him as He is.

Job 19:25 For I know that my Redeemer lives, And He shall stand at last on the earth;

THE PURPOSE OF THE RAPTURE.

1. For Christ to receive the saints of all past ages to Himself [John 14:1-3].

2. To resurrect the dead "in Christ" from among the wicked dead [1 Thess 4:13-17].

3. To take the saints to heaven where they will receive judgment for works done in the body; receive their rewards; and partake in the marriage supper [John 14:1-3, 2 Cor 5:10, Rev 19:1-11].

4. To bring great joy to soul winners [1 Thess 2:19-20].

5. To change the saints from mortality to immortality [1 Cor 15:51-56, Phil 3:21].

6. To permit the revelation of the Antichrist [2 Thess 2:1-8].

7. To present the Church to Himself [Eph 5:27].

8. To give the saints a crown of righteousness [2 Tim 4:8].

9. To give the saints the reality of the blessed hope [Titus 2:13].

10. To make the saints like Christ [1 John 3:2].

11. To take the saints out of the earth for the duration of the Tribulation [2 Thess 2:1-3].

12. To end the Church age and make it possible for God to

deal more exclusively with Israel to fulfill, with them, the last day prophecies [Dan 9:27, Matt 24 & 25].

N.B. If there were no Rapture until the Second Coming of Christ then all of these purposes would be cancelled.

THE PURPOSE OF THE SECOND COMING OF CHRIST.

1.   Christ is coming to judge the living nations [Matt 25:31-46].

2.   He is coming to defeat the Antichrist and his armies at Armageddon [Rev 19:11-21, Jude 14,15, and 2 Thess 2:7,8].

3.   He is coming to execute righteousness and justice on earth [Isa 11:3-9, Jer 23:5-6].

4.   He is coming to reign over all nations [Rev 19:11-21].

5.   He is coming to establish the raptured saints as kings and priests [Matt 19:28, Rev 20:4-6].

6.   He is coming to put down all rebellion on earth [1 Cor 15:24-28].

7.   He is coming to remove every curse from the earth [Romans 8:19-22].

8.   He is coming to bring universal peace and prosperity [Isa 2:2-4, Mic 4:1-7].

9. He is coming to establish Jerusalem as the capital of the world [Jer 3:17, Zech 14].

10. He is coming to cast the Antichrist and the false prophet into the lake of fire [Rev 19:20].

CONTRASTS BETWEEN:

RAPTURE OF THE CHURCH.	SECOND COMING OF CHRIST
1. It occurs before the Tribulation [Luke 21:36].	1. It occurs after the Tribulation [Matt 24:29,30].
2. Christ comes for the saints [1 Thess 4:13-17].	2. Christ comes with the saints [Jude 14, Rev 19:11-21].
3. Christ takes the saints to heaven [John 14:3].	3. Christ brings the saints back to earth [Zech 14:4,5, Rev 19:14].
4. Christ returns to the clouds [1 Thess 4:17].	4. Christ returns to the earth [Zech 14:4,5].
5. Christ is not seen [1 Cor 15:52].	5. Every eye shall see Christ [Rev 1:7].
6. It is the blessed hope of the Church [Titus 2:13].	6. It is the great day of His wrath [Rev 19:15].
7. At the Rapture Christ does not come to destroy the Antichrist but to remove the Church, so that the Antichrist can be revealed [2 Thess 2:1-8].	7. At the Second Coming, Christ comes back to the earth with all the saints of all the ages to destroy the Antichrist and his forces [Rev 19:11-21].

8. At the Rapture there will be no Battle of Armageddon [1 Thess 4:16].

8. At the Second Coming Armageddon will be fought [Zech 14].

9. At the time of the Rapture no man on earth will know who the Antichrist is [2 Thess 2:7,8].

9. At the Second Coming all men on earth will know who He is [Rev 13:16-18].

10. There will be a 7 year period of Tribulation after the Rapture [Dan 9:27].

10. There will be no Tribulation at all after the Second Coming , for this ends all Tribulation.

11. The Rapture is a mystery that is not revealed in the Old Testament Scriptures.

11. The Second Coming is revealed in both the Old and the New Testaments.

12. After the Rapture the saints will be rewarded in heaven at the Judgment Seat of Christ according to their works.

12. After the Second Coming, Christ judges the living nations here on the earth.

GUARD YOURSELF AGAINST OTHER FALSE TEACHINGS...

PROPHETIC DATE-SETTING.

Many prophecy teachers have attempted, and they are still trying, to predict the dates for the Rapture and the Second Coming of Christ! DON'T SET DATES - the Bible absolutely forbids it - Matt 24:36 and Mark 13:32,33.

> Mark 13:32,33 "But of that day and hour no one knows, neither the angels in heaven, nor the Son, but only the Father.
> 33 Take heed, watch and pray; for you do not know when the time is.

THE 144,000

Some are teaching that God has already selected and is preparing the 144,000 born again Jewish evangelists for their special assignment during the Tribulation! This is false because if they are born again and being prepared today then they would go up in the Rapture.

Child of God, the only way you can avoid deception and stay out of false doctrine is by **staying in** God's Word and **staying with** God's Word! What the Bible teaches is paramount, forget about some man's teaching based on guesswork, sensationalism, speculation or complex mathematical calculations!!

Stay with the Bible and you will live free from deception.

> 2 John 9,10 Whoever transgresses and does not abide in the doctrine of Christ does not have God. He who abides in the doctrine of Christ has both the Father and the Son.
> 10 If anyone comes to you and does not bring this doctrine, do not receive him into your house nor greet him;

CHAPTER 12:
WHY THE CHURCH MUST BE RAPTURED BEFORE THE TRIBULATION.

The Pre-Tribulation Rapture defined: holds that the Church, the Body of Christ in its entirety, will, by resurrection and translation, be removed from the earth before any part of the seven year Tribulation period.

1 Cor 15:51-54 Behold, I tell you a mystery; We shall not all sleep, but we shall all be changed -
52 in a moment, in the twinkling of an eye, at the last trumpet. For the trumpet will sound, and the dead will be raised incorruptible, and we shall be changed.
53 For this corruptible must put on incorruption, and this mortal must put on immortality.
54 So when this corruptible has put on incorruption, and this mortal has put on immortality, then shall be brought to pass the saying that is written: "Death is swallowed up in victory."

1 Thess 4:16-18 For the Lord Himself will descend from heaven with a shout, with the voice of an archangel, and with the trumpet of God. And the dead in Christ will rise first.
17 Then we who are alive and remain shall be caught up together with them in the clouds to meet the Lord in the air. And thus we shall always be with the Lord.
18 Therefore comfort one another with these words.

Titus 2:13 looking for the blessed hope and glorious appearing of our great God and Saviour Jesus Christ,

Child of God, you must understand that the Church has to be caught up, otherwise there will never be a Tribulation period, there will never be an Antichrist, there will never be a mark of the Beast.

8 REASONS WHY THE CHURCH MUST BE RAPTURED BEFORE THE 7 YEAR TRIBULATION PERIOD.

1. Because of the Nature and Character of Our Heavenly Father.

     Psalm 145:8,9 The Lord is gracious and full of compassion, Slow to anger and great in mercy.
     9   The Lord is good to all, And His tender mercies are over all His good works.

As I look at God's Character revealed in His Word, I just cannot see a great and loving God pouring out His wrath upon His own children - children bought and saved through the power of His Son's blood shed at Calvary. It doesn't make sense.

Since the Church is the Body of Christ, of which Jesus is the Head [Eph 1:22, 5:23, Col 1:18], the Bride, of which He is the Bridegroom [1 Cor 11:3, Eph 5:23], the object of His love [Eph 5:25], the branch of which He is the Root and Stem [John 15:5], the building of which He is the Foundation and Cornerstone [1 Cor 3:9, Eph 2:19-22], there exists between the believer and the Lord a union and a unity. The believer is brought into the closest oneness with Him. If the Church is in the 70th week, she is subject to wrath, judgments and the horrendous plagues which characterises the period. This **absolutely** contradicts the character of God our

Heavenly Father in relation to His own Covenant Children.

2.   Because we are Christ's Ambassadors.

2 Cor 5:20 tells us that the Christian is an ambassador for Christ. Before a nation declares war on another nation, it first calls it's ambassadors home. God will call us home via the Rapture before He begins to pour out His wrath on this sin-cursed earth. God took Lot out of Sodom before He poured out the fire and the brimstone. The TRIBULATION is that period of time in which GOD'S WRATH is POURED OUT on the earth prior to the 1,000 year reign of Christ.

> **Rev 6:15-17   And the kings of the earth, the great men, the rich men, the commanders, the mighty men, every slave and every free man, hid themselves in the caves and in the rocks of the mountains,**
> **16   and said to the mountains and rocks, "Fall on us and hide us from the face of Him who sits on the throne and from the wrath of the Lamb!**
> **17   "For the great day of His wrath has come, and who is able to stand?"**

Chapters 6 through 19 of Revelation give a detailed description of the Tribulation, but the Church is not mentioned once in any of these chapters. **Why?** Simply because God has called His Ambassadors home!

3.   Because the Bible teaches that God never Judges and Destroys the Righteous with the Unrighteous.

> 1] The flood - Righteous Noah and his family were not judged or destroyed with the wicked.

2] Righteous Lot was taken out of Sodom before
the wicked were judged and destroyed.

Mal 3:6   For I am the Lord, I do not change;

Hebrews 13:8   Jesus Christ is the same yesterday, today and
forever.

4.   Because of the Evidence that the words "Church" and "Churches" are not mentioned again after Rev 3:22.

After **Rev 3:22**, the words "Church" and "Churches" do not
again appear as referring to a Church present on earth. If the
Church were to be present on earth during the Tribulation
period, surely it would be mentioned in the Word of God
after the third chapter of Revelation. But **it is not** mentioned!
Doesn't it seem strange, if the Church of the living God were
to be present during the Tribulation, that God would have
mentioned it in His Word? He speaks at great length about
the Church during the first 3 chapters. Why is the subject
suddenly dropped if the Church is to play a prominent role
during this period? The answer? Of course, the Church will
not be on earth during the Tribulation!

Study Matt 16:18, Mark 16:17,18, Acts 2:4, James 4:7 etc. and
ask yourself where in Rev 6-19 is God's army, the "Church",
resisting the devil, healing the sick, speaking in tongues,
using the Name of Jesus, raising the dead and casting out
demons. That supernatural body of Christ is nowhere in
evidence on the earth during the Tribulation period because
it has already been transferred to heaven!

On the other hand, after Rev 4:1, the evidence of Israel is
seen everywhere in the book of Revelation. If you will
notice, Israel is not mentioned at all during the first three

chapters. This clarifies that two particular groups are being dealt with in the different parts of this book. First, the Church is talked about up to the time of the end of Chapter 3, which marks the instant of the Rapture. After this, the references to the Church cease and great attention is given to Israel. Reference to Israel fills the book of Revelation in Chapters 4 through 19.

The Tribulation period is not a Church period, but is the final week of Daniel's vision regarding God dealing with Israel: Seventy weeks are determined upon THY people and upon THY HOLY CITY, to finish the transgression, and to make an end of sins, and to make reconciliation for iniquity, and to bring in everlasting righteousness..." [Dan 9:24, also 25-27]. The Tribulation period is called by Jeremiah "Jacob's trouble" [Jer 30:4-7].
In actuality, the Tribulation period will principally involve Israel, and it will continue through Revelation - especially from chapters 6 through 19. Focus your attention on Israel as you read these chapters. Study the Hebrew character of the Book of Revelation after chapter 3.

Child of God, its an interesting thought that if you read and study the Epistles, the letters to the Churches;

i]   There is no mention of the Church going through the Tribulation.

ii] There are no survival instructions given to the Church for that time. The reason is quite simple ... THE CHURCH WILL BE IN HEAVEN AT THAT TIME AND NOT ON THE EARTH.

5.   Because of God's definite Promises to the Church.

There are certain passages of Scripture which definitely promise the removal of the Church before the 7 year Tribulation.

> **Rev 3:10** "Because you have kept My command to persevere, I also will keep you from the hour of trial [the Tribulation], which shall come upon the whole world, to test those who dwell on the earth".

Thayer says that, from the Greek used here it would indicate that John is promising a removal from the sphere of testing, not a preservation through it. This is further substantiated by the use of the words, "the hour". God is not only guarding us from the trials but from the very hour itself when these trials will come upon the earth dwellers.

> **1 Thess 5:9 [Amp]** "For God has not appointed us to incur His wrath - He did not select us to condemn us - but that we might obtain salvation and deliverance through our Lord Jesus Christ".

> **Nahum 1:2(b),3(a)**   The Lord will take vengeance on His adversaries, And He reserves wrath for His enemies; The Lord is slow to anger and great in power, And will not at all acquit the wicked.

6.   **2 Thessalonians 2:6-8 offers Clear Proof that the Church must be Raptured before the Tribulation begins.**

This Scripture leaves no doubt whatsoever as to when the Rapture will take place:

> **2 Thess 2:6-8** And now you know what is restraining, that he may

be revealed in his own time.

7   For the mystery of lawlessness is already at work; only he who now restrains will do so until he is taken out of the way.

8   And then the lawless one will be revealed, whom the Lord will consume with the breath of His mouth and destroy with the brightness of His coming.

The question here is this: What restrains or hinders the powers of darkness from having full sway today? What **prevents** the powers of darkness from revealing the Antichrist at this time? There are **three** forces I can think of which impede the revelation of the Antichrist. These are governments, the Church and the Holy Spirit. The hindrance mentioned here **has** to come from one of these three sources.

Obviously, the governments of the world will not be removed from the earth because they will become even **more** prominent during the period of the Tribulation. [Governments will not really **hinder** the Antichrist, they will, in fact, aid and abet his programmes.] The Holy Spirit will obviously not be taken out of the world during the Tribulation because Rev 7:9-17 establishes that multitudes will be saved during this period. John 3:5-8, Rom 8:9 and Eph 2:18 attest that no man is saved **except** through the ministry of the Holy Spirit.

Acts 2:17-21 also clearly states that during the Tribulation the Holy Spirit will be present on earth. I am well aware that some believe [and teach] that the Holy Spirit **will** be removed, but prayerful reading of these [and other] Scriptures should confirm that this is **not** the case. So, with two of the three constraining factors **present** during the Tribulation, we must conclude that it is the third factor which is removed. And what is the third factor? The Church, of course!

The Church then WILL be removed and, upon its removal, the Antichrist will be revealed. Careful reading of this Scripture should convince even the most sceptical that it is the Church pointed to in this particular segment of the Word of God, and that it is only **after** the withdrawal of the Church that the Antichrist will be revealed ... and allowed to pursue his vicious ends.

So the evidence of 2 Thess 2:1-8 proves that the Church must be raptured before the Tribulation can begin and the Antichrist revealed.

In Matt 5:13,14 - the Church is likened to the salt of the earth - salt prevents corruption taking place and gives flavour and savour [2 Cor 2:14].

The Church is also likened to the Light of the World - light dispels darkness. With the removal of the Church, the forces of darkness and corruption take over - the Antichrist can then be revealed!

7.   **Because of the Evidence of the 24 Elders in Heaven before the Tribulation begins.**

In Revelation chapters 4 and 5, the apostle John describes the Church in heaven. They are represented by the 24 Elders. Why 24 Elders representing the Church? 12 to represent the righteous tribes of 'srael and 12 to represent the New Testament saints. The New Jerusalem described in Revelation 21 includes both companies [Rev 21:12,14]. The full description of these 24 elders fits every believer. They have to be representatives because the number 24 is itself a symbolic figure. But even without the number 24 being symbolic of the Church, the word ELDER alone is enough to indicate that this passage does not refer literally to 24 men.

In the New Testament an ELDER always represents the Church before God. The 24 elders are not a company complete within themselves; they are just representatives of the Church which is in heaven.

> **Rev 4:4 "Around the throne were twenty-four thrones, and on the thrones I saw twenty-four elders sitting, clothed in white robes; and they had crowns of gold on their heads.**

The name ELDER is never applied to angels, neither do angels have "crowns" and sit on "thrones". Only redeemed MEN are promised "thrones" and "crowns". Rev 3:21, 1 Peter 5:2-4, 2 Tim 4:8. These "ELDERS" then must be representative of the Old and New Testament saints, that have been redeemed by the BLOOD OF CHRIST.

That these Elders were REDEEMED MEN is further evidenced by the "SONG" they sing:

> **Rev 5:9,10 And they sang a new song, saying: "You are worthy to take the scroll, And to open its seals; For You were slain, And You have redeemed us to God by Your blood Out of every tribe and tongue and people and nation, And have made us kings and priests to our God; And we shall reign on the earth."**

Now, this could not be said of angels, or any other created heavenly beings, for they have not been redeemed by the blood of the Lamb, nor are they to be "kings" and "priests" on the earth.

The word "Elder" in the majority of places where it is used in the Scriptures means the representative head of a city, family, tribe or nation, so the "four and twenty Elders" are representative of the redeemed human race.
The "Elders" are representative of both the Old and the New Testament saints. The Old Testament saints are represented by the 12 tribes of Israel and the New Testament saints by the 12 Apostles of the Lamb. They together make up 24 representative characters. This distinction is clearly brought out in the description of the New Jerusalem, where the 12 foundation stones are named after the 12 Apostles of the Lamb, and the 12 gates after the 12 tribes of Israel [Rev 21:10-14].

So these 24 representative characters [Elders] seen in heaven rejoicing in Revelation chapters 4 and 5 is additional evidence that the Rapture of the Church takes place before the Tribulation.
N.B. The Tribulation cannot commence until Jesus, The Lamb, opens the seals of Revelation chapter 6;
-    seal one releases the Antichrist
-    seal two releases the Russian Invasion of Israel.

8.   Because the "Pre-Tribulation Rapture" is the Blessed Hope of the Church.

The believers in the early Church were constantly expecting the imminent return of Jesus. They looked forward to the time when Jesus would make His personal appearance in the air and they would be translated into His presence. Paul describes this as, "The Blessed Hope of the Church" [Titus 2:13]. Writing to the church at Thessalonica, Paul described what would happen at the Rapture, the event which they looked for [1 Thess 4:13-17].

In verse 18 he told them to "COMFORT ONE ANOTHER WITH THESE WORDS". [COMFORT = EDIFY, ENCOURAGE, BUILD UP EACH OTHER WITH THIS GOOD NEWS!!]
The Church was looking forward to the Rapture, WE DO NOT FIND THEM LOOKING FOR THE TRIBULATION. They were expecting Christ to make His appearance, NOT the Antichrist.

If the Church must pass through the Tribulation THEN HOW CAN WE POSSIBLY, "COMFORT ONE ANOTHER" KNOWING THE SEVEN YEARS OF HORROR THAT LIES AHEAD - "THE BLESSED HOPE" LOSES ITS POWER OF COMFORT.

Paul assures believers in 1 Thess 5:9 that they are not marked out for the Tribulation...
> "For God hath not appointed us to wrath but to obtain salvation by our Lord Jesus Christ".

The Church has an appointment with Jesus in the air at the Rapture, NOT an appointment with God's wrath during the 7 year Tribulation period on earth!

??? PRE - OR MID - OR POST TRIBULATION RAPTURE ???

POST-TRIBULATION RAPTURE - IMPOSSIBLE!!!

It is often argued by those who teach the Post Tribulation Rapture that the Church must be raptured to return instantly

and immediately with the Lord to the earth, thus denying
and making impossible any interval between the Rapture
and the Return. **Certain events predicted for the Church
after her translation make such an interpretation [post
Tribulation Rapture] impossible.**
These events are ;

i]   the Judgment Seat of Christ,
ii] the Presentation of the Church to Christ,
iii] the Marriage Supper of the Lamb. 2 Cor 5:10,
     1 Cor 3:11-16, Rev 19:6-9.

MID TRIBULATION RAPTURE POSITION -
IMPOSSIBLE!!!

From 2 Thess 2:3-8 it is clear that the Antichrist cannot
possibly be revealed until after the Church is taken out of
the way. Now comes the question of whether the Antichrist
will be revealed at the beginning or at the middle of the
Tribulation. If it can be proved that he will be revealed at the
beginning instead of at the middle of the 7 year Tribulation
[Daniel's 70th week], then it can also be proved that the
Church is raptured before the beginning and not in the
middle of the Tribulation.

i]   In Dan 9:27 we have one indisputable argument that he
is revealed at the beginning of the Week, for he makes a
covenant for 7 years with Israel and NOT for $3\frac{1}{2}$ years. The
breaking of the covenant in the middle of the week is not a
revelation of him on the scene of action, but an unfolding of
what he is to do in the middle of the Week, $3\frac{1}{2}$ years after
his revelation.
[Daniel's 70th Week, which is the same as the Tribulation
period, is exactly 7 years in length. This is proved by Dan

9:27 and also Ezek 39:9 which describes the 7 years involved in burning fuel supplies that Israel takes after Russia's conquest by God! N.B. Russia invades Israel at the beginning of the 7 year Tribulation].

ii]   Also, if the Church is raptured in the middle of Daniel's 70th Week, there is a definite time set for the Rapture and we need to stop looking for the Rapture at any time and look for the events which mark the appearance of the 70th Week. If the Church goes through the terrible events or the Seals and Trumpets, then Paul's teaching that the Church is caught up before the revelation of the Antichrist is contradicted, for the Antichrist is here $3\frac{1}{2}$ years before the middle of the Week.

CHAPTER 13:
WHEN THE SAINTS GO
MARCHING IN.

The next event on God's prophetic timetable is **the Rapture** which is the appearing of Jesus and the catching up of the Church.

> **1 Thess 4:16,17 For the Lord Himself will descend from heaven with a shout, with the voice of an archangel, and with the trumpet of God. And the dead in Christ will rise first.**
>
> **17 Then we who are alive and remain shall be caught up together with them in the clouds to meet the Lord in the air. And thus we shall always be with the Lord.**

The Rapture is the supernatural removal of the Body of Christ from the earth to meet Jesus in the air when He appears for us.

> **John 14:3 "And if I go and prepare a place for you, I will come again and receive you to Myself; that where I am, there you may be also."**

At the Rapture our bodies will be changed and glorified and made identical to the resurrection body of our Lord Jesus Christ. Think about having a strong physical body that will last **forever.** No tooth decay, no eyeglasses, no wrinkles, no blemishes, no balding heads for the men, no walking sticks. The aging process will stop and our bodies will not be subject to wear and tear!

KEY FUTURE EVENTS.

1. THE RAPTURE - JESUS COMES FOR US IN THE AIR.

7 YEARS IN HEAVEN.

a] Resurrection of the dead in Christ, re-united with their spirits and souls.

b] Translation of living believers in Christ.

c] Judgment Seat of Christ in heaven for rewards or loss.

d] Marriage Supper of the Lamb - Heaven's wedding feast!

2. 7 YEAR TRIBULATION ON EARTH DETAILED IN REVELATION 6-19.

3. THE SECOND COMING - JESUS COMES BACK TO THE EARTH WITH US.

*   Battle of Armageddon and the Antichrist's defeat.
*   Satan bound for 1,000 years in the abyss.
*   1,000 year reign of Christ on earth [Millennium].
*   Satan loosed to deceive the nations.
*   Battle of Gog and Magog.
*   Satan cast into the lake of fire forever.
*   Great White Throne Judgment.
*   New Heavens and New Earth.

The Challenge of the Rapture.

Paul and other Apostles taught the Bible believing Christians in their day to look for the IMMINENT, IMMEDIATE COMING OF JESUS! They fully expected Jesus to come before they died! This means that there are no signs or prophecies yet to be fulfilled that might postpone the Rapture!

Jesus could come instantaneously tonight - how important it is to be ready!

The Word of God is very clear and very specific concerning how the Christian should be living in these last days, in view of the nearness of the Rapture.

i] The Christian is instructed to live a godly, separated life that brings glory to Jesus.

Titus 2:11-13   For the grace of God that brings salvation has appeared to all men,
12 teaching us that, denying ungodliness and worldly lusts, we should live soberly, righteously, and godly in the present age,
13 looking for the blessed hope and glorious appearing of our great God and Saviour, Jesus Christ.

1 Cor 16:13,14 Watch, stand fast in the faith, be brave, be strong.
14 Let all that you do be done with love.

ii] The Christian is to stay spiritually awake and not allow his spiritual condition to become weak, lukewarm or spiritually sluggish.

1 Thess 5:6 Therefore let us not sleep, as others do, but let us watch and be sober.

Eph 6:10 [Amp] In conclusion, be strong in the Lord - be

empowered through your union with Him; draw your strength
from Him - that strength which His [boundless] might provides.

iii] The child of God is to win souls.

James 5:20 Let him know that he who turns a sinner from the
error of his way will save a soul from death and cover a multitude
of sins.

iv] The child of God is to be committed to a local church
that exalts Jesus and to regularly attend the church
services.

Heb 10:25 Not forsaking the assembling of ourselves together,
as is the manner of some, but exhorting one another, and so much
the more as you see the Day approaching.

v] The child of God is to continue, daily, in the renewing
of his mind through the Word of God.

Romans 12:2 And do not be conformed to this world, but be
transformed by the renewing of your mind, that you may prove
what is that good and acceptable and perfect will of God.

vi] The Christian must have a strong, consistent prayer
life.

Matt 26:41 [Amp] All of you must keep awake [give strict
attention, be cautious] and watch and pray that you may not come
into temptation. The spirit is indeed willing but the flesh is weak.

vii] The Christian is to live free from the lusts of the flesh.

Romans 13:12-14 The night is far spent, the day is at hand.

Therefore let us cast aside the works of darkness, and let us put
on the armour of light.

13 Let us walk properly, as in the day, not in revelry and
drunkenness, not in licentiousness and lewdness, not in strife
and envy.

14 But put on the Lord Jesus Christ, and make no provision for
the flesh, to fulfill its lusts.

viii] The Christian is to observe the Lord's Supper and partake of Communion with the Rapture in mind.

1 Cor 11:26 For as often as you eat of this bread and drink this cup,
you proclaim the Lord's death till he comes.

4 KEY QUESTIONS EACH CHRISTIAN MUST ASK HIMSELF ...

Q : 1]   WHAT and WHO am I living for?

Q : 2]   ARE my priorities in life, God's priorities?

Q : 3]   IS Jesus Christ Lord of every aspect of my life?

Q : 4]   IF the Rapture was to take place in the next 7 days
and I knew about it, what changes would I make in
my life?

WHAT HAPPENS AFTER THE RAPTURE?

2 Cor 5:10 For we must all appear before the judgment seat of
Christ, that each one may receive the things done in the body,
according to what he has done, whether good or bad.

Romans 14:12 So then each of us shall give account of himself to
God.

Once the saints of God have been raptured into heaven each one of us must stand before God and personally give an account of our lives as born again believers.

Since the time that you were born again you have been establishing and accumulating works as a believer in Christ - you will stand before Jesus one day in the future judgment and give an account of your deeds.

> 1 Cor 3:8-15 Now he who plants and he who waters are one, and each one will receive his own reward according to his own labour.
>
> 9   For we are God's fellow workers; you are God's field, you are God's building.
>
> 10   According to the grace of God which was given to me, as a wise master builder I have laid the foundation, and another builds on it. But let each one take heed how he builds on it.
>
> 11   For no other foundation can anyone lay than that which is laid, which is Christ Jesus.
>
> 12   Now if anyone builds on this foundation with gold, silver, precious stones, wood, hay, straw,
>
> 13   Each one's work will become manifest; for the Day will declare it, because it will be revealed by fire; and the fire will test each one's work, of what sort it is.
>
> 14   If anyone's work which he has built on it endures, he will receive a reward.
>
> 15   If anyone's work is burned, he will suffer loss; but he himself will be saved, yet so as through fire.

JUDGMENT OF BELIEVERS WORKS.

Subjects   : Every born again believer [2 Cor 5:10].

Time :   Between the Rapture and the Second Coming.

Place :   Heaven.

Basis :   Works both good or bad analysed.

Result :   Reward/crowns or nothing at all.

Having become sons of God through faith in Jesus Christ, then, believers have a responsibility for their present conduct.

The Judgment Seat of Christ does not involve the question of sin and salvation, rather it is judgment of the believer's works from the time he was saved until he goes to be with Christ.

This judgment will not be in the sense of a trial to determine the believer's future destiny because our eternal destiny is already decided and sealed during our life on earth at the moment we accept the free gift of God's salvation.

Immediately after the Rapture of the Church, the Judgment Seat of Christ will take place involving:

i]   the inspection of the believer's works,

ii]   the judgment of the counsels of the hearts of the believers - attitudes and motives.

iii]   the rewards for faithful service [1 Cor 3:11-15].

The refining fire of this judgment will test the quality of each believer's works and our bad and dead works, represented by wood, hay and stubble, will be consumed and only our good works shall remain.

All believers will be judged concerning:

1. **Things that affect our relationship with God:** Disobedience, refusal to walk in the light, failure to co-operate and yield to the Spirit etc.

2. **Things that affect themselves:** Personal ambition, pride, lusts of the flesh, neglected opportunities, talents wasted, lukewarmness etc.

3. **Things that affect our relationship with others:** Wrong dealings, broken promises, slander, quarrels etc.

7 THINGS THAT WILL BE EXPOSED AND JUDGED ON THAT DAY.

1] **IDLE WORDS** - Gossip, slander. lying, backbiting, critical tongue [Matt 12:34-37].

2] **DOCTRINE** - Sound doctrine, human opinions, religious tradition, error, what you believe and why you believe it.

James 3:1 [Amp] "Not many of you should become teachers my brethren, for you know that we [teachers] will be judged by a higher standard and with greater severity [than other people]. - Thus we assume the greater accountability and the more condemnation.

3] **CARNAL LIVING** – Strife, sowing discord, disharmony and division amongst the brethren.

1 Cor 3:3 "For you are still carnal. For where there are envy, strife and divisions among you, are you not carnal and behaving like mere men?"

The Greek says ... "... Mere UNCHANGED MEN ..." Carnal Christian living can be seen in believers lives in the following ways,

* Causing strife and division,
* Lack of respect for ministry gifts in the Church,
* Compromising, worldly living [Gal 5:19-21],
* Dishonesty in business / Wrong dealings,
* Broken promises and vows [beware of lying to the Holy Spirit], Acts 5 : Ecclesiastes 5:4,5,
* Busy-bodies who are slack, [2 Thess 3:10-12], idle, lazy and unemployed,
* Yielding to the lusts of the flesh.

4] **FINANCIAL STEWARDSHIP**

Luke 12:42-44 - Financial commitment to God's Work and God's Kingdom.
Mal 3:10. Abuse / misuse / mal-practice of God's money! Stinginess and robbing God.

5] **HEART ATTITUDE AND MOTIVES**

- 1 Cor 4:1-5, Matt 6:6-18

6]   QUALITY OF YOUR PERSONAL CHRISTIAN LIFE.

- Living as a true disciple, maintaining
  your spiritual life, reading your Bible,
  prayer life, faithfulness in serving Jesus,
  Praise Life, regular Church attendance
  and involvement etc.

7] **TALENTS** - Failure or faithfulness to use your God
-given talents! [Matt 25:14-30].

REWARDS FOR THE BELIEVER.

The following rewards have been promised for faithful
service to the Lord:

1   **VICTOR'S CROWN.**   1 Cor 9:25-27.

2] **CROWN OF RIGHTEOUSNESS**   2 Tim 4:8.

3] **CROWN OF REJOICING**   [Soulwinners
                                                          crown] 1 Thess
                                                          2:19.

4] **CROWN OF LIFE**   James 1:12.

5] **CROWN OF GLORY**   1 Peter 5:4.

6] **CROWN OF GOLD**   Rev 4:4.

7] **THE OVERCOMER'S REWARD**   Revelation
                                                          Chapters 2 & 3.

God's Word informs us that the saints will be given a mansion in which to live eternally [John 14:2], and Christ also will determine the amount of earthly rulership given to each saint on the basis of his faithfulness to God in this present life - [Luke 19:12-26]; for we shall reign as kings and priests with Christ forever [Rev 1:6, Rev 5:10].

Child of God, I encourage you and I challenge you now to get rid of anything that is holding you back from serving Jesus 100%.

> **Rev 16:15**   **"Behold, I am coming as a thief. Blessed is he who watches, and keeps his garments, lest he walk naked and they see his shame."**

Today make a fresh commitmentment of your life to Christ – take personal inventory of your life. Get rid of all the "excess" baggage and go forward in God!

CHAPTER 14:
AN INTRODUCTION TO THE
BOOK OF REVELATION.

Rev 1:3 Blessed is he who reads and those who hear the words of this prophecy, and keep those things which are written in it; for the time is near.

The book of Revelation completes the inspired Word of God. Without this book the Bible would be incomplete. Many interesting and important questions concerning the future are revealed in it. Questions regarding Eschatology [End-time events] abound in the minds of people. These questions concern the Rapture, the Great Tribulation, the Antichrist, the Millennium and other related events. The book of Revelation will help fulfill that quest for understanding as it deals with a multitude of vital end time concerns.

The message of the entire book of Revelation was given to John who faithfully wrote it down. The aging apostle recorded in Revelation the hope of the Church and of Israel in the message that was revealed to him. This occurred in about 95-96 A.D when the Roman Emperor, Domitian, was persecuting the Christian Community and the practice was to send the Christians into exile. John writes this epistle from exile in Patmos. Patmos was a rock quarry island about 6 miles wide and 10 miles long, approximately 25 miles off the coast of Asia Minor, due west of Miletus. It was an ideal place to confine political prisoners.

This last book of the Bible is called "the Revelation" being derived from the Greek word **apokalupsis**. The term is a combination of **kalupto**, meaning "to unveil," and **apo**, meaning "from". Hence the meaning, "to remove the veil" or "reveal". The book of Revelation is not some mysterious, confusing book that cannot be understood. To clearly comprehend and come to a correct understanding of the book of Revelation, **proper principles of interpretation must be followed**:

First of all, give the same meaning to the words of prophecy as are given to the words of history. Give the word its basic and true meaning. Simply because it is prophecy does not mean that it has some mystical meaning and cannot be understood in the literal sense. Of course, there are metaphors, types or examples that are used but these should be easily recognised.

In the **second** place, the literal meaning should not be changed to a spiritual or symbolic one when it is not called for. For example, in studying the 6th seal in Revelation 6:12-17, reference is made to an earthquake. This is not to be interpreted as meaning the break up of society, as some have suggested, instead of a literal earthquake. When reading the Bible, and especially when it comes to prophecy, don't seek to find some hidden meaning in the words of Scripture or try to add anything to them. Be satisfied with what God has said.

Regarding the book of Revelation, many attempts have been made to identify the Antichrist by taking the name of the individual and translating it into the Greek and using the numerical value of the letters to see if they equal 666. Much confusion has come out of these efforts! Some have taken the letters "u-s-a" out of the name of Jerusalem to make some prophecies pertain to the United States!

Realise that prophecy can be understood. It is literally history written beforehand. And, prophecy can be understood before it is fulfilled. Don't attempt to interpret God's own interpretation of symbols or change the meaning from that which is plain and clear. If it is a symbol or figure of speech, it usually will harmonise with other Scriptures on the same subject. Give Scripture the plain and literal meaning unless it is made clear that a double meaning is to be understood.

> **Rev 1:19 Write the things which you have seen, and the things which are, and the things which will take place after this.**

One basic key in understanding this great book is to recognise that it is divided into three parts.

THE FIRST PART involves the things that have already happened, i.e. that which is in the past. Christ is in the midst of the 7 candlesticks [1:12-18,20] as seen by John before he began to write. John had been with Jesus during His three and a half year ministry. Now he sees the resurrected and glorified Christ in this vision.

THE SECOND PART The things which are, constitute the second part and include Revelation 2 and 3. This concerns the churches in existence at that time. The messages to these churches are, of course, relevant for all churches that would exist throughout the Church age until the Rapture.

THE THIRD PART involves "the things which will take place after this" [from the Greek words **meta tauta**, literally "after these things"]. This is the major portion of the book of Revelation. It is a prophetic look at God's programme "after these things", i.e. "after the Church Age."

By reading through the book of Revelation it can be clearly seen and noted that,

*   Rev 1-3 deals primarily with the Church on earth.

*   Rev 4-5 pictures the Church and the Old Testament saints with God in heaven after the Rapture, represented by the 24 elders.

*   Rev 6-19 deals mainly with Israel under the oppression of the Gentiles with the 7 year Tribulation on earth.

*   Rev 19-22 deals with the Second Coming of Christ, the Millennium [1000 year reign of Christ on earth], the Great White Throne Judgment and the New Heaven and the New Earth.

This book is generally called, "The Revelation of John" but in fact the very first expression in Chapter 1 verse 1 indicates God's title. It is, "The Revelation of Jesus Christ". The words "Revelation" and "Apocalypse" are synonymous. They come from the Greek word **apokalupsis** meaning to "unveil, reveal or uncover". God gave the book of Revelation for us to understand. This is an unveiling and an uncovering of the events that are going to take place. The object and purpose of Revelation is simply to reveal, or make known the things that will come to pass in the future.

THE THEME OF REVELATION

Rev 1:7,8 Behold, He is coming with clouds, and every eye will see Him, and they also who pierced Him. And all the tribes of the earth will mourn because of Him. Even so, Amen.

8 "I am the Alpha and the Omega, the Beginning and the End," says the Lord, "who is and who was and who is to come, the Almighty."

The Second Coming of Jesus Christ is the main theme of the book of Revelation. The events involving the seals, trumpets, bowls and other things in the plan of God are preparatory to Christ's Coming. The Coming of Jesus is announced at the beginning [1:7], in the middle [11:15-18], and at the end of the prophecy [22:20]. The Second Coming of Christ is vividly described in Rev 19:11-16. Jesus is coming back again crowned King of kings and Lord of lords.

Jesus is saying that He is the Alpha and the Omega, the Beginning and the End. He claims equality with the Father in eternity, in His state of being, in power and in Lordship [Rev 1:4, 4;8, 11:17, 15:3, 16:7,14, 19:6,15, 21:22].

Immediately following the vision of Christ in the midst of the 7 lampstands, messages are given to the churches. This is the beginning of the second part of the book of Revelation and has to do with "the things which are". This part includes chapters 2 and 3 and contains the things concerning the Church on earth until its Rapture. Regarding the letters to the churches, the messages are given to the local churches that existed in Asia in that day and that were addressed in this letter. John knew these churches. There is much speculation as to the additional meaning and application of these messages. Some Bible teachers have tried to say that the 7 churches in Asia to which John was writing have dispensational application. That means that they portray 7 church periods or 7 phases of church history. According to this theory, we are now in the Philadelphian or Laodicean church. This is not the case. Actually the conditions that existed in the Ephesian church, which some say would be the period ending with the apostles, still exist in churches today. Conditions in all of the 7 churches which are described continue to exist even in churches in this day and age and will as long as the Church is upon the earth.

AN OVERVIEW OF THE BOOK OF REVELATION.

REVELATION CHAPTER 1 Introduction and John's vision of the resurrected Christ.

REVELATION CHAPTER 2 & 3 God's message for the 7 churches and for the church today.

REVELATION CHAPTER 4 & 5 A picture of the Raptured Church and Old Testament saints in heaven worshipping the Lord.

REVELATION CHAPTER 6 TO 19 Detailed information concerning the events on earth of the 7 year Tribulation.

REVELATION CHAPTER 19 The marriage supper of the Lamb, the Second Coming of Christ and the Battle of Armageddon.

REVELATION CHAPTER 20   The 1000 year reign of Christ on earth and the Great White Throne Judgment in Heaven.

REVELATION 21 & 22   Discusses the future heaven and the new earth.

KEY EVENTS OF THE TRIBULATION.

The future 7 year Tribulation period on earth is known as Daniel's 70th Week and is biblically divided into two halves;

FIRST $3\frac{1}{2}$ YEARS TRIBULATION   Matthew 24:9-14

SECOND $3\frac{1}{2}$ YEARS GREAT TRIBULATION
Matthew 24:15-26

Matthew 24:27-51 describes the **Second Coming of Christ**. The Tribulation is a time on earth of the most horrific and horrendous plagues and calamities in the history of mankind as seen by the releasing of the 7 seals, the 7 trumpet judgments and the 7 bowl judgments.

> **Matt 24:22** "And unless those days were shortened, no flesh would be saved; but for the elect's sake those days will be shortened."

SEVEN SEAL JUDGMENTS.

FIRST SEAL   Rise of the Antichrist [Rev 6:1,2].

SECOND SEAL   War [Rev 6:3,4].

THIRD SEAL	Famine and economic chaos [Rev 6:5,6].
FOURTH SEAL	Pestilence, death and hell [Rev 6:7,8].
FIFTH SEAL	Tribulation saints martyred by the Antichrist [Rev 6:9-11].
SIXTH SEAL	Wrath of God releases upheaval of nature [Rev 6:12-17].
SEVENTH SEAL	Silence in heaven for half an hour [Rev 8:1].

SEVEN TRUMPET JUDGMENTS
[REV CH 8,9 & 11]

FIRST TRUMPET	Hail, fire and blood rained from heaven [Rev 8:7].
SECOND TRUMPET	ONE THIRD of the oceans and seas turned to blood [Rev 8:8,9].
THIRD TRUMPET	ONE THIRD of domestic drinking water is poisoned! [Rev 8:10,11].
FOURTH TRUMPET	ONE THIRD of the planets - sun, moon and stars are darkened [Rev 8:12].
FIFTH TRUMPET	Men tormented by plague of demonic locusts [Rev 9:1-11].

SIXTH TRUMPET   ONE THIRD of mankind killed by 200 million strong Oriental army [Rev 9:13-19, 16:12].

SEVENTH TRUMPET Satan and fallen angels cast down from heavenlies [Rev 11:15-19, 12:7-12].

SEVEN BOWL JUDGMENTS [REV CH 16]

FIRST BOWL   Boils and horrible sores come upon every person who has taken the mark of the Beast [Rev 16:1,2].

SECOND BOWL   Sea turned to blood [Rev 16:3].

THIRD BOWL   Rivers and domestic drinking water turned to blood [Rev 16:4].

FOURTH BOWL   Men scorched with the intensified heat of the sun [Rev 16:8,9].

FIFTH BOWL   Antichrist's kingdom is covered by darkness [Rev 16:10,11].

SIXTH BOWL   The river Euphrates is dried up preparing the way for the Oriental army in it's march to Armageddon [Rev 16:12, 9:13-19].

SEVENTH BOWL   A great earthquake and upheaval of nature - 120 lb hailstones! [Rev 16:17-21].

The horrendous events of the Tribulation period will be so severe and so intense that men will pray and plead for the rocks to fall on them.

> Rev 6:15-17 And the kings of the earth, the great men, the rich men, the commanders, the mighty men, every slave and every free man, hid themselves in the caves and in the rocks of the mountains,
> 16 and said to the mountains and rocks, "Fall on us and hide us from the face of Him who sits on the throne and from the wrath of the Lamb!"
> 17 "For the great day of His wrath has come, and who is able to stand?"

ARMAGEDDON AND THE SECOND COMING OF CHRIST [REV 19:11-21]

On the final day of the great Tribulation there will occur a tremendous earthquake and upheaval of nature. [Rev 6:12-17, 11:13-19, 16:16-21].

Can you visualise the terror and destruction with the combination of a massive cyclone, hurricane, typhoon, tornado and a great earthquake plus hailstones raining upon the earth weighing 120 lbs [Rev 16:21] ALL HAPPENING AT THE SAME TIME?

In the valley of Megiddo there is the Antichrist and the combined armies of his ten nation kingdom [Rev 17:12-14] plus his allies and the 200 million strong demon-controlled oriental army [Rev 9:13-19, Rev 16:12,16] are gathered for the battle of Armageddon -[please study Zech 14].

As these armies gather to do battle suddenly CHRIST returns at the Second Coming [Rev 19:11-21, Jude 14,15]. Jesus Christ returns to the earth as King of kings and Lord of lords with the angels and millions of His saints to defeat the Antichrist and his forces at Armageddon.

> **Matt 24:30** "And then shall appear the sign of the Son of Man in heaven: and then shall all the tribes of the earth mourn, and they shall see the Son of Man coming in the clouds of heaven with power and great glory."

This is called the "Second Coming of the Lord" which is totally different from the Rapture.

After the Battle of Armageddon, the Bible informs us that Satan is chained by an angel from heaven and then imprisoned in the bottomless pit for 1,000 years [Rev 20:1-3]. Then our Lord Jesus Christ establishes His Millennial Kingdom on earth.

THE MILLENNIUM - THE 1,000 YEAR REIGN OF CHRIST [REV 20:1-6]

See also Isa 9:6 and Jer 23:5,6

This planet and its inhabitants will experience 1,000 years of divine government with Jesus Christ as King of kings reigning from Jerusalem. The Millennium will be marked as an age of,

*   Perfect righteousness.
*   Perfect health - no sickness, deformity or disease - no AIDS!
*   Perfect prosperity.

* Perfect environment - Curse lifted from the earth.
* Perfect peace - no crime, no wars.
* Perfect government.

THE FINAL WORLD WAR [REV 20:7-10].

At the end of Christ's 1,000 year reign Satan is loosed for a short season resulting in the battle of Gog and Magog. The last judgment or Great White Throne Judgment takes place after Satan is cast into the Lake of Fire at the end of the 1,000 years. God sits on this throne and every lost sinner stands before Him to receive sentence and punishment in the Lake of Fire.

THE GREATEST REVIVAL IS YET TO COME!

HOW THE GOSPEL WILL BE PREACHED DURING THE SEVEN YEAR TRIBULATION.

Matt 24:14 "And this gospel of the kingdom will be preached in all the world as a witness to all the nations and then the end will come."

First of all let me say that when the Rapture of the Church takes place the Holy Spirit **DOES NOT** leave the earth but remains in the earth for the entire duration of the 7 year Tribulation, the 1,000 year Millennial reign of Christ and for the rest of eternity - **He is not going to leave!**

The Holy Spirit is the agent of salvation and is the One who produces the miracle of the New Birth in the heart of every sinner who repents and believes in the Gospel of Christ. So

therefore, how can He leave the earth when the Church is raptured? If the Holy Spirit leaves at the Rapture then no-one will be or could be born again during the Tribulation - but understanding end time Scriptures we know that the greatest revival and harvest of souls, in all history, is during the Tribulation!

God will use FOUR VEHICLES in preaching the gospel and in getting people born again during the Tribulation.

1. The ministry of the 144,000 born again Jewish evangelists.
2. The testimony of the Tribulation converts.
3. The end time ministry of angels.
4. The ministry of the two witnesses [Enoch and Elijah].

I believe the greatest revival will break out upon this earth only minutes after the Rapture of the Church...
How will the presidents, prime-ministers and politicians of nations explain away the Rapture?
How will the television newscasters explain the following facts?

* Multiplied millions of people have been instantly removed from the earth?

* Millions of graves have been emptied of their corpses?

* Pilots of aircraft and jumbo-jets, in flight, have disappeared?

* The confusion and chaos of trains and cars without drivers?

*   Millions of babies and infants around the world have
      suddenly disappeared?

*   Born again medical doctors and surgeons have dis-
      appeared whilst operating and/or attending patients?

*   World famous people in sport/television/politics/
      theatre/ALL walks of life have just disappeared without
      a trace?

HOW CAN ALL THIS BE EXPLAINED AWAY? Can you
imagine the headlines of the newspapers? On that day I
believe, millions of sinners will be touched by the Holy
Spirit and make Jesus their Lord - especially your relatives,
friends and people at work who said you were crazy when
you witnessed to them about Jesus!

FOUR VEHICLES IN PREACHING THE GOSPEL.

1. The Preaching of the 144,000.

Within a few days or few weeks after the global impact of
the Rapture, Russia and its allies will invade the tiny nation
of Israel. According to Bible prophecy God Himself will
personally intervene and defend Israel, destroying all the
armies of Russia and its allied forces PLUS He will wipe out
the nation of Russia in one day.
Think about the impact of the Rapture and then think about
the effect of Russia's defeat and destruction especially the
great impression upon the nation of Israel and the Jewish
people.

Rom 11:26,27 And so all Israel will be saved, as it is written: "The

Deliverer will come out of Zion, And He will turn away ungodliness from Jacob; For this is My covenant with them, When I take away their sins".

Millions of Jews will recognise the "Divine Intervention of God" and will receive Jesus Christ as Lord and Saviour. From that great company of born again Jewish people God will select and seal [Revelation 7] 144,000 born again Jewish men, make them evangelists and send them forth to preach the Gospel around the world.

Zech 8:23 "Thus says the Lord of hosts: 'In those days ten men from every language of the nations shall grasp the sleeve of a Jewish man, saying "Let us go with you, for we have heard that God is with you."'"

2.   The Tribulation Converts.

Rev 7:9,14[b]   After these things I looked, and behold, a great multitude which no-one could number, of all nations, tribes, peoples and tongues, standing before the throne and before the Lamb, clothed with white robes, with palm branches in their hands,
14 ..."These are the ones who came out of the great tribulation, and washed their robes and made them white in the blood of the Lamb."

This great multitude of Born Again Believers came as a result of the impact of the Rapture and the preaching of the 144,000. When the Gospel of Christ is proclaimed people always get saved, then they go out and share their testimony with other people who in turn get saved!

3. The End Time Ministry of Angels.

Rev 14:6 Then I saw another angel flying in the midst of heaven, having the everlasting gospel to preach to those who dwell on the earth - to every nation, tribe, tongue, people -

In this present Church age angels are NOT permitted to preach the Gospel. They can only lead sinners to Christian workers or they can lead soul winners to sinners. So angels in this present dispensation are not allowed to preach the gospel but this changes during the Tribulation. Can you imagine an angel flying down from heaven and preaching the Gospel in your city during peak hour traffic?
This will have a great influence on the salvation of many people.

4. The Ministry of the Two Witnesses.

Rev 11:3 "And I will give power to My two witnesses, and they will prophesy one thousand two hundred and sixty days, clothed in sackcloth".

Rev 11:5,6 And if anyone wants to harm them, fire proceeds from their mouth and devours their enemies. And if anyone wants to harm them, he must be killed in this manner.
6 These have power to shut heaven, so that no rain falls in the days of their prophecy; and they have power over waters to turn them to blood, and to strike the earth with all the plagues as often as they desire.

At Mid-Tribulation God will send down to the earth two special end-time agents; Enoch and Elijah who did not die [Heb 9:27] but were raptured into heaven during Old

Testament times. The Antichrist, his armies and his followers will bitterly hate these two agents of God because they will cause havoc in the Antichrist's 10 nation Empire. They will preach the Gospel for three and a half years and they cannot be stopped or killed for God Himself will Divinely protect them until the final week of the Great Tribulation.

> **Rev 11:7-10** Now when they finish their testimony, the beast that ascends out of the bottomless pit will make war against them, overcome them and kill them.
>
> 8   And their dead bodies will lie in the street of the great city which spiritually is called Sodom and Egypt, where also our Lord was crucified.
>
> 9   Then those from the peoples, tribes, tongues and nations will see their dead bodies three and a half days, and not allow their dead bodies to be put into graves.
>
> 10   Then those who dwell on the earth will rejoice over them, make merry, and send gifts to one another, because these two prophets tormented those who dwell on the earth.

So God's two dynamic witnesses are slain in the final week of the 7 year Tribulation and their dead bodies lie in the streets of Jerusalem for three and a half days while the Antichrist and his followers have a huge celebration.

HOW MANY OF YOU KNOW THAT GOD ALWAYS HAS THE FINAL WORD?

> **Rev 11:11,12** Now after three and a half days the breath of life from God entered them, and they stood on their feet, and great fear fell on those who saw them.
>
> 12   And they heard a loud voice from heaven saying to them, "Come up here." And they ascended to heaven in a cloud and their enemies saw them.

Right in front of the Antichrist and his followers and the T.V. networks of the world, God resurrects His two witnesses then raptures them into heaven!

THE FOUR HORSEMEN OF THE APOCALYPSE

REVELATION 6v1-8

SEAL 1   WHITE HORSE
Antichrist revealed and
begins his seven year
satanic assignment

SEAL 2   RED HORSE
War (Russia and her allies
invade Israel)

SEAL 3   BLACK HORSE
Food shortage, famine and
economic chaos

SEAL 4   PALE HORSE
Pestilence – death and hell

THESE FOUR HORSEMEN WILL RUN FOR
THE DURATION OF THE SEVEN YEAR
TRIBULATION, AS A RESULT, ONE
QUARTER OF THE EARTH'S POPULATION
WILL DIE

FOUR WAYS THE GOSPEL IS PREACHED DURING THE SEVEN YEAR TRIBULATION

(1)   The ministry of the 144,000
born-again Jewish men,
unmarried and sealed by God
(Revelation 7)

(2)   The testimony of the Tribulation
converts — people born
again during the Tribulation
will witness for Christ
(Revelation 7)

(3)   The end-time ministry of
Angels
(Revelation 14v6,7)

(4)   God's two dynamic witnesses —
Enoch and Elijah
(Revelation 11)

CHAPTER 15:
THE RUSSIAN INVASION OF
ISRAEL.

Ezek 38:1-3 Now the word of the Lord came to me, saying,
2 Son of man, set your face against Gog [Russian Premier - Gorbachev], **of the land of Magog**[U.S.S.R.], **the prince of Rosh** [Mikhail Gorbachev - Russia's leader], **Meshech** [Modern day Moscow], **and Tubal** [Modern day city of Tobolsk], **and prophesy against him,**
3 "and say, 'Thus says the Lord God: "Behold, I am against you, O Gog, the prince of Rosh, Meshech and Tubal"'".

This prophecy and vision of Ezekiel was given around 650 B.C. and accurately predicts the time, method and result of the next world war when Russia and its allies invade Israel.

BACKGROUND INFORMATION.

Modern Day Identification of Ancient Biblical Peoples and Nations.

We must realise that geographical areas DO NOT CHANGE, they are fixed. However names of places DO CHANGE!

In Ezek 38:1-3 Ezekiel speaks concerning a specific geographical area of the earth. His prophecy to that area, its people and its leaders, refers to the same geographical locations that now include the nation of Russia. On old biblical maps, the territories of Gog and Magog and the provinces of Meshech and Tubal are all found within the confines of the geographical region known today as Russia.

Magog, Meshech and Tubal according to Genesis 10 were all grandsons of NOAH and their descendants migrated out of the Middle East northwards and filled the area that we know today as U.S.S.R. The descendants of Magog, Meshech and Tubal settled in a vast area of Northern Europe and Asia known as Scythia, which lies completely within the geographical boundaries of the SOVIET UNION. Persia [Iraq, Iran and Afghanistan], Ethiopia, Libya, Gomer [Eastern Europe], and Togarmah [Turkey], today are being swallowed up by the Soviet Union [Ezek 38:5,6].

The province of Meshech included the geographical location of the present city of Moscow. In the province of Tubal there now exists the Russian city of Tobolsk. Togarmah's descendants were to occupy the southern part of the nation we know as Russia, along with Rumania, Bulgaria and Turkey. The geographical area that we know as eastern Europe - East Germany, Poland, Hungary and Czechoslovakia - was originally settled by the descendants of Gomer. The use of modern names to identify nations does no damage to the scriptural account.

Gog is the symbolic name of the nation's leader and Magog his land. He is also the prince of the ancient people who were called Rosh, Meshech and Tubal. In the biblical chapter, commonly called the "Table of Nations" by scholars, these names are mentioned [see Genesis 10]. They are described as the grandsons of Noah through his son Japheth, with the exception of Rosh [Genesis 10:1,2]. Magog is the second son; Tubal is the fifth son; and Meshech is the sixth son.

Wilhélm Gesenius, a great Hebrew scholar of the early 19th

Century said "Meshech was founder of the Moschi, a
barbarous people, who dwelt in the Moschian mountains".
This scholar went on to say that the Greek name, "Moschi",
derived from the Hebrew name Meshech is the source of the
name for the city of MOSCOW. In discussing Tubal he said,
"Tubal is the son of Rapheth, founder of the Tibereni, a
people dwelling on the Black Sea to the west of Moschi".
Gesenius concludes that these people undoubtedly make
up the modern Russian people. Gesenius also identified
"Meshech" as Moscow, the capital of modern Russia.
"Tubal" he identified as Tobolisk, the earliest province in
Asiatic Russia to be colonised, and, also, the name of the city
wherein Peter the Great built the old fortress after the
pattern of the Kremlin in Moscow.

Quote from the Biblical and Theological Dictionary:

"Magog signifies the country or people, and Gog the king of
that country; the general name of the northern nations of
Europe and Asia, or the districts north of the Caucasus or
Mount Taurus."

Dr. Gesenius in his Hebrew Lexicon says,... "Rosh was a
designation for the tribes then north of the Taurus mountains,
dwelling in the neighbourhood of the Volga". He concluded
that in this name and tribe we have the first historical trace
of the Russ or Russian nation.

More evidence for identifying the land of Magog as Russia
lies in its geographical location from Israel. Ezekiel puts
great stress on this, by saying three times, that this great
enemy of Israel would come from the far north. The Hebrew
word that qualifies "north" means either "uttermost" or
"extreme". You only need to take a globe to verify this exact

geographical fix. There is only one nation to the "uttermost north" of Israel - the U.S.S.R. Ezek 38:2 "Gog" identifies the Russian leader.

Ezek 38:5,6 "Persia [Iran, Iraq and Afghanistan], **Ethiopia, and Libya are with them, all of them with shield and helmet;**
6 "**Gomer** [East Germany, Poland, Hungary, Czechoslovakia] **and all its troops; the house of Togarmah** [Bulgaria, Rumania, Turkey] **from the far north and all its troops - many people are with you.**

Examining ancient biblical maps, we find that Gomer lies in Eastern Europe, particularly the area we now know as East Germany, Poland, Hungary and Czechoslovakia.

It is no coincidence that Germany was divided at the close of World War II. This became necessary that there might be a satellite of Russia in that part of the world to fulfill this passage of Scripture.

The province of Togarmah is south of Meshech, or Moscow, covering much of the highly industrialised area of the nation of Russia, plus Rumania, Bulgaria and Turkey.

Gomer was the eldest son of Japheth, and the father of Ashkenaz, Riphath and Togarmah. These people make up an extremely important part of the future Russian invasion force. Dr. Young, citing the best of the most recent archaeological finds, says of Gomer and his hordes, "They settled on the north of the Black Sea and then spread themselves westward and southward to the extremities of Europe". Gesenius speaks of part of Gomer's hordes as being Ashkenaz..."the proper name of a region and a nation in northern Asia, sprung from the Cimmerians who are the ancient people of Gomer." Josephus called the sons of Ashkenaz, "the Rheginians" and a map of the ancient Roman Empire places them in the area of modern Poland, Czechoslovakia and East Germany to the banks of the Danube River. The conclusion is that Gomer and its hordes are part of the vast area of modern Eastern Europe which is totally behind the Iron Curtain. This includes East Germany and the Slovak countries.

Ezek 38:7 says that the Russian ruler is to equip his allies with arms and to assume command. Ezekiel catalogues the ancient names of the peoples and nations who would be confederates of Russia in Ezek 38:5,6.

All authorities agree on who Persia is today. It is modern Iran, Iraq and Afghanistan.

Ethiopia is a translation of the Hebrew word, Cush. Cush was the first son of Ham, one of the sons of Noah.

Dr. Gesenius tells us,
1.   The Cushites were black men.
2.   They migrated first to the Arabian peninsula and then across the Red Sea to the area south of Egypt.

Libya is the translation of the original Hebrew word, Put. Put was the third son of Ham [Gen 10:6]. The descendants of Put migrated to the land west of Egypt and became the source of the North African Arab nations, such as Libya, Algeria, Tunisia and Morocco.

UPGRADING TERMINOLOGY.

Ezek 38:4,9 "I will turn you around, put hooks in your jaws, and

lead you out, with all your army, horses and horsemen [tanks, mechanised equipment], **all splendidly clothed, a great company with bucklers and shield, all of them handling swords** [weapons of warfare].
9   You will ascend coming like a storm, covering the land like a cloud [This describes an airborne attack], **you and all your troops and many people with you."**

Interpretation must remain consistent; therefore, the use of modern names to identify nations must be applied, as well, to weapons of warfare and modes of transportation. Today's armies do not use shield, helmets, bows and arrows; nor do they travel on horseback.

Contrary to what some prophetic teachers say, Russia is NOT importing horses to invade Israel on horseback! [Check this out in the **Newsweek and Time** magazines.]

Russia **does not** fight on horseback, nor with shield and swords. We must realize that Ezekiel was using terminology to describe armies of his day. The modern horse is heavy armoured vehicles, high powered mechanized equipment with great fire power. The tank is a mechanized horse. The sword represents an implement of military warfare.

WHY RUSSIA WILL INVADE ISRAEL.

Ezek 38:10,12   "Thus says the Lord God: "On that day it shall come to pass that thoughts will arise in your mind, and you will make an evil plan [Russia's invasion plans].
12   "to take plunder and to take a spoil [Russia seeks the strategic position of the Middle East plus its food and oil supplies], **to stretch out your hand against the waste places that are again inhabited,**

and against a people gathered from the nations, who have acquired livestock and goods, who dwell in the midst of the land."

Firstly the Middle East happens to be the most s rategic military spot on the earth. The Middle East is the key geographical area that links Asia to both Europe and to Africa. When in control of that area, a nation is sitting in a key military position. Israel stands in Russia's way. Israel is the only force keeping Russia from controlling the Middle East right now. If it had not been for Israel, Russia would already be there. The Arabs with their lack of unity would be no opposition for her. Israel is the thorn in Russia's side.

Secondly Russia needs the vast supply of untapped natural resources that are housed in the Middle East. Israel is a fabulous food basket - and Russia needs food!

Ezek 38:12 predicts that Russia will come against Israel for food. Russia has troubles which continue to increase. Industrially and socially, she is underdeveloped. Agriculturally she is in trouble. Over the past 19 growing seasons, Russia has experienced 16 crop failures. While some were small, others were immense. The 1981 crop failure was one of the worst.

Why is Russia having so much trouble with agriculture? Simply because nature is not co-operating. In Ezek 38:3. Remember, God said, "I am against you Russia!" The upheaval of nature in Russia has been extremely severe through the years, especially within the past 5 or 6 years. Her supply of food has been drastically affected. She is being hard pressed to see that all her people are fed properly. Russia is in serious trouble because of a growing population and a food production decrease. Each year Russia is forced

to import many million metric tonnes of grain from the
U.S.A. and Canada.

At the future military confrontation between Russia and
her satellite allies against Israel, nuclear weapons will not
be used as nuclear warfare would destroy the farming land
of Israel and its abundant produce. Russia will use
conventional weapons.

Thirdly if Russia can successfully "takeover" and control
the Middle East then it will be controlling the largest oil
resource in the world.

WHEN WILL RUSSIA INVADE ISRAEL?

Ezek 38:8,16 "After many days you will be visited. In the latter
years you will come into the land of those brought back from the
sword and gathered from many people on the mountains of
Israel, which had long been desolate; they were brought out of
the nations, and now all of them dwell safely.
16 You will come up against My people Israel like a cloud
[airborne invasion - rapid deployment forces], to cover the land. It
will be in the latter days that I will bring you against My land, so
that the nations may know Me, when I am hallowed in you, O
Gog, before their eyes."

God identifies the time for us in Ezek 38.
EZEKIEL 38:8 says THE LATTER YEARS,
EZEKIEL 38:16 says THE LATTER DAYS.

In the latter years, northern lands shall come down upon
Israel, a people brought back from the sword. Israel - a
persecuted people for 2,000 years - would be attacked from

the north in their own land where they had come to dwell in safety.

Russia will invade and attack Israel at a time when there is peace in the Middle East between Israel and her 5 surrounding Arab neighbours; Egypt, Saudi Arabia, Syria, Jordan and Lebanon. From Ezek 38:8,11,14 we see that Russia makes no move against Israel UNTIL the restored nation of Israel is at rest and at peace in the Middle East.

Ezek 38:11 "Walls, bars and gates" refer to heavy defenses to keep out enemies **therefore** at this time Israel must be at peace and safety with her surrounding Arab nations.

The Russian invasion of Israel described by Ezek in Chapters 38 and 39 is also covered by the Apostle John in Revelation 6 with the Lord Jesus Christ opening the book with the seven seals [Rev 6:1-4].

SEAL No 1. releases the Antichrist.

SEAL No 2. releases the Red Horse which identifies the attack of the Red Army [combined military forces of the U.S.S.R.] on Israel. This Red Horse represents the **first act** of war in the Tribulation period which may take place within days after the appearing of Jesus Christ and the catching away of the Church to meet Him in the air [including **all** born again believers in Russia!] The Russian Christians will be raptured **before** God destroys the U.S.S.R.

RUSSIA AND CHINA WILL NOT ENGAGE IN A MAJOR WAR.

Both Russia and China are geared for world conquest. As

far as political and military science are concerned, they are on a collision course. However, they will never collide. Such an event is not in the plan of God. The prophetic Scriptures do not reveal it.

There will never be a major military confrontation between Russia and China. Both will have their "Waterloos", but these "Waterloos" will be separated by 7 years.

Russia's defeat comes at the very beginning of the Tribulation period. China's military forces, after great success in the Orient and in Asia, are to arrive at the back door of Israel. They will cross the dried up river Euphrates, turn south into the state of Israel, and arrive at the battle site of Armageddon, where they will meet their "Waterloo".
 Within one hour China and ten other massive European and Mediterranean armies will be dissolved into a pool of blood that covers an area of 200 miles [Rev 14].

RUSSIA'S INVASION OF ISRAEL IS NOT THE BATTLE OF ARMAGEDDON.

Do not confuse these two battles. They are separate affairs. Take note that the battle discussed in Ezek 38 & 39 is fought in the mountains of Israel far to the north of Jerusalem, between Russia and her satellites and Israel and her allies. The victor is Israel. The defeated foe is Russia.

It will take Israel 7 months to bury the Russian dead and 7 years to use up the fuel supplies brought by Russia into the field of battle [Ezek 39:9]. This 7 year period is significant in that it is the same amount of time given in the scriptures to the Tribulation period, and is also the period of time that separates the fulfillment of Ezek 38 & 39 from the Battle of Armageddon.

Armageddon takes place on the final day of the Tribulation period. The Battle of Armageddon is fought in the plains of Megiddo, outside of Jerusalem. This battle is fought between the Antichrist and his armies and the Lord Jesus Christ and his heavenly host.

After Armageddon, Jesus sets up a kingdom here on the earth for a thousand years. So there are marked differences between the two battles.

THE RUSSIAN ALLIED FORCES.

Ezek 38:5-7   Persia [Iran, Iraq and Afghanistan], **Ethiopia and Libya are all with them, all of them with shield and helmet;**
6   "**Gomer** [East Germany, Poland, Hungary and Czechoslo-·vakia] **and all its troops; the house of Togarmah** [Bulgaria, Rumania and Turkey] **from the far north and all its troops - many people are with you.**
7   "**Prepare yourself and be ready, you and all your companies that are gathered about you; and be a guard for them".**

Persia which was in Ezekiel's time is today made up of Iran, Iraq and Afghanistan. At the time of this invasion all three will be under total Russian control

* IRAQ is already under Russian control by reason of military treaties in 1972.

* IRAN is all set for a communist take-over - it is destined to join the atheist communists of Russia to come against Israel.

*   AFGHANISTAN in 1979 was invaded by Russia and is
     in the process of coming under Russian domination.

*   ETHIOPIA has been under Russian control since 1977.

*   LIBYA in northern Africa on the Mediterranean Sea is
     closely linked to Russia by reason of military treaties
     since 1952.

GOMER and ALL HIS BANDS identifies ;

*   East Germany,
*   Poland,
*   Hungary,
*   Czechoslovakia.

THE HOUSE OF TOGARMAH and ALL HIS BANDS
identifies,

*   Rumania and Bulgaria which have been under Russian
     control since the end of World War II.
*   Turkey forms a major region once known as
     "Togarmah" and is set for communist take-over.

> **Ezek 38:9** **"You will ascend, coming like a storm, covering the
> land like a cloud,** [This describes an airborne attack], **you and all
> your troops and many peoples with you."**

The Russian alliance consists of Iran, Iraq, Afghanistan,
Ethiopia, Libya, East Germany, Poland, Hungary,
Czechoslovakia, Rumania, Bulgaria, Turkey and the Arab
states hostile to Israel.

All these nations are under Russian domination or else are

currently in the process of being brought under the control of the U.S.S.R. in time for Israel's invasion.

Ezek 38:7 informs us that Russia will arm and equip this vast confederacy of nations for the attack on the restored nation of Israel.

Child of God ... WATCH THE NEWS HEADLINES FOR DEVELOPMENTS IN THE MIDDLE EAST especially,

1. Iran and Turkey in relation to Russia.
2. Israel and her Arab neighbours [5 nations] making peace.

I believe significant things will soon be happening there.

The good news concerning Africa is that with the exception of 2 nations, Libya and Ethiopia, the Russian plans for a communist take-over in Africa will totally fail!

RUSSIA'S MILITARY STRATEGY FOR THE INVASION OF ISRAEL. [Ezek 38:4,9,15,16].

From these Scriptures we see that the Russians plan to come by air and take Israel using their "Rapid Deployment" forces.

This would be a swift action opening the way for a secondary action by their armoured divisions and infantry. Russia WILL NOT use her nuclear power as she has no wish to destroy the land or delay occupying that area.

It is Russia who first developed "Rapid Deployment Forces"

and they are experts at it.

DEFINITION: RAPID DEPLOYMENT FORCE: By air-borne attack you airlift vast armies into the surrounding territory you wish to invade.

This area has already been heavily stockpiled with military hardware waiting in readiness for the battle.

Using Rapid Deployment strategy Russia took Ethiopia in November 1977 and invaded Afghanistan in December 1979. [In November 1977 Russia deployed 3 of her armies from Russia to Ethiopia in just over 10 hours!].

WHO WILL SUPPORT ISRAEL?

Ezek 38:13 "**Sheba, Dedan** [Israel's 5 Arab nations at peace - Syria, Jordan, Lebanon, Saudi Arabia, Egypt], **the merchants of Tarshish** [U.S.A., South Africa, Canada, New Zealand, Australia], **and all their young lions will say to you, 'Have you come to take plunder? Have you gathered your army to take booty, to carry away silver and gold, to take away livestock and goods, to take great plunder?'"'**

Scripture reveals that Israel has some committed allies and they too recognise Russia's desires to conquer Israel and control the middle East: These allies, Sheba and Dedan, identify Israel's 5 Arab neighbours that are sympathetic toward the nation of Israel, quite likely the ones at peace with Israel.[Egypt, Lebanon, Jordan, Syria and Saudi Arabia.]

These major allies of Israel are found by examination of the merchants of Tarshish and the young lions thereof. The

Merchants of Tarshish receive their name from the ancient city of Tarshish on the Mediterranean Sea, where they once traded their goods. These merchantmen represented all of the nations that would one day become the Roman Empire, whose existence would fade away with the total collapse of the Roman Empire.

Out of the Merchants of Tarshish came the colonial Empires. The most successful of these was Great Britain. The symbol of Great Britain is a lion. That symbol exists to this day and no other empire had more young lions than Great Britain. The present young lions are, Canada, Australia, New Zealand, South Africa and the United States.

These five "Young Lion" nations that came out of the British Empire - Canada, South Africa, Australia, New Zealand and U.S.A. have much in common;

1.   Each is a committed sponsor of Israel - giving the nation of Israel full support.

2.   Each is destined by God to play a vital role in Bible prophecy in these last days as they will come to the aid of Israel when Russia attacks.

3.   Genesis 12:3 is being fulfilled in these nations as we see that they are, along with Israel, the most blessed nations in the world. Economically, materially, and spiritually!

N.B. Only 6 nations in the world today are self-sufficient food- wise; They are Israel and the 5 Young Lion nations. **ISRAEL'S ALLIES [EZEK 38:13,14]** are ...
U.S.A. Canada, Australia, New Zealand, South Africa, Egypt, Saudi Arabia, Syria, Jordan and Lebanon.

THE DESTRUCTION OF RUSSIA IN ONE DAY BATTLE.

The prophecy of Ezek 38 is totally dependant upon the existing state of Israel. At the time Ezekiel was setting forth these things, most of Israel was already in captivity and the captivity [Ezek 1:1] was soon to be completed. There was no state of Israel from that time until May of 1948. The stage was then set for this very prophecy to begin to unfold and come to pass.

More than 2,600 years ago, God spoke through Ezekiel and predicted the rise of Russia and its threats to the new nation of Israel and even revealed the battle plans that Russia would use.

Ezek 38:9 "You will ascend, coming like a storm, covering the land like a cloud [airborne attack], you and all your troops and many people with you."

Ezek 38:14,15 "Therefore, son of man prophesy and say to Gog, 'Thus says the Lord God:"On that day when My people Israel dwell safely, will not you know it?
15 Then you will come from your place out of the far north, you and many peoples with you, all of them riding on horses, a great company and a mighty army."

Ezek 38:16 "You will come up against My people Israel like a cloud [airborne invasion - rapid deployment forces], to cover the land. It will be in the latter days that I will bring you against My land, so that the nations may know Me, when I am hallowed in you, O Gog, before their eyes." [God will become filled with wrath against Russia as she moves against Israel.]

Ezek 38:18,19 "And it will come to pass at the same time, when

Gog comes against the land of Israel," says the Lord God, "that My fury will show in My face. [God is totally against communism.] 19 For in My jealousy and in the fire of My wrath I have spoken: 'Surely in that day there shall be a great earthquake in the land of Israel."

Ezek 38:21-23 "I will call for a sword [weapons of warfare] against Gog throughout all My mountains [Israel's allied forces - the Young Lion nations]," says the Lord God. "Every man's sword will be against his brother. [Mutiny and confusion among the Russian troops].
22 And I will bring him to judgment with pestilence and bloodshed; I will rain down upon him, on his troops, and on the many peoples who are with him, flooding rain, great hailstones, fire and brimstone.
23 Thus I will magnify Myself and sanctify Myself, and I will be known in the eyes of many nations. They shall know that I am the Lord."

As the Russians are making their initial move to launch a devastating blow, God unleashes nature and a plague of illness against them.

Ezek 39:1-4 "And you son of man, prophesy against Gog, and say, 'Thus says the Lord God: "Behold I am against you, O Gog, the prince of Rosh, Meshech and Tubal [When God is against you then you are in BIG trouble!]
2   and I will turn you around and lead you on, bringing you up from the far north, and bring you against the mountains of Israel.
3   Then I will knock the bow out of your left hand, and cause the arrows to fall out of your right hand [Russia's armies immobilised].
4   You shall fall upon the mountains of Israel, you and all your troops and the peoples who are with you; I will give you to birds

of prey of every sort and to the beasts of the fields to be devoured."

The upheaval of nature is such that an earthquake of major intensity rocks the mountains north of Israel **all the way through the interior of Russia**. The effect on that area is cataclysmic.

> **Ezek 39:6** **"And I will send fire** [earthquake] **on Magog and on those who live in security in the coastlands.** [The great earthquake goes right through the U.S.S.R.] **" Then they shall know that I am the Lord.**

Along with the earthquake comes the overflowing rain with hail. Such an action of nature not only hinders the movement of the armies, but prevents the use of aircraft and intercontinental ballistic missiles.

The massive earthquake ripping through the U.S.S.R. will crush Russian missiles in their underground silos, exploding them and bringing destruction to Russia.

Ezek 39 :3   declares that the Russian soldiers will be unable to fire their guns or even hold them in their hands because of the plague that God sends upon them. God sends physical pestilence, a strange sickness, to every man involved in the military, and they are unable to handle or fire their weapons. The Russian army, navy and airforce are totally affected and wiped out.

Notice that God has said He would call for a sword against Russia from all of his mountains [Ezek 38:21]. Ezekiel is not describing a natural mountain, but using a figure of speech, oft times used in Scripture to designate kingdoms. This is the occasion for the allies of Israel to rise to her defence.

Israel will use her nuclear warheads, the U.S.A. will send her ICBMs on their way to Russian targets. The final outcome will be that in ONE 24 hour day period the entire Russian forces **plus** all of her allied forces will be destroyed, not one soldier will escape. Not one Israeli soldier will be killed or any of her allies. In that same day the nation of Russia will be destroyed and all of the Russian population killed. There will be no **survivors** because of the great earthquake and the nuclear strikes against the Russian cities.

In one day World War III will be over and Russia will cease to exist as a nation.

> **Ezek 39:7-9 "So I will make My Holy name known in the midst of My people Israel, and I will not let them profane My holy name any more. Then the nations shall know that I am the Lord, the Holy One of Israel.**
>
> **8   Surely it is coming, and it shall be done," says the Lord God. "This is the day of which I have spoken.**
>
> **9   Then those who dwell in the cities of Israel will go out and set on fire and burn the weapons, both the shields and bucklers, the bows and arrows, the javelins and spears; and they will make fires with them for seven years.** [Length of the Tribulation... this World War III takes place at the beginning of the 7 year Tribulation].

CONCLUSION

The Russian armies plus all of Russia's allied forces and the entire nation of the U.S.S.R. will be destroyed as a result of,

1.   A mighty earthquake right up into the U.S.S.R. [Ezek 38:19,20,39:6].

2. Confusion and mutiny amongst the Russian forces
    [Ezek 38:21].

3. A pestilence among the Russian troops [Ezek 38:22].

4. Great hailstones, fire and brimstone coming down
    from heaven [Ezek 38:22].

God always has the final word and World War III is no
exception - this will be God's conquest of Russia and an
action replay of David [Israel] and Goliath [U.S.S.R.].

THREE FUTURE WORLD WARS

(1)   WORLD WAR THREE
Russian invasion of Israel
Ezekiel 38, 39 ; Revelation 6v3,4

(2)   WORLD WAR FOUR
Battle of Armageddon
Revelation 14v14-20 ; 19v15 ;
Zechariah 14 Combined ten nation
forces of Antichrist, plus two
hundred million oriental army.
Revelation 9v13-19 ; 16v12,16

(3)   WORLD WAR FIVE
This final World War is the Battle
of Gog and Magog and takes place
at the end of one thousand year reign
of Christ. Satan leads all the
ungodly millenial people against
Christ and the Saints.
Revelation 20v7-10

DANIELS PROPHECY OF WORLD EMPIRES

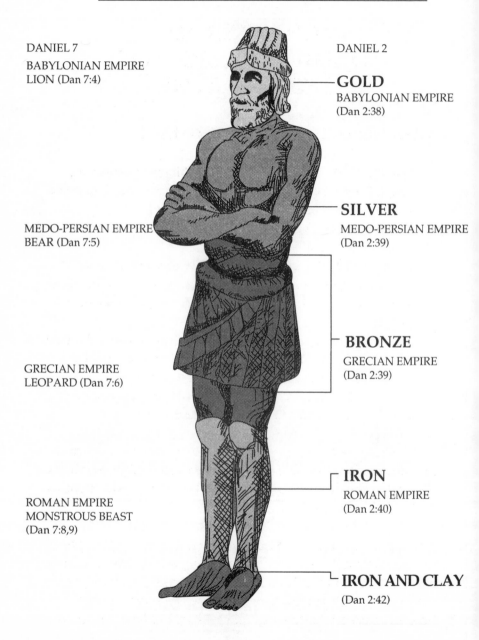

DANIEL 7

BABYLONIAN EMPIRE
LION (Dan 7:4)

DANIEL 2

GOLD
BABYLONIAN EMPIRE
(Dan 2:38)

SILVER
MEDO-PERSIAN EMPIRE
(Dan 2:39)

MEDO-PERSIAN EMPIRE
BEAR (Dan 7:5)

BRONZE
GRECIAN EMPIRE
(Dan 2:39)

GRECIAN EMPIRE
LEOPARD (Dan 7:6)

IRON
ROMAN EMPIRE
(Dan 2:40)

ROMAN EMPIRE
MONSTROUS BEAST
(Dan 7:8,9)

IRON AND CLAY
(Dan 2:42)

CHAPTER 16:
DANIEL'S VISION OF
THE END TIME.

KING NEBUCHADNEZZAR'S IMAGE

Daniel 2:31-35 "You, O king, were watching; and behold, a great image! This great image, whose splendour was excellent, stood before you; and its form was awesome.

32 This image's head was of fine gold, its chest and arms of silver, its belly and thighs of bronze,

33 its legs of iron, its feet partly of iron and partly of clay.

34 You watched while a stone was cut without hands, which struck the image on its feet of iron and clay, and broke them in pieces.

35 Then the iron, the clay, the bronze, the silver, and the gold were crushed together, and became like chaff from the summer threshing floors; the wind carried them away so that no trace of them was found. And the stone that struck the image became a great mountain and filled the whole earth."

King Nebuchadnezzar was given a dream so that he might know the things that would take place in his kingdom after his death. The dream was also a revelation of world empires that would come after him.

The great image that Nebuchadnezzar saw had five parts, each containing a specific metal: gold, silver, bronze, iron, and clay. A stone not made with the hands appeared and smote the image on the feet, breaking them into pieces. The broken pieces became like chaff, carried away with the wind. Jesus Christ is that stone made without hands [Isa 8:14, Ps 118:22, Acts 4:11]. Notice that the stone did not strike the head, which represented King Nebuchadnezzar and the Babylonian Empire. Nor did it strike the body of silver. Rather it struck the feet of iron and clay. The prophet Daniel revealed to King Nebuchadnezzar the meaning of the dream.

THE INTERPRETATION OF NEBUCHADNEZZAR'S DREAM.

Daniel 2:38[b]-45   You, O king ... you are the head of gold. But after you shall arise another kingdom inferior to yours; then another, a third kingdom of bronze, which shall rule over all the earth.

40   And the fourth kingdom shall be as strong as iron, inasmuch as iron breaks in pieces and shatters all things; and like iron that crushes, that kingdom will break in pieces and crush all the others.

41   Whereas you saw the feet and toes, partly of potter's clay and partly of iron, the kingdom shall be divided; yet the strength of the iron shall be in it, just as you saw the iron mixed with the ceramic clay.

42   And as the toes of the feet were partly of iron and partly of clay, so the kingdom shall be partly strong and partly fragile.

43   As you saw iron mixed with ceramic clay, they will mingle with the seed of men; but they will not adhere to one another, just as iron does not mix with clay.

44   And in the days of these kings the God of heaven will set up a kingdom which shall never be destroyed; and the kingdom shall not be left to other people; it shall break in pieces and consume all these kingdoms, and it shall stand forever.

45   Inasmuch as you saw that the stone was cut out of the

mountain without hands, and that it broke in pieces the iron, the bronze, the clay, the silver and the gold - the great God has made known to the king what will come to pass after this. The dream is certain and its interpretation is sure."

The great image of King Nebuchadnezzar consisted of five different substances, representing five different world empires:
1. **gold** [Babylonian Empire],
2. **silver** [Medo-Persian Empire],
3. **bronze** [Grecian Empire]
4. **iron** [Roman Empire],
5. **iron and clay** [Revised Roman Empire]. This last, the Revised Roman Empire, corresponding to the 10 toes of King Nebuchadnezzar's image will be composed of 10 kingdoms.

1. GOLD [Dan 2:32,35,38] - Babylon.

During his extended reign, King Nebuchadnezzar sieged Jerusalem, the Holy City, three times. He destroyed her walls, destroyed her great Temple, carted away her great treasures and carried away her people. He also defeated the Moabites, the Philistines, the Amorites, the Assyrians; besieged Tyre; and invaded Egypt. He made Babylon one of the wonders of the ancient world. Nebuchadnezzar's great military genius and great wealth, which he extracted from conquered land, brought him to the zenith of a world empire.

According to the historian Herodotus, Babylon was situated in a great plain. The city was square, with each side about 14 miles long, making a circuit of nearly 56 miles, covering an area of nearly 196 square miles. Around the city was a deep and broad moat [canal], full of water. Then came the wall, which was 50 royal cubits thick and 200 cubits high. The regular cubit being a little over 18 inches, the wall was more than 300 feet high. Considering that a royal cubit is equal to 21 inches, the thickness of the wall was 87 feet! Each of the wall's 100 gateways had a brass gate. The 250 towers on the wall served as guard rooms for the soldiers.

The Euphrates River divided the city into two almost equal parts. Both banks of the river were guarded by brick walls, with 25 gates connecting streets and ferry boats. There was one bridge a mile and a half long and 30 feet wide, on stone piers, with drawbridges that were removed at night. Under the river was a tunnel 15 feet wide and 12 feet high. Recent excavations have fairly well verified the fabulous accounts of the ancient historians.

Many other amazing structures and phenomenal features characterised Babylon, which was a most remarkable and outstanding city. Israel was oppressed by Babylon for 70 years. But this place of great glory, the beauty of the Chaldean's pride, was destined to be desolate. Its destruction was prophesied [Isa 13:17-22, Jer 51:37-43].

2.   SILVER [Dan 2:32,35,39] - Medo-Persia.

The Medes and the Persians succeeded Babylon as a world empire at the end of the 70 year captivity for the Jews. The two nations making up the dual kingdom are symbolised in Nebuchadnezzar's image by the two arms. This kingdom was inferior to Babylon, just as sil.·er is inferior to gold.

3.   BRONZE [Dan 2:32,35,39] - Greece.

The Greek empire came to world empire status in about 331

B.C. with Alexander the Great as its head. Alexander conquered all the territory that had belonged to both Babylon and Medo-Persia, along with India. When Alexander died at the age of 32, his empire was divided into 4 parts, each of 4 generals taking a share: Ptolemy [Egypt], Seleucus I, [Syria and Persia], Lysimachus [Asia Minor], and Cassander [Macedonia]. This was foretold in Dan 7:6, 8:8,22.

4. IRON [Dan 2:33-35,40] - Rome.

The Old Roman Empire [the fourth kingdom of the dream to oppress Israel in the time of the Gentiles] [Dan 2:40, 7:23,24, 9:26, Luke 2:1, 20:20-24] is depicted in Nebuchadnezzar's dream as the legs of iron in the image. It followed Greece in domination of Israel as the outstanding world power. We can assume this kingdom was stronger than all the previous kingdoms since iron is stronger than gold, silver or bronze.

The two legs of iron represent the eastern and western divisions of the Old Roman Empire. This kingdom continued in power until about 476 A.D.

5. IRON AND CLAY [Dan 2:33-35,41] - Revised Roman Empire.

This is man's last world empire, made up of 10 kingdoms, symbolised by 10 toes in King Nebuchadnezzar's image. It will arise out of the old Roman Empire territory, which includes the modern day countries of England, France, Belgium, Switzerland, Holland, Spain, Portugal, Italy, Austria, Hungary, Romania, Yugoslavia, Bulgaria, Albania,

Greece, Turkey, Syria, Lebanon, Egypt, Iraq, Iran, Libya, Algeria, Tunisia and Morocco. These many countries will be reduced to a 10-kingdom confederacy once the Antichrist is revealed [Dan 7:7, 8:23,24, Rev 17:10-13]. Inside the Old Roman Territory, ten kingdoms will be formed and ruled by ten kings [Dan 2:44,45, 7:7,8,23,24]. The ten kingdoms represented by the ten toes will be in existence in the last days before the Second Coming of Christ, at which time He will destroy them at His Coming [Rev 17:8,17, 19:11-21]. The ten kings will rule during the first three and a half years of the 70th Week but then the Antichrist will be in complete command for the last three and a half years [Dan 2:44,45, 7:7-25, 2 Thess 2:1-12, Rev 13:1-18, 17:8-17].

The five kingdoms seen in Nebuchadnezzar's dream involve:
Babylon [606-538 B.C.],
Medo-Persia [538-331 B.C.],
Greece [331-168 B.C.],
Rome [168 B.C.- 476 A.D.],
and the **future Revised Roman Empire**.
The feet of iron and clay will not exist until the time of the Tribulation. [The years given for Babylon, Medo-Persia, Greece and Rome are not intended to cover the entire history of these nations, but only those periods during which each of these great powers exercised world dominance.]

THE STONE [Dan 2:34-35,44-45]. The stone smiting the image symbolises the kingdom of heaven headed by the Lord Jesus Christ. He will, at His Second Coming, destroy the kingdoms of this world [Dan 2:35,44,45, 7:13-27, Zech 14:1-21, Matt 24:29-31, 25:31-46, 2 Thess 1:7-11, 2:4-8, Jude 14, Rev 11:15, 19:11-20:7]. Jesus Himself is called a "stone" [Ps 118:22, Matt 21:44, Eph 2:19-22, 1 Pet 2:6-8].

The phrase, "without hands" emphasises that Jesus' coming will not be due to human instrumentality, but rather an act of God. The kingdom of God will be set up in the time of Jesus' Second Coming and it will never be destroyed.

Jesus is coming back again. He will smite the world systems and pulverise them into powder. The wickedness, rot, dirt and hell of the world today will be completely defeated by the power of His greatness and glory. The evil leaders of the world will be finished. That last kingdom under the Antichrist will be destroyed. The stone that Nebuchadnezzar saw will grow into a huge mountain that will fill and cover the entire earth. Praise the Lord!

DANIEL'S PROPHECY OF THE SEVENTY WEEKS.

The prophecy of the 70 Weeks of Years was given under unusual circumstances. The prophet Daniel and his people had been taken into Babylonian captivity and the Holy City, Jerusalem, had been desecrated and sacked [2 Chron 36:17-21]. The prophet Daniel had learned from studying the parchments that the prophet Jeremiah, years ago, had twice written in his prophecy that Israel would be in captivity for 70 years [Jer 25:11,12, 29:10]. Calculating from the fall of Jerusalem and the carrying away of captives to his present day, Daniel discovered that the 70 years were almost ended and it was time for his people to be returned to their homeland.

Immediately upon realizing the significance of this revelation for his people, the Jewish Nation, and for the Holy City, Jerusalem, Daniel set himself to prayer and supplication before God, confessing his sins and the sins of his people, which had resulted in this great calamity. While Daniel was seeking the face of God, through prayer and supplication, the Angel Gabriel appeared to him and began to reveal God's plan for the future of Israel from that present time right into the Millennium.

> Dan 9:23   "At the beginning of your supplications the commandment went out, and I have come to tell you, for you are greatly beloved; therefore consider the matter, and understand the vision."

He went on to tell him:

> Dan 9:24-27 "Seventy weeks are determined For your people and for your holy city, To finish the transgression, To make an end of sins, To make reconciliation for iniquity, To bring in everlasting righteousness, To seal up vision and prophecy, And to anoint the Most Holy.
> 25   "Know therefore and understand, That from the going forth of the command To restore and rebuild Jerusalem Until the Messiah the Prince, There shall be seven weeks and sixty-two weeks; The street shall be built again and the wall, Even in troublesome times.
> 26   "And after the sixty-two weeks Messiah shall be cut off but not for Himself; And the people of the prince who is to come Shall destroy the city and the sanctuary. The end of it shall be with a flood, And till the end of the war desolations are determined.
> 27   Then he shall confirm a covenant with many for one week; But in the middle of the week He shall bring an end to sacrifice and offering. And on the wings of abominations shall be one who makes desolate, Even until the consummation which is determined, Is poured out on the desolate."

The **first** thing that we notice is that ...

"seventy weeks are determined."

In other words, they have been fixed and planned by God, and therefore cannot be changed.
The **second** thing we notice is that the weeks concern ...

"your people and ... your holy city"

No Gentiles are mentioned here. In other words, this does not in any way concern the Church, but it relates specifically to the restoration of Israel to the Promised Land.

The next thing that we need to understand is the meaning of the term **seventy weeks** in Dan 9:24. The Hebrew word for WEEKS is "SHABUA" and literally means a "SEVEN". So then, in the Hebrew, the idea of seventy weeks is seventy sevens or seventy segments of seven.
The Hebrew word for DETERMINED is "CHATHAK" and literally means "CUT OUT" or "MARKED OFF".

There are several reasons for believing that the 70 weeks of Daniel are in fact 70 segments of seven years.

Reasons;

1.   We have established that the events of verse 24 concerning the Jews and Jerusalem take place in the Millennium. The Millennium hasn't arrived yet and if it was just 70 weeks then we should be living in the Millennium now - [which obviously is not the case].

2.   According to the opening of this chapter in Dan 9:2, Daniel had been thinking in terms of years NOT days, NOT weeks, but years. Thus we are not discussing days, or weeks but years.

3.   According to Dan 9:25 the time period involved in rebuilding Jerusalem is 7 weeks which if it were 7 segments of 7 days = 49 days, or if it were 7 segments of 7 weeks = 49 weeks. Of course this is physically impossible!

So, what then is the true meaning of the 70 weeks? The time period is seventy segments of seven years = 490 years.

Each week represents 7 years;

70 weeks represents 70 x 7 = 490 years.

Therefore, what God is saying in Dan 9:24 is that **70 WEEKS OF TIME** or **490 YEARS** is **CUT OUT** or **MARKED OFF** for the Jewish people until the beginning of the Millennium.

The Bible is God's Prophetic Textbook and blueprint for these last days and end time prophetic events! The seventy weeks of God's determined dealings and plan for Israel is prophesied in Dan 9:21-27. God's determined plan for Israel is a period of time of 490 years i.e. "70 weeks".

As we study this more closely we find there was a break/gap, in the fulfillment of this prophetic plan for Israel, between the end of week 69 and the beginning of week 70. During this break/gap God brought in the Church Age of approximately 2,000 years so that the Church Age is **sandwiched** in between week 69 and week 70.

6 THINGS THAT MUST BE FULFILLED BY THE END OF THE 70 WEEKS.

1.   To finish Transgression [unfulfilled].

SEVENTIETH WEEK OF DANIEL

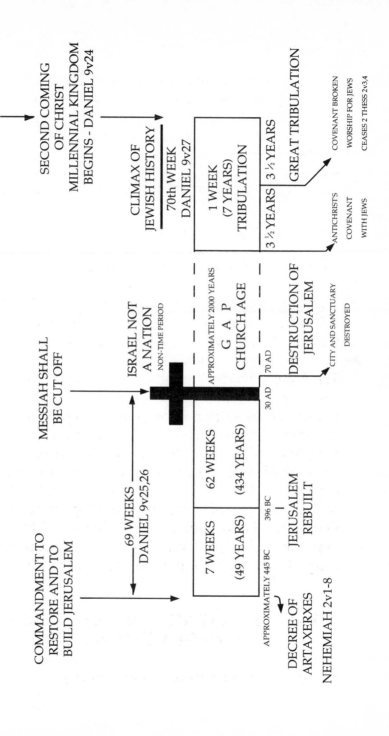

SOUND THE ALARM

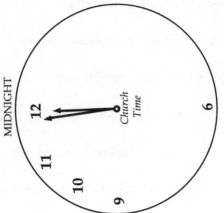

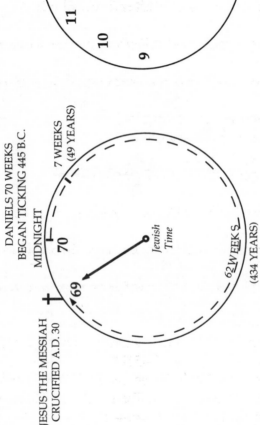

DANIELS 70 WEEKS
BEGAN TICKING 445 B.C.

7 WEEKS
(49 YEARS)

MIDNIGHT

70

69

JESUS THE MESSIAH
CRUCIFIED A.D. 30

Jewish Time

62 WEEKS
(434 YEARS)

The Jewish clock stopped at calvary.
It will re-start after the Rapture of
the Church when Daniels 70th Week
begins!

MIDNIGHT

12

11

10

9

6

Church Time

The Church Clock began ticking
on the day of Pentecost.
Time is running out fast-
The Rapture is IMMINENT!!
The clock will stop at the Rapture.
Church Time is between Daniels
69th & 70th week.

2. To make an end of sins [unfulfilled].

3. To make reconciliation for iniquity [unfulfilled].

4. To bring in EVERLASTING righteousness [unfulfilled].

5. To seal up the prophetic Scriptures [unfulfilled].

6. To "anoint" the Holy of Holies [unfulfilled].

These 6 things can **only** be fulfilled during the Millenium.

Notice carefully that the weeks are divided into a trilogy of events:
1. seven weeks of years [49 years],
2. 62 weeks of years [434 years],
3. one week of years [7 years],
... a total of 70 weeks of years [490 years].

The prophecy of the 70 weeks of years begins with,

"the commandment to restore and build Jerusalem."

Three decrees for the restoration of Jerusalem were actually given.

1. The **first** decree was given in the first year King Cyrus of Persia [Ezra 1:1-4, 3:8, Isa 45:1-4, 46:11]. Cyrus reigned for 9 years and then was succeeded by his son, Cambyses, who reigned for 7 years. During Cambyses' reign work on the Temple ceased [Ezra 4:1-24].

2. The **second** decree was given by Darius the Mede, who reigned for 35 years. In the second year of his reign he

reactivated Cyrus' decree. Consequently the Temple was completed in the sixth year of Darius but the city was not restored.

3.   The **third** decree was given by Artaxerxes about 20 years into his reign [@ 445 B.C.]. It was at this time that Nehemiah rebuilt the walls of Jerusalem which had fallen down.

And so, we begin the calculation of the 490 years from the time of the decree to rebuild Jerusalem was issued to Nehemiah in 445 B.C. [Neh 2:1-9]. It was hearing of the broken down walls and burned gates of Jerusalem that stirred Nehemiah to a state of prayer and fasting for Jerusalem and the nation. As the Jewish cupbearer for King Artaxerxes, Nehemiah petitioned the king's favour [Neh 2:1-8].

At his request the king gave Nehemiah an official letter to give to the provisional governor of Jerusalem allowing him safe passage and another letter permitting him timber to rebuild the walls.

The most significant part here, besides the command to build the city, is that it took place in the 20th year of Artaxerxes. History tells us that the date of Artaxerxes' ascension to the throne of Persia was 465 B.C. The 20 th year of his reign would place the date of this decree at 445 B.C. Here we have the beginning of the 70 weeks. The angel told Daniel:

> Dan 9:25 "Know therefore and understand, That from the going forth of the command To restore and build Jerusalem Until the Messiah the Prince, There shall be seven weeks and sixty-two

weeks; The street shall be built again, and the wall, Even in troublesome times.

Again keep in mind that Daniel's 70 weeks of years are divided into three divisions:
1.   7 weeks of years = 49 years.
2.   62 weeks of years = 434 years.
3.   1 week of years = 7 years.
70 weeks of years = 490 years.

First Period of Time = 49 years.

Dating from the month of [March] NISAN, 445 B.C. the date the building permit was issued to Nehemiah until the rebuilding of Jerusalem and the walls of the city took 49 years, and was completed in 396 B.C.

Second Period of Time = 434 years.

Dan 9:26 "And after the sixty-two weeks Messiah shall be cut off, but not for Himself; And the people of the prince who is to come Shall destroy the city and the sanctuary. The end of it shall be with a flood, And till the end of the war desolations are determined.

This second period began in 396 B.C. immediately after the rebuilding of Jerusalem and continued for 434 years until Messiah the Prince was "cut off" - crucified in A.D. 30 at Calvary.

At the cross Jesus, the Messiah, was cut off in death "BUT NOT FOR HIMSELF".

Isa 53:5   But He was wounded for our transgressions, He was bruised for our iniquities; The chastisement for our peace was upon Him, And by His stripes we are healed.

1 Peter 3:18 For Christ also suffered once for sins, the just for the unjust, that He might bring us to God, being put to death in the flesh but made alive in the Spirit.

2 Cor 5:21 For He made Him who knew no sin to be sin for us, that we might become the righteousness of God in Him.

At the end of Daniel's 69th week Jesus was crucified which was in A.D. 30. Thus this prophecy of Daniel accurately pinpointed and predicted the time of Christ's crucifixion - a prophecy given over 500 years before the birth of Christ, once again showing that the Bible is the infallible, inspired Word of God.

Dan 9:26 "... And the people of the prince who is to come Shall destroy the city and the sanctuary."

Who are the people of the prince?
Which people is Daniel discussing here?

This has reference to the Romans. They fulfilled the prophecy of the destruction of the city and the temple and brought the desolations of verse 26. Roman soldiers under Titus destroyed the city and temple in 70 A.D.

Luke 21:20 "But when you see Jerusalem surrounded by armies, then know that its desolation is near."
Luke 21:24 "And they will fall by the edge of the sword, and be led away captive to all nations. And Jerusalem will be trampled by Gentiles until the times of the Gentiles are fulfilled."

Luke 19:43,44 "For the days will come upon you when your enemies will build an embankment around you, surround you and close you in on every side,

**44   and level you, and your children within you, to the ground;
and they will not leave in you one stone upon another, because
you did not know the time of your visitation."**

The reference made to, "the prince that shall come" [v26] is
a reference to the future Antichrist, who will come from the
territory of the Roman Empire. He will come from the
people who destroyed the city and the temple of Israel in 70
A.D. [Luke 21:20-24]. He will come from among the ten
kingdoms of the Revised Roman Empire that are yet to be
formed with the territory of the Old Roman Empire [v26,27].

First, the crucifixion of Christ came at the end of the 69th
week [v26]. Secondly, the destruction of Jerusalem and the
temple by the Romans came between the crucifixion, at the
end of the 69th week and the 70th week [v26,27]. The third
event concerns a war between the Romans and Israel
between the 69th and 70th weeks. Israel was defeated and
scattered among the nations at the end of this war. This is
that which is described as a flood unto the end of the war,
which carried them away [v26,27, Luke 21:24].

Jerusalem was destroyed about 40 years after the crucifixion
of Christ, which ended the 69th week. The next event to be
noted between the 69th and 70th weeks is that the prince
"who was to come" would do so after the destruction and
desolation of Jerusalem [v26,27]. The Jews were led away
captive among all the nations about 70 A.D.,so the prince
who shall come would not be able to confirm the covenant
with the Jews to fulfill verse 27 until they [the Jews] would
be back together in their own land. Also, it must be pointed
out that Jerusalem and the sanctuary that was destroyed
must be restored before the 7 year covenant of verse 27 can

be made. The temple is to be made desolate again in the midst of the 7 years. It has never been restored from 70 A.D until now, so the fulfillment of verse 27 must still be future.

We must clearly understand that between the 69th week and the 70th week the prophetic time clock with Israel was suspended. The intervening period, between the Crucifixion and the Tribulation has been the Church age or a period when God no longer has dealt with Israel as a nation. Jerusalem was destroyed in A.D 70 by the Roman army. Since that time Israel has been dispersed among the nations of the world, and God has been calling out a Church, the Body of Christ, to fulfill His divine plan. When the Church is raptured, God once again will deal with national Israel in the last unfulfilled week of Daniel's prophecy, commonly called the Tribulation:

> Jer 30:7   Alas! For that day is great, So that none is like it; And it is the time of Jacob's trouble, But he shall be saved out of it.

Third Period of Time = 7 years.

This is the final week of years which is yet to be fulfilled in the future and is known as Daniel's 70th Week.

> Daniel 9:27   "Then he shall confirm a covenant with many for one week; But in the middle of the week He shall bring an end to sacrifice and offering, And on the wing of abominations shall be one who makes desolate, Even until the consummation which is determined, Is poured out on the desolate."

Who is the "he" of Dan 9:27?

It cannot be Jesus Christ because He did not confirm a

covenant with anyone according to the Bible or secular history. It could not be General Titus or Emperor Nero. Titus did not confirm a covenant with the Jews and then break it in the middle of the "week". Furthermore, the Jews were scattered throughout the world after the Roman destruction of the Holy City. So, the "prince" could not confirm a covenant with the Jews until they are brought back into their Land.

According to Dan 9:27, the Temple will again be desolate in the middle of the "week". Since A.D. 70 the Temple has never been restored. So the fulfillment of Dan 9:27 must still be future.

It is obvious, then, that the 70th week remains to be fulfilled when God again deals with Israel as a nation [Ezek 37]. Then, in order for the events of Dan 9:27 to transpire, it would be necessary for the Jews to be established in their land and for the Temple to be in operation.

The "he" of Dan 9:27 is the "prince that shall come" of verse 26, the coming deceiver of Israel, the Antichrist. He will not appear before the world until the ten kingdoms [Dan 7:23,24] are formed within the old Roman Empire and until after the Rapture of the Church [2 Thess 2:6-8]. His "week" will be the last of Daniel's 70 weeks of years - the 70th week. This "week" will comprise the time between the Rapture and the Second Coming of Christ, that time known as the Tribulation.

In the middle of this "week", or after three and a half years, the Antichrist will break covenant with Israel. He will invade Jerusalem, defile the Temple, and set himself up as god in the temple in Jerusalem.

The cutting off of the Messiah and the events of the 69 weeks are behind. The events of the 70th week remain for the future. They will be realised in the age of the Tribulation of seven years just prior to the Second Coming of Christ and ushering in of "everlasting righteousness" [Dan 9:24]. Between the 69th and the 70th weeks there is a long uncharted lapse of time. It was not revealed to Daniel or any of the Old Testament prophets. The intervening time span incorporates the Age of the Church in which we are now living. So the Church Age is sandwiched between the end of the 69th week and the start of Daniel's 70th week - a period of almost 2,000 years. Other gaps in Scripture that may be mentioned for study are Isa 9:6, Zech 9:9,10, and Acts 2:16-21.

UNDERSTANDING THE 3 TIME PERIODS OF DANIELS 70 WEEKS

DANIEL 9v25-27

DANIEL 9v25 : FIRST TIME PERIOD
7 weeks of years = 49years

DANIEL 9v26 : SECOND TIME PERIOD
62 weeks of years = 434 years

TOTAL = 69 weeks of years = 483 years

Jesus the Messiah was "cut off" at calvary (crucified) - as our substitute at the end of the second time period after 69 weeks of this prophecy was fulfilled

"AFTER" THE END OF THE 69 WEEKS

(1) Jesus the Messiah was crucified **AD 30**

(2) Romans destroyed the temple and Jerusalem **AD 70**

(3) Jewish people were carried into slavery and scattered amongst the nations **AD 70**

DANIEL 9v27 : THIRD TIME PERIOD
1 week is yet future

Daniels 70th week
can only take place during the tribulation period

DANIEL 9v26

After Jesus was "cut off" and crucified in Jerusalem God then brought in the Church age

The Church age is sandwiched in between week 69 and week 70

The Church age is now rapidly coming to a close as we see the **prophetic signposts** around us being fulfilled

We are now approaching the time when God will bring in Daniels 70th week and complete the last 7 years of His plan for Israel

After 69 weeks/483 years of God's determined dealings with Israel Jesus Christ is crucified and God puts the "pause button" on Israel and introduces the church age which runs for approximately 2 000 years and terminates at the rapture

Immediately following the rapture God re-starts His programme and dealings with Israel for the final week/seven years during the tribulation period

CHAPTER 17:
THE TRUTH ABOUT THE
COMING ANTICHRIST.

Most of the teaching about the Antichrist magnifies Satan's programme and is unsound Biblically. It merely releases **doom**, **gloom** and **fear** on the people, [Remember that fear is Satan's number one tool]. This usually produces large altar calls with a good number of psychological and emotional decisions but without true salvation taking place in people's hearts.

Satan's agent, the Antichrist, begins his 7 year satanic assignment only at the beginning of the Tribulation by negotiating and making a peace treaty with Israel [Dan 9:27].

2 Thess 2:1-8 and Rev 6:1,2 tell us that the Antichrist can only be revealed AFTER the Rapture of the Church. In other words nobody can know the personal identity of the Antichrist until the 7 year Tribulation begins, immediately following the Rapture, although we do know that the Antichrist is alive today, active in politics and being prepared for his work.

The Bible states that no-one today can accurately name or identify the Antichrist, however this has not prevented misguided prophetic teachers trying to guess and speculate who they believe the Antichrist is. The "guesswork" list is endless and books by the thousands have been sold over the years. Here is a sample of those suggested;

— Judas Iscariot resurrected
— Adolf Hitler
— Mussolini
— John F. Kennedy
— The Pope
— Henry Kissinger
— King Juan Carlos of Spain
— Ronald[6], Wilson[6], Reagan[6]...[666!]

There is a scriptural and a specific time for the Antichrist to be revealed and his identity discovered which is with the opening of the first seal of Revelation 6 marking the beginning of the 7 year Tribulation period [2 Thess 2:3 & 6-8].
The presence of the Church in the earth today [the salt and the light] is holding in check and preventing the revelation of the Antichrist.
Only once the "Hinderer of Lawlessness" [the glorious and victorious Church] of 2 Thess 2 has been supernaturally removed from the earth, can satan's agent the Antichrist come forth.

For Bible information about the Antichrist please read and study, Daniel chapters 7,8 & 11 and Revelation chapters 13 & 17.

THE NAMES AND TITLES OF THE ANTICHRIST.

Many names and titles are given to this individual in the Scriptures. He is called,

"the Assyrian" .... Isa 10:5-12

"the King of Babylon" .... Isa 14:4

"the Spoiler" ....Isa 16:4-5

"the Little Horn" ....Daniel 7:8

"the Prince that shall come" ....Daniel 9:26

"the Vile Person" ....Daniel 11:21

"the Wilful King" ....Daniel 11:36

"the Man of Sin" ....2 Thess 2:3

"the Son of Perdition" ....2 Thess 2:3

"the Beast" ....Rev 13:1

"the King of Fierce Countenance" .....Daniel 8:23

"the King of the North" ....Daniel 11:36-45

SCRIPTURAL TRUTHS ABOUT THE FUTURE ANTICHRIST.

The Scriptures have much to say about the person and work of the future Antichrist:

1] He will appear on the scene in the "LAST YEARS" of Israel's history [Dan 8:23].

2] His manifestation is being hindered by the True Church, "the Restrainer" [2 Thess 2:6,7].

3] The Antichrist will be a demon possessed, satanically -

controlled man and a spiritualist medium of the highest order, well able to communicate with the devil [Dan 8:23-25]. With Satan's ability to lie and deceive, he will perform lying signs and wonders causing many to worship him as god! [2 Thess 2:9-12].

4] One of the traits of the Antichrist is that he will be a homosexual [Dan 11:37].

5] His rise comes through his peace programme [Dan 8:25, Dan 11:21].

6] As the head of a 10 nation empire, he makes a 7 year covenant with Israel [Dan 9:27] which is broken after three and a half years at Mid-Tribulation [Dan 9:27].

7] He introduces idolatrous worship in which he sets himself up as "god" [Dan 11:36,37, 2 Thess 2:4, Rev 13:5].

8] The Antichrist cannot be revealed until after the Rapture of the Church as proved in 2 Thess 2:1-8.

9] The Antichrist will not come from Russia as some teach, because the entire nation of Russia will be destroyed in one day at the opening of the second seal of Revelation chapter 6. God supernaturally conquers Russia when Russia and her allies invade Israel [Ezek 38 & 39].

10] He is energised by Satan [Rev 13:4], receives his authority from him, and is controlled by the pride of the devil [Dan 8:25].

11] His rule will be terminated by a direct judgment from

God and he will be cast into the lake of fire [Rev 19:20]. This judgment will take place at the Second Coming of Christ [2 Thess 2:8, Dan 7:22].

12] NOT ONE VERSE OF SCRIPTURE CAN BE PRODUCED THAT TEACHES US THAT.....

*   the Antichrist will rule the world as DICTATOR;
*   there will be a ONE WORLD GOVERNMENT with the Antichrist as its head;
*   there will be a ONE WORLD MONETARY SYSTEM;
*   the Beast is a MASSIVE COMPUTER SYSTEM [See Rev 19:19,20].

All these statements are guesswork and speculation and, as I have stated so often in this book, we must stay with the information in God's Word!

THE MARK OF THE BEAST.

·When the Antichrist [the Beast] comes into full power and authority, he will be able to exercise all the power of a fully-fledged dictator, and even more, all the power of a sorcerer or medium. He will make many demands of the people. He will command their allegiance, their worship and in effect, their livelihood. He will exercise total control of those whom he governs in his ten nation empire.

Midway in the Tribulation he will require all his subjects to receive a mark on their right hand or on their forehead in order to buy or sell [Rev 13:16-18]. Some people, of course, will refuse, and for this they will be executed [Rev 7:9-17, 13:7, 14:13, 15:2,3, 20:4].

In a way that we do not fully understand, this mark will be tied in with occult worship, so that in taking the mark a person commits apostasy, and can never be saved. To take this mark the individual must totally deny Jesus Christ and, in so many words, sell his soul to the devil. There are three features of this adherence to the Beast:

1   **MARK OF THE BEAST**. This is different from the name of the Beast or the number of his name. We do not know what the mark will be, but it must be an emblem, like a tattoo or lazer image, imprinted on or under the skin that stands for the kingdom of the Antichrist [Rev 13:16].

2   **NAME OF THE BEAST**. We do not know the name of the Beast, but during the Tribulation, of course, he will ultimately be identified. Instead of receiving a mark, a person may receive his name. Like the mark it may be tattooed or imprinted on the body [Rev 13:17].

3   **NUMBER OF THE BEAST**. Rev 13:17 says, "number of his name", and Rev 13:8 says, "number of the beast". Like the emblem and the name, it must be an ID number that can be tattooed or imprinted on the right hand or forehead. His number is 666.

Many people have tried to calculate the number of the Beast. Someone has said it refers to the Latin Kingdom [Romanism], which has been tallied 666. Others have said the Greek letters of the alphabet have numerical meaning, and as such may be tallied to a sum total. We do not really know at this point in time what the number of the Beast means, even though we are told it is 666.

CHAPTER 18:
THE SECOND COMING OF
CHRIST.

The Second Coming of Christ takes place seven years after the Rapture. At that time Christ will come to the earth. He will bring the saints with Him. He will fight the armies of the Antichrist and set up the Millennial Kingdom. This event cannot take place until after the events of Revelation 4 through to 19 are fulfilled.

When Christ comes He will make no secret of His arrival. Rather, it will be like a huge bolt of lightning that illuminates the night sky: obvious and magnificent [Matt 24:27]. In fact, Jesus will come back to earth at His Second Coming in exactly the same way that He departed from the earth when He went to the right hand of the Father. Two men [presumably angels who looked like men] in "white apparel" revealed this to the Apostles: "'Men of Galilee, why do you stand gazing up into heaven? This same Jesus, who was taken up from you into heaven, will so come in like manner as you saw Him go into heaven'" [Acts 1:10,11].

This means that Christ's return will be a **bodily** one. It will not be some sort of spiritual return - it will be the real thing. Christ had a real body when He was on earth [1 John 1:1], and He will come in a real body when He returns to earth. At the Second Coming, Jesus will return in the clouds. "He was taken up, and a cloud received Him out of their sight" [Acts 1:9]. Although He will be clearly visible as He comes, He will also be surrounded by clouds.

Jesus at His return will be in the full view of the people. "Now when He had spoken these things, while they watched, He was taken up" [Acts 1:9]. Like the tourists at Cape Canaveral who follow the course of a rocket launch until it disappears from view, the Apostles followed Christ as He ascended into heaven until the clouds obscured their view. In the same way, those on the earth at the end of the Tribulation will be able to see Christ return and follow Him as He descends from heaven to earth with His armies.

Jesus Christ will at His Second Coming return to the Mount of Olives. He ascended into heaven from the Mount of Olives [Acts 1:12], and at His Second Coming He will return to the Mount of Olives [Zech 14:4]. This event will cause an earthquake that will split the mount and open up "a very large valley; half the mountain shall move toward the north and half of it toward the south" [Zech 14:4].

We are also given a description of His magnificent appearance as He descends. Like a Roman general riding in triumph, Christ will lead the armies of heaven to the earth. He will be riding a white stallion as our triumphant King of kings and Lord of lords.

> Rev 19:11-16 Then I saw heaven opened, and behold, a white horse. And He who sat on Him was called Faithful and True, and in righteousness He judges and makes war.
> 12 His eyes were like a flame of fire, and on His head were many crowns. He had a name written that no one knew except Himself.
> 13 He was clothed with a robe dipped in blood, and His name is called The Word of God.
> 14 And the armies in heaven, clothed in fine linen, white and clean, followed Him on white horses.
> 15 Now out of His mouth goes a sharp sword, that with it He

should strike the nations. And He Himself will rule them with a rod of iron. He Himself treads the winepress of the fierceness and wrath of Almighty God. And He has on His robe and on His thigh a name written:

KING OF KINGS AND LORD OF LORDS.

When Jesus came the first time, He came as the Lamb of God; when He comes the second time, He will come as the Lion of the Tribe of Judah.

As the Man of Galilee, He rode on the foal of an ass; as King of kings and Lord of lords, He will ride on a white stallion.

He came as a servant in humility; He will come as a Judge in power.

He came as a Saviour to die; He will come as a King to reign.

He came the first time to wear a crown of thorns; He will come again to wear the Royal Diadem.

When He came the first time, He was beaten with rods; when He comes the second time, He will rule the nations with a rod of iron.

When He came the first time, He came to die on a cruel cross; He will come to reign on a glorious Throne.

When He came the first time, His own received Him not; when He comes the second time, every knee shall bow, and every tongue shall confess that Jesus Christ is Lord to the glory of God the Father.

BIBLE REFERENCES TO THE SECOND COMING.

Dan 2:44,45 "And in the days of these kings the God of heaven will set up a kingdom which shall never be destroyed; and the kingdom shall not be left to other people; it shall break in pieces and consume all these kingdoms, and it shall stand forever.
45 Inasmuch as you saw that the stone was cut out of the mountain without hands, and that it broke in pieces the iron, the bronze, the clay, the silver, and the gold - the great God has made known to the king what will come to pass after this. The dream is certain, and its interpretation is sure."

Dan 7:13,14 "I was watching in the night visions, And behold, One like the Son of Man, Coming with the clouds of heaven! He came to the Ancient of Days, And they brought Him near before Him.
14 Then to Him was given dominion and glory and a kingdom, That all the peoples, nations and languages should serve Him. His dominion is an everlasting dominion, Which shall not pass away, And His kingdom the one which shall not be destroyed.

Zech 14:4 And in that day His feet will stand on the Mount of Olives, Which faces Jerusalem on the east. And the Mount of Olives shall be split in two, From east to west, Making a very large valley; Half of the mountain shall move toward the north And half of it toward the south.

Matt 24:29,30 "Immediately after the tribulation of those days the sun will be darkened, and the moon will not give its light; the stars will fall from heaven, and the powers of the heavens will be shaken.
30 Then the sign of the Son of Man will appear in heaven, and then all the tribes of the earth will mourn, and they will see the

Son of Man coming on the clouds of heaven with power and great glory."

Matt 25:31 "When the Son of Man comes in His glory, and all the holy angels with Him, then He will sit on the throne of His glory."

2 Thess 1:7-10 And to give you who are troubled rest with us when the Lord Jesus is revealed from heaven with His mighty angels,
8 in flaming fire taking vengeance on those who do not know God, and on those who do not obey the gospel of our Lord Jesus Christ.
9 These shall be punished with everlasting destruction from the presence of the Lord and from the glory of His power,
10 when He comes, in that Day to be glorified in His saints and to be admired among all those who believe, because our testimony among you was believed.

2 Thess 2:8 And then the lawless one will be revealed, whom the Lord will consume with the breath of His mouth and destroy with the brightness of His coming.

Jude 14,15 Now Enoch, the seventh from Adam, prophesied about these men also, saying, "Behold, the Lord comes with ten thousands of His saints,
15 to execute judgment on all to convict all who are ungodly among them of all their ungodly deeds which they have committed in an ungodly way, and of all the harsh things which ungodly sinners have spoken against Him".

Isa 63:4,5 For the day of vengeance is in My heart, And the year of My redeemed has come.
5 I looked, but there was no one to help, And I wondered that

there was no one to uphold; Therefore My own arm brought salvation for Me; And My own fury, it sustained Me.

Joel 3:16   The Lord also will roar from Zion, And utter His voice from Jerusalem; The heavens and earth will shake; But the Lord will be a shelter for His people, And the strength of the children of Israel.

Rev 1:7   Behold, He is coming with the clouds, and every eye will see Him, and they also who pierced Him. And all the tribes of the earth will mourn because of Him. Even so, Amen.

Rev 19:11-21   "And I saw heaven opened, and behold a white horse; and He that sat upon him was called Faithful and True, and in righteousness He judges and makes war ... And the armies in heaven, clothed in fine linen, white and clean, followed Him on white horses."

DIFFERENT FROM THE RAPTURE.

According to 1 Thess 4:13-18, the next event on God's End Time calendar is the Rapture not the Second Coming of Christ. The **Rapture of the Church** is the sudden supernatural removal of the Body of Christ from the earth to meet Jesus when He appears for us in the atmosphere.

The Rapture is the appearing of Jesus and the catching up of the Church. The Rapture involves a two fold operation;

1.   The resurrection of the SAVED DEAD - to be reunited with their spirit/soul in the atmosphere.
2.   The translation [catching up] of every Born Again Believer living at that time.

WHY THE CHURCH WILL BE RAPTURED <u>BEFORE</u> THE TRIBULATION BEGINS

(1)   <u>Because</u> of God's character
(Psalm 145v8,9)

(2)   <u>Because</u> in the Bible God never judges the righteous with the wicked
(Nahum 1v2,3)

(3)   <u>Because</u> God has made definite promises to the Church
(1 Thessalonians 5v9)

(4)   <u>Because</u> the Church is not mentioned again in God's Word after Revelation 3v22

(5)   <u>Because</u> in Revelation chapter 4 & 5 the raptured saints are already in heaven before the tribulation begins in chapter 6
(Revelation 5v9)

(6)   <u>Because</u> the Antichrist cannot begin his assignment until the Church has been removed
(2 Thessalonians 2v1-8)

(7)   <u>Because</u> the rapture is called in scripture the "Blessed Hope" of the Church
(Titus 2v13)

THE BELIEVERS REWARDS

REVELATION 22v12
"And behold, I am coming quickly, and My reward
is with Me, to give to everyone according
to his work."

(1)   ## THE VICTORS CROWN
This is given to those who overcome the flesh
1 Corinthians 9v25-27

(2)   ## THE SOULWINNERS CROWN
This is the crown of rejoicing given to those who
win the lost at any cost
1 Thessalonians 2v19

(3)   ## THE CROWN OF GLORY
This is given to faithful pastors and teachers
1 Peter 5v2-4

(4)   ## THE CROWN OF RIGHTEOUSNESS
Given to those who live their lives in
expectation of the rapture
2 Timothy 4v8

(5)   ## THE CROWN OF LIFE
Given to those believers who successfully
overcome temptation, tests, trials and persecutions
for the gospel's sake
James 1v12 : Revelation 2v10

(6)   ## THE CROWN OF GOLD
Revelation 4v4

(7)   ## THE OVERCOMERS INHERITANCE
Revelation Chapters 2&3

DIFFERENCES BETWEEN THE RAPTURE AND THE SECOND COMING.

1. The Church will meet Christ in the air [1 Thess 4:17].

1. The Church will return to the earth with Christ [Zech 14:4].

2. The Church will be taken to heaven [1 Thess 4:17, John 14:3].

2. The Church will return to the earth from heaven [Jude 14, Matt 25:31].

3. Christ will come for His saints [2 Thess 2:1].

3. Christ will come with His saints [Rev 19:14].

4. The Rapture is a "MYSTERY" - a truth unknown in Old Testament times [1 Cor 15:51].

4. The Second Coming is NOT a mystery but is the subject of many Old Testament prophecies [Isa 11, Zech 14].

5. Satan will not be bound [Rev 13:2].

5. Satan will be bound [Rev 20:3].

6. The righteous will be removed [1 Thess 4:17].

6. The wicked will be removed [Matt 25:40,41].

7. No signs will lead to the Rapture [2 Pet 3:10].

7. Signs will precede the Second Coming [Matt 24:24].

8. It occurs BEFORE the Tribulation [Rev 4].

8. It occurs AFTER the Tribulation [Matt24:29,30].

THE MANNER OF HIS SECOND COMING.

Many phrases, words and expressions are used in Scripture to describe the manner of the Second Coming of Christ.

1.   His Coming will be Swift.

Matt 24:27 "For as lightning comes from the east and flashes to the west, so also will the coming of the Son of Man be."

2.   His Coming will be with Power and Great Glory.

Matt 24:30   "Then the sign of the Son of Man will appear in heaven, and then all the tribes of the earth will mourn, and they will see the Son of Man coming on the clouds of heaven with power and great glory."

3.   His Coming will be with Brightness and Fire .

2 Thess 1:7,8,10 "The Lord Jesus shall be revealed from heaven with His mighty angels, In flaming fire taking vengeance on them that know not God ... when He shall come."

4.   His Coming will be with Vengeance and Great Wrath.

Micah 5:10,15 "And it shall be in that day ", says the Lord, "That I will cut off your horses from your midst And destroy your chariots.
15 And I will execute vengeance in anger and fury On the nations that have not heard."

5.   His Coming will be as Judge and King.

Matt 25:31 "When the Son of Man comes in His glory, and all the holy angels with Him, then He will sit on the throne of His glory."

6. His Coming will be with Saints and Angels.

Zech 14:5 ... Thus the Lord my God will come, And all the saints with You.

Matt 24:31 "And He will send His angels with a great sound of a trumpet, and they will gather together His elect from the four winds, from one end of heaven to the other."

7. His Coming will be Sudden.

1 Thess 5:2,3 For you yourselves know perfectly that the day of the Lord so comes as a thief in the night.
3 For when they say, "Peace and safety!" then sudden destruction comes upon them, as labour pains upon a pregnant woman. And they shall not escape.

8. His Coming will be literal.

Zech 14:4 And in that day His feet will stand on the Mount of Olives, Which faces Jerusalem on the east. And the Mount of Olives shall be split in two, from east to west, making a very large valley; Half of the mountain shall move toward the north And half of it toward the south.

9. His Coming will be Visible.

Rev 1:7 Behold, He is coming with the clouds, and every eye shall see Him, and they also who pierced Him. And all the tribes of the earth will mourn because of Him. Even so, Amen.

10. His Coming will be with the Clouds.

Matt 26:64 Jesus said to him, "It is as you said. Nevertheless, I

say to you hereafter you will see the Son of Man sitting at the
right hand of the Power, and coming on the clouds of heaven."

A LITERAL COMING.

The Second Coming of Christ will coincide with the other
events on the prophetic agenda. It will be a day of horrible
destruction, in which the Battle of Armageddon will be
fought. It will also be a day of national repentance, as Israel
learns that the Son of Man, Jesus Christ of Nazareth, is truly
her long-awaited Messiah. It will also be a day of judgment
upon the earth and catastrophic changes in the earth's
surface.

Just prior to Christ's return, Jerusalem will be taken by the
Antichrist, the houses will be rifled, the women will be
ravished, and the city will go into captivity [Zech 14:1,2,
Matt 24]. Suddenly Christ will appear from heaven, with
His armies and defeat the Antichrist forces in a one-day
battle. At this time He will take over the kingdoms of this
world and set up His own Kingdom, to reign eternally.

The feet of Jesus Christ - with the nailprints in them - will
literally touch down on the Mount of Olives, near Jerusalem.
The mountain will split into east and west, creating a great
valley [Zech 14:4]. Israel will flee as she fled before the
earthquake in the days of Uzziah, king of Judah.

The landscape will be so altered that a new river will emerge
out of Jerusalem. Half of it will flow toward the "former
sea" [the Dead Sea] and half of it will flow toward the
"hinder sea' [the Mediterranean Sea], all year long, "in
summer and in winter" [Zech 14:8]. Much of the great

desert south of Jerusalem will become a great plain [Isa 35] and will be inhabited. Jerusalem itself will be raised [Zech 14:10].

The realisation that this same Jesus has defeated the Antichrist forces and brought about salvation for the Jews will be eye- opening! In that day when Jesus comes with His armies to take over the kingdoms of this world, Israel will turn to Him with a whole heart, with fasting, with weeping, with mourning, with national repentance.

THE TIME OF HIS SECOND COMING.

At this point in time we cannot say exactly **when** Christ will return. But we do know that,

1, according to Matt 24:34 all the signs of His coming will be fulfilled in one generation and
2, according to Matt 24:36 the exact date of His coming is unknown.

We also know that His coming will mark the timing of, or coincide with, certain other events. Thus we can say from Scripture that,

1. He will come at the end of the Tribulation.

Matt 24:29,30 "immediately after the tribulation of those days the sun will be darkened, and the moon will not give its light; the stars will fall from heaven, and the powers of the heavens will be shaken.
30 Then the sign of the Son of Man will appear in heaven, and then all the tribes of the earth will mourn, and they will see the

Son of Man coming on the clouds of heaven with power and great glory."

2. He will come after the reign of the Antichrist.

2 Thess 2:8 And then the lawless one will be revealed, whom the Lord will consume with the breath of His mouth and destroy with the brightness of His coming.

3. He will come in days like Lot's and Noah's.

Matt 24:37 "But as the days of Noah were, so also will the coming of the Son of Man be."

4. He will come when Jerusalem is surrounded by armies.

Luke 21:20,27 "But when you see Jerusalem surrounded by armies, then know that its desolation is near.
27 Then they will see the Son of Man coming in a cloud with power and great glory."

5. He will come when the 10 kingdoms are formed inside the Old Roman Empire.

Dan 2:44,45 "And in the days of these kings shall God set up a kingdom, which shall never be destroyed."

6. He will come when the Gospel is preached in all the world.

Matt 24:14 "And this gospel of the kingdom will be preached in all the world as a witness to all the nations, and then the end will come."

7. He will come in such an hour as ye think not!

Matt 24:44   "Therefore you also be ready, for the Son of Man is coming at an hour when you do not expect Him".

8.   He will come when the powers of heaven are shaken.

Mark 13:25,26   "The stars of heaven shall fall, and the powers that are in heaven shall be shaken. And then shall they see the Son of Man coming in the clouds with great power and glory."

Although we cannot know the hour or the day of Christ's coming again, we can know the times and the seasons. We do know that the Second Coming will be 7 years after the Rapture and just prior to the 1,000 year reign of Christ on earth. Jesus used the fig tree as an illustration, saying that when the branch is tender and puts forth leaves, we know that it is time for His return [read Mark 13:28,29].

Current world events point to the End Times. Signs indicate the nearness of the Rapture, the Tribulation, Armageddon and the Second Coming. Jesus said that "generation" or "race" or "lineage" would not pass away until "all" these things would be fulfilled [Mark 13:30-33]. Ever since the restoration of Israel to the Promised Land in 1948 we have witnessed that "generation". This is the time to be looking, working and waiting for His return!

AT THE SECOND COMING WHO WILL BE TAKEN AND WHO WILL BE LEFT?

THE BIBLE ANSWER TO MATT 24:40,41 "ONE TAKEN AND ONE LEFT".

In Matt 24:40-42 we have 3 verses that are the most misunderstood in the Bible by some, because they interpret the passage as referring to the Rapture instead of the events at the time of the Second Coming of Christ. It is clear from the context that the Rapture is NOT referred to. Again we repeat, the Rapture is not involved in the questions of the disciples [Matt 24:1-3]. These verses are connected to the "coming of the Son of Man" or the Second Coming by the word "then". "Then [at the Second Coming of Christ to earth with His saints] shall two be in the field; the one shall be taken, and the other left ... Watch therefore; for you know not what hour your Lord is coming."

Why should we take these verses out of their proper setting which is at the coming of Christ to the earth **with** the saints, and make them refer to the coming of Christ in the air **for** the saints? The Bible is very clear that there will be a large number of people, both RIGHTEOUS and UNRIGHTEOUS who will survive the 7 year Tribulation and will enter the Millennium with natural bodies and that they will reproduce and re-populate the earth.

The Bible informs us that during the 1,000 year reign of Christ on earth that He will rule with "A ROD OF IRON" meaning FIRM AUTHORITY! If the only people entering the Millennium were born again, righteous believers then why would Jesus have to rule with **A ROD OF IRON**?

WHO WILL THE TRIBULATION SURVIVORS BE?

1.   Isa 19:23-25 Egyptians, Assyrians and Israeli's.

2.   Zech 14:6 tells us there will be survivors of the nations who came against Jerusalem, i.e. 10 European nations under the Antichrist plus Oriental nations [which means those people who did not take the mark of the Beast or worship his image].

3.   According to Zech 14:16-19 there must also be millions of Tribulation survivors of the nations who did not come against Israel e.g. U.S.A., African nations, Australia, Canada, South America, New Zealand etc.

The Bible speaks to us clearly in Matt 25:31-46 about the Judgment of the "Living Nations" which takes place at the Second Coming of Christ.

The purpose of this judgment is to separate the sheep and goats and determine who shall enter the Millennium and who shall receive the Judgment of hell.

THE JUDGMENT OF THE NATIONS
[MATT 25:31-46, JOEL 3:1,2].

1.   **Subjects** : Gentile Nations [Matt 25:32].

2.   **Time**   : At the Second Coming of Christ before the Millennium [Matt 25:31-46].

3.   **Place**   : Israel [Zech 14, Matt 25:31, Rev 19:11-21].

4.   **Basis**   : Their treatment of Christ's brethren, the Jews [Matt 25:31-46].

5.   **Result**   : Some permitted to go into the Millenium and some destroyed [Matt 25:34,41,46, Zech 14, Joel 3].

A study of Matt 25:31-46 with Rev 20:11-15 will reveal that this judgment is entirely different from the Great White Throne Judgment.

JUDGMENT OF THE NATIONS.	GREAT WHITE THRONE JUDGMENT
1. Living nations [Matt 25:31-46].	1. Wicked dead resurrected [Rev 20:11-15].
2. Before the Millennium [Matt 25:41-46].	2. After the Millennium [Rev 20:11-15].
3. Christ the Judge [Matt 25:31].	3. God the Judge [Rev 20:11-15].
4. On earth [Matt 25:31-46, Zech 14].	4. In heaven [Rev 20:11-15].
5. Two classes - sheep and goat nations [Matt 25:31-46].	5. One class - all UNSAVED people [Rev 20:11-15].
6. Some saved [Matt 25:34].	6. None saved [Rev 20:11-15].
7. Some punished [Matt 25:41-46].	7. All punished [Rev 20:11-15].
8. No resurrection [Matt 25:32, Zech 14].	8. A resurrection [Rev 20:11-15].
9. No books opened [Matt 25:31-46].	9. Books opened [Rev 20:11-15].
10. One generation [Matt 25:31-46].	10. All generations [Rev 20:11-15, Acts 17:31].
11. Gentiles only [Matt 25:32].	11. Jews and Gentiles [Rev 20:11-15, Acts 17:31].
12. Angels help in this judgment [Matt 25:31].	12. No angels mentioned in this judgment.

The basis of this judgment is that God will curse or bless according to how men have dealt with Israel in Daniel's 70th Week.

THE SHEEP NATIONS will be those nations who favoured, supported and assisted Israel especially during Daniel's 70th Week.

THE GOAT NATIONS will be those nations who persecuted, fought against, oppressed and were enemies of Israel especially during Daniel's 70th Week.

The amazing fact is that there will be many survivors from the goat nations who will be allowed to enter the Millenium [Zech 14:16-19].
In these verses we have an explanation of what will happen to those who are left of all the nations who will fight against Jerusalem under the Antichrist. If they have not taken the mark of the Beast [Rev 14:9-11], and if they have not persecuted Christ's brethren, the Jews [Matt 25:31-46], they are worthy of entrance into the kingdom,then they will be left here to live as natural men on earth. They will be permitted to establish themselves in the earth and live through the entire 1,000 years. They will be required to go up [at least representatives] to Jerusalem to worship the King, the Lord of Hosts, and to keep the feast of the Tabernacles yearly [v 16]; and if they do not go up as required, there will be no rain in their land [v 17-19]. If any rebel with the Satan at the end of the 1,000 years, then fire will come down from God out of heaven and devour them [Rev 20:7-10].

Christ and His armies will land in Jerusalem at His Second Coming and fight the Battle of Armageddon on the first day of His arrival [Zech 14, Rev 19:11-21]. Then the nations will be gathered to judgment to determine who is worthy of death for mistreatment of Israel - not every person in every nation of earth, but those responsible who have had dealings with Israel in the last days [Matt 25:31-46].

NOTE: There is no statement in Scripture saying that all men who enter the Millennium will be righteous or born again. We cannot teach this from Matt 25:34 because the righteousness of that passage consists of doing right by Israel, whether one is born again or not. Any man can feed, clothe, visit and do other things said regarding the sheep nations of Matt 25:31-46 who enter the Millenium, without being born again.

The judgment of the nations, as in Matt 25, will be to determine who is worthy of entrance into the kingdom; and being born again is not stated as a qualification either here or elsewhere.

GOAT NATION SURVIVORS.

I believe that during the 7 year Tribulation there will be many people [men, women and children], living in the "goat" nations who will refuse to accept the mark of the Beast and will not enlist in the armed forces against Israel. These people will be permitted to enter the Millennium and will escape the punishment of hell at this time.

The "righteous" company of Matt 25:46 who receive eternal life **could be** any number of Tribulation survivors that accept Jesus Christ as Lord at the Second Coming.

All Tribulation people who:

1. took the mark of the Beast,
2. worshipped the image of the Beast,
3. persecuted and fought against Israel,
   will be judged and sentenced to hell.

So Matt 24:37-41 is a prophetic picture that tells us that at the Second Coming of Christ there will be two groups of people living on the earth [Tribulation survivors] and one group will be taken away and sentenced to hell. The other group will be left behind, escaping the judgment of hell and enter the Millennium to repopulate the earth.

Because millions of Tribulation survivors are allowed to become the Millennial people and live on earth throughout the 1,000 year reign of Christ we can scripturally say that, there are millions of people living today who will outlive Methuselah [969 years]!

CHAPTER 19:
LIFE ON EARTH DURING
THE MILLENNIUM.

The Millennium will be a 1000 year period in which Christ will set up His kingdom and rule over the entire earth [Rev 20:4].

Our English word "millennium" does not appear in the Bible. "Millennium" comes from two Latin words, **mille**, meaning "thousand" and annum, meaning "years"; hence 1,000 years. The doctrine of the Millennial Reign is strongly substantiated in Scripture. It is referred to as ...

1. **The 1,000 year Reign of Christ** [Rev 20:4,6].

2. **The Dispensation of the Fullness of Time** [Eph 1:10].

3. **The Age to Come** [Matt 12:32, Mark 10:30, Luke 18:30, Eph 1:21, 2:7].

4. **The Kingdom of Christ and of God** [Eph 5:5, Matt 20:21, 2 Tim 4:1].

5. **The Times of the Restitution of All Things** [Acts 3:20,21].

THREE VIEWS ON THE MILLENNIUM.

1. **Post-Millennialism teaches,**
    Christ will come to establish His Kingdom on earth

after [post] the 1,000 years [Millennium].

The earth will get better and better through the spread of the Gospel, and Christ will come to claim His Kingdom after 1,000 years of peace has transpired.

This theory is anti-scriptural and naive. The earth is not getting better; and the Bible does not teach that it is [2 Tim 3:1-7].

2. **A Millennialism teaches,**
    There will be NO future earthly 1,000 year reign [Millennium]. [In the Greek "A" at the beginning of a word means "no".]
    They teach that the millennium is NOW! Peace on earth exists in the Church; and Satan is NOW bound so that he cannot prevent the spread of the Gospel.

The Bible and world conditions totally refute this false doctrine. Rev 20:3 says that Satan goes to prison "that he should deceive the nations no more." Look at Cuba, China, Russia and the state of the world today - Satan is certainly not NOW in prison!

3. **Pre-Millennialism teaches,**
    Christ will come personally to judge the nations and to establish the Kingdom before [pre] the 1,000 years [Millennium] begins.

This is the teaching of the Bible. Christ will come [Rev 19:11-21] and then the Kingdom will be set up [Rev 20].

CHARACTERISTICS OF THE MILLENNIUM.

The term "ONE THOUSAND YEARS" appears 6 times in

the first seven verses of Revelation 20:

BEFORE the Millennium begins Satan is expelled from the earth.

DURING the Millennium Satan is bound.

AFTER the Millennium Satan is released for a short period.

When we think about this great future age of 1,000 years that lies ahead many questions come to our minds ...

What kind of government will there be?
What will living conditions be like during the Millennium?
What will be the spiritual conditions during this age?

In order to answer these questions and others let us study the characteristics of the Millennial Kingdom from God's Word.

A LITERAL KINGDOM ON EARTH.

The Millennial Kingdom will be a literal, earthly Kingdom - it will be just as real as any other that has been on the earth such as Egypt, Greece, Babylon, Rome etc.

The "TERRITORIAL" extent of the Millennial Kingdom will be worldwide. Speaking of the Lord Jesus Christ, Dan 7:14 says;

> **Dan 7:14 Then to Him was given dominion and glory and a kingdom, That all peoples, nations, and languages should serve Him. His dominion is an everlasting dominion, Which shall not**

pass away, And His Kingdom the one which shall not be destroyed.

The 1,000 year reign will begin when the Lord Jesus Christ returns to the earth with all of the saints, interrupting the Battle of Armageddon, sets His feet upon the Mount of Olives, and establishes His Kingdom in the Holy City, Jerusalem, Israel. The Millennial Kingdom will be a literal kingdom, with the Lord Jesus Christ reigning in Jerusalem. Just as all preceding kingdoms have been literal, so this one will be literal as well [Isa 9:6,7, Dan 2:44,45 Dan 7:13, Zech 14].

GOVERNMENT IN THE MILLENNIUM.

The form of government during the Millennium will be a "THEOCRACY".

Now don't let that word scare you. It simply means **"The direct rule of God in the affairs of men"**.

God Himself will rule over the earth in the person of Jesus Christ, the Son of David.

> Jer 23:5 "Behold, the days are coming" says the Lord, "That I will raise to David a Branch of righteousness; A King shall reign and prosper, And execute judgment and righteousness in the earth.

> Isa 9:6,7 And the government will be upon His shoulder. And His name shall be called Wonderful, Counsellor, Mighty God, Everlasting Father, Prince of Peace.
> 7   Of the increase of His government and peace There shall be no end upon the throne of David and over His kingdom, To order

it and establish it with judgment and justice From that time forward, even forever.

Jerusalem is to be the seat of government. Israel will have the first place among the nations and Jerusalem will be the world capital from which KING JESUS rules.

Isa 2:2,3 Now it shall come to pass in the latter days That the mountain of the Lord's house Shall be established on the top of the mountains, And shall be exalted above the hills; And all nations shall flow to it.

3 Many people shall come and say, "Come and let us go up to the mountain of the Lord, To the house of the God of Jacob; He will teach us His ways, And we shall walk in His paths." For out of Zion shall go forth the law, And the word of the Lord from Jerusalem.

The coming one-world kingdom will exist under the personal rulership of the Lord Jesus Christ. He will be the universal King and His throne and headquarters will be in Jerusalem.

The government will not be a monarchy, democracy or autocracy but a theocracy, meaning that God Himself will be its head. God will reign through the Lord Jesus Christ [Matt 25:31-46, Luke 1:32-35, Rev 11:15], through King David, who will actually rule the nation of Israel [Jer 30:9, Ezek 34:24, Hosea 3:4,5] and through redeemed saints [Rev 5:10].

SICKNESS IS BANISHED.

The Millennium will mean the END OF DISEASE AND DEFORMITY - All those with infirmities will experience immediate healing.

> Isa 35:5,6 "Then the eyes of the blind shall be opened, And the ears of the deaf shall be unstopped. Then shall the lame man leap as the deer, And the tongue of the dumb will shout for joy."

Man's lifespan will be greatly lengthened and premature death will not be a part of the MILLENNIAL AGE. Total health and an **extra-long** life will be the order of the day.

> Isa 65:20 "No longer will there be an infant who lives but a few days, Or an old man who does not live out his days."

> Isa 65:22 ..."For as the lifetime of a tree, So shall be the days of My people..."

LONGEVITY DURING THE MILLENNIUM.

During this time human life will be prolonged [Isa 65:20, Zech 8:4]. The glorified saints ruling with Christ at this time, of course, will be immortal, but natural people will continue to live. They will be able to live a thousand years; and if they do not align with Satan to rebel against God at the end, they will live forever and ever.

Man was made to live a long time. Adam lived 900 years and Methuselah lived 969 years. Enoch lived 365 years on the earth, and has lived for over 5,000 years in heaven in his natural body! The human body virtually replenishes itself every 7 years and should live on indefinitely, and will during this time.

INCREASE OF LIGHT.

There will be an increase of light [Isa 30:26, Isa 60:18-22] to the extent that it will be increased 7 times, and the light of the moon will be as the light of the sun today:

> Isa 30:26 Moreover the light of the moon will be as the light of the sun, And the light of the sun will be sevenfold, As the light of seven days, In the day that the Lord binds up the bruise of His people And heals the stroke of their wound.

Light has healing and restorative powers, and this also may relate to man's longevity.

NO MORE WARS AND NO MORE CRIME.

Another aspect of the Millennial Kingdom will be

UNIVERSAL PEACE AND JUSTICE.

The psalmist says of the Messiahs return as King that,

> Ps 46:9 He makes wars cease to the end of the earth; He breaks the bow and cuts the spear in two; He burns the chariot in the fire.

The prophet Hosea recorded God's pledge,

> Hos 2:18 "I will break the bow and the sword and the battle out of the earth."

> Micah 4:3 "Neither shall they learn war any more."

All of these prophetic statements speak of the coming Millennial Age when peace will reign supreme over the earth. Man's efforts to bring lasting peace on the earth have been totally unsuccessful.

The LEAGUE OF NATIONS could not bring about a warless world. The UNITED NATIONS have failed miserably.

In the Millenium, the Lord Jesus Christ will rule with absolute authority. He will guarantee security to every country upon the face of the earth and there will be TOTAL INTERNATIONAL PEACE! No terrorists and crime will be a thing of the past, colour prejudice and class distinctions will be non-existent and justice will be enforced [Isa 11:3-5].

Living conditions during the Millennium will be most wonderful. There will be no tempter, as Satan will be bound! There will be universal peace [Isa 2:4, Isa 9:6,7, Micah 4:3,4].

> **Micah 4:3,4** **He shall judge between many peoples, And rebuke strong nations afar off; They shall beat their swords into ploughshares, And their spears into pruning hooks; Nation shall not lift up sword against nation, Neither shall they learn war any more.**
>
> **4** **But everyone shall sit under his vine and under his fig tree, And no-one shall make them afraid; For the mouth of the Lord of Hosts has spoken.**

There will be no harbouring of prejudices and national ills. Spiritual revivals will break out in every land; and as people turn to God, they will be united in serving Christ. Attention will not be focused on wars, recessions and depressions. People will live in full satisfaction with peace and prosperity, knowing the goodness and blessings of God in His wonderful reign.

There will be neither need nor want, as man feeds on universal prosperity [Isa 65:24, Micah 4:4,5]. Unemployment and poverty will cease to be because there will not be great amounts of money spent on evils as in our present day.

Sexual Reproduction will exist.

Those who live through the Tribulation period and enter the Millennium in their natural bodies will be able to have children through out the 1,000 year age. In fact the population of the earth will once again become great.
But it must be kept in mind that those who are born during the 1,000 year Millennial Age will have a sin nature and it will be necessary for them to accept Christ if they are to participate in the final and continuing eternity that begins after this 1,000 year period.

UNIVERSAL WORSHIP.

Another characteristic of the Messiah's Kingdom is that people throughout the earth will worship the one true God.

> Mal 1:11 "For from the rising of the sun, even unto the going down of the same, My name shall be great among the gentiles, And in every place incense shall be offered unto My name, And a pure offering; For My name shall be great among the nations," Says the Lord of Hosts.

> Isa 11:9 ... The earth shall be full of the knowledge of the Lord, As the waters cover the sea."

This **does not** mean that every individual person will be born again and saved! The majority will be saved and truly serve God however many will not. The Bible teaches that there will still be SIN and DEATH on earth during the Millennium [Isa 65:20]. The Lord will not force anyone to be saved, **BUT** there will be no communism and no rebellious anti-God movements. There will be no cults nor will anyone be allowed to establish false religious systems.

Everybody will go to church and have a Bible in their own language. Everyone will "hear" the Gospel of Salvation. The Lord Jesus will rule with a "rod of iron". No false teaching or worship of false gods will be allowed.

Pilgrimages from **ALL** the nations of the earth will make their way annually to the city of Jerusalem - the centre of worship.

After the Battle of Armageddon and the return of Jesus Christ, there will be many persons left of all nations of the earth. These will go up from year to year to worship the Lord of hosts and to keep the feast of Tabernacles. It is these people and their children who will populate the earth during the Millennium.

> **Zech 14:16 And it shall come to pass that everyone who is left of all the nations which came against Jerusalem shall go up from year to year to worship the King, the Lord of hosts, and to keep the feasts of Tabernacles.**

See also Isa 2:2,3.

The Holy Spirit will be poured out as never before during the Millennial Reign [Joel 2:28,29]. God's promise of a worldwide universal spiritual awakening - even with the salvation of millions of persons today and the infilling of the Holy Spirit - has not been fully fulfilled and will not be fully fulfilled until the Millennium.

During the Millennium multiplied hundreds of millions of people will be saved by the blood of Jesus Christ - just as is happening today. Then millions of people will be baptised in the Holy Spirit as recorded by the prophet Joel [Joel 2:28,29].

When the Messiah comes to bring universal peace and prosperity to all, there will be universal knowledge of the Lord.

Isa 11:9 For the earth shall be full of the knowledge of the Lord, As the waters cover the sea.

Habakkuk 2:14 For the earth will be filled with the knowledge of the glory of the Lord, As the waters cover the sea.

There will be required universal worship of the King of kings and Lord of lords.

Phil 2:9-11 Therefore God also has highly exalted Him and given Him the name which is above every name,
10 that at the name of Jesus every knee should bow, of those in heaven, and of those on the earth, and of those under the earth,
11 and that every tongue should confess that Jesus Christ is Lord to the glory of God the Father.

As a result of the great missionary programme, millions upon millions of people will be brought into the Kingdom of God. Denominations, sects and doctrinal differences will be a thing of the past. There will be one Lord and one faith.

WORLD WIDE PROSPERITY.

In the coming Millennial Age there will be NO UNEMPLOY-

MENT, NO-ONE JOBLESS, NO ECONOMIC DEPRES-
SIONS, NO INFLATION, NO POVERTY, THERE WILL BE
NO NEED TO RAISE CHARITY FUNDS. NO LONGER
WILL THE POOR BE EXPLOITED BY THE RICH. NO ONE
WILL BE ALLOWED TO TAKE ADVANTAGE OF ANY-
ONE ELSE.
There will be NO ENERGY CRISIS.
There will be NO THREAT OF WORLD FAMINE.
There will be plenty of trees, grass, cattle, crops, fruit,
vegetables, sheep, gold, silver and other material blessings.

> Isa 51:3 For the Lord will comfort Zion, He will comfort all her
> waste places; He will make her wilderness like Eden, And her
> desert like the garden of the Lord; Joy and gladness will be found
> in it, Thanksgiving and the voice of melody.

> Isa 65:21,23 They shall build houses and inhabit them; They
> shall plant vineyards and eat their fruit.
> 23 They shall not labour in vain, Nor bring forth children for
> trouble; For they shall be the descendants of the blessed of the
> Lord, And their offspring with them.

In the coming Kingdom Age everyone will share in the
abundance of earth's resources.

NATURE TRANSFORMED.

The world of creation is at present under the curse of sin and
for that reason tornados, hurricanes, earthquakes, droughts,
noxious weeds and harmful insects plague us. But when
King Jesus establishes His Kingdom on earth, the curse will
be lifted and nature's beauty will be restored, and even the
deserts will become fruitful gardens.

Isa 35:6,7 ... For water shall burst forth in the wilderness, And the streams in the desert.

7 The parched ground shall become a pool, And the thirsty land springs of water...

Isa 35:1 The wilderness and the wasteland shall be glad for them, And the desert shall rejoice and blossom as the rose.

Isa 55:13 Instead of the thorn shall come up the cyprus tree, And instead of the briar shall come up the myrtle tree;

During the Millennium this reign of peace and prosperity will extend to the animal kingdom as well [Isa 11:6-8, 65:17-25, Rom 8:18-23]. Their very nature will be transformed. No longer will they be fierce; they will not kill; they will not be poisonous.

Isa 11:6-9 "The wolf also shall dwell with the lamb, The leopard shall lie down with the young goat, The calf and the young lion and the fatling together; And a little child shall lead them.

7 The cow and the bear shall graze; Their young ones shall lie down together; And the lion shall eat straw like the ox.

8 The nursing child shall play by the cobra's hole, And the weaned child shall put his hand in the viper's den.

9 They shall not hurt nor destroy in all My holy mountain, For the earth shall be full of the knowledge of the Lord As the waters cover the sea."

This means that the carnivorous nature of the wild beast will be gone. Even naturally ferocious beasts, like the lion, will become vegetarian, and "shall eat straw like the ox". Not only will the beasts be at peace between themselves, but they will be at peace with man. The baby, the toddler, the little schoolchild will be safe from all harm even if he puts his hand into a nest of rattlesnakes!

What glorious prospects and wonderful times lie ahead for those who know and love the Lord.

JERUSALEM - CAPITAL OF THE KINGDOM.

Jerusalem will be the centre of worship and government. It will have been rebuilt and restored, having great and marvellous splendour [Ps 48:8, Isa 2:2-4, 11:11 through to 12:6, Jer 17:25, Ezek 34:1-31, 43:7, Joel 3:17,20].

Jesus will return from heaven [as promised in Acts 1:11] and His feet will literally touch down on the Mount of Olives [Zech 14:4].

> **Isa 60:13,14   ... I will make the place of My feet glorious.**
> **14 ... and all those who despised you shall fall prostrate at the soles of your feet; And they shall call you the City of the Lord, Zion of the Holy One of Israel.**

Jerusalem will become the headquarters of the King and the Kingdom. Jesus Himself called it ... "the city of the great King" [Matt 5:35]. Jerusalem is the Holy City, a glorious city, where once Jesus was rejected as King and Lord. But **someday** He will be hailed as King Jesus. Throngs of worshippers will come daily to the world capital, Jerusalem, to worship King Jesus.

LAWS OF THE KINGDOM.

Those who have been truly born again and fully committed to the Lord, and who have fellowship with God during the 1,000 years, will not rebel, but there will be sinners alive during the Millennium. For this reason the Kingdom will have laws and regulations. The sinners will be people who have survived the Tribulation, but who did not take the mark of the Beast. They will not be saved when the Millennium begins, but will be allowed to live through it. Many will not be changed by the transforming power of the Gospel. Some of these may even be executed because of committing sins worthy of the death penalty.

> Isa 11:2-5 The Spirit of the Lord shall rest upon Him, The Spirit of wisdom and understanding, The Spirit of counsel and might, The Spirit of knowledge and fear of the Lord.
> 3   His delight is in the fear of the Lord, And He shall not judge by the sight of His eyes, Nor decide by the hearing of His ears;
> 4   But with righteousness He shall judge the poor, And decide with equity for the meek of the earth; He shall strike the earth with the rod of His mouth, And with the breath of His lips He shall slay the wicked.
> 5   Righteousness shall be the belt of His loins, And faithfulness the belt of His waist.

> Isa 65:20-22   No more shall an infant from there live but a few days, Nor an old man who has not fulfilled his days; For the child shall die one hundred years old, But the sinner being one hundred years old shall be accursed.
> 21 They shall build houses and inhabit them; They shall plant vineyards and eat their fruit.
> 22 They shall not build and another inhabit; They shall not plant and another eat; For as the days of a tree, so shall the days of My people, And My elect shall long enjoy the work of their hands.

There will be laws to govern and to keep order. Quick action will be instituted for refusal to follow the rules and laws of

God. Even though the Millennium will be a righteous reign, and even though Satan will be bound for 1,000 years, man still will be sinful without giving his heart to the Lord Jesus Christ and being born again. The Good news is that multitudes of people will be saved, healed and delivered during this glorious reign of Jesus Christ.

The laws of the Kingdom will include those given to Israel as an eternal standard of holiness [Isa 2:2-4, Micah 4:1,2, Ezek 40:1 through to 48:35] and the laws of the New Covenant given by Jesus Christ. Some of Israel's feasts will be required of all nationalities. If they do not participate, God will withdraw His providence from those nations.

> **Zech 14:16-19** And it shall come to pass that everyone who is left of all the nations which came against Jerusalem shall go up from year to year to worship the King, the Lord of hosts, and to keep the Feast of Tabernacles.
> **17** And it shall be that whichever of the families of the earth do not come up to Jerusalem to worship the King, the Lord of hosts, on them their will be no rain.
> **18** If the family of Egypt will not come up and enter in, they shall have no rain; they shall receive a plague with which the Lord strikes the nations who do not come up to keep the Feast of Tabernacles.
> **19** This shall be the punishment of Egypt and the punishment of all the nations that do not come up to keep the Feast of Tabernacles.

Presently the rule of the earth is in the hands of the devil, under his influence, and not under the command of the saints. But during the Millennium the rule of the earth will be exclusively in the hands of the Lord of lords and His saints with Him.

Isa 9:6,7 ... and the government shall be upon His shoulder. And His name shall be called Wonderful, Counsellor, Mighty God, Everlasting Father, Prince of Peace.

7   Of the increase of His government and peace There will be no end, Upon the throne of David and over His Kingdom, To order it and establish it with judgment and justice. From that time forward, even forever. The zeal of the Lord of hosts will perform this.

Today we have a choice to serve God or not to serve God. But in that day men will be obliged to accept and obey God's laws or else be smitten and punished on the spot! Millions of people from all over the world will hear the Word of God and will obey the laws of the King of kings. Lawbreaking immediately will be stopped and justice and righteousness will prevail.

SATAN IS BOUND.

Rev 20:1-3   Then I saw an angel coming down from heaven, having the key to the bottomless pit and a great chain in his hand.

2   He laid hold of the dragon, that serpent of old, who is the Devil and Satan, and bound him for a thousand years;

3   and he cast him into the bottomless pit, and shut him up, and set a seal on him, so that he should deceive the nations no more till the thousand years were finished. But after these things he must be released for a little while.

After the Battle of Armageddon, upon the initiation of the Millennial Reign, Satan will be bound in chains and cast into the bottomless pit. No human being ever goes to the bottomless pit. The pit is not the Lake of Fire [Gehenna], where Satan - along with wicked men, demons, fallen angels and all rebellious creatures - will finally be sentenced to eternal torment.

The object of this binding and imprisonment of Satan and his legions will be the temporary end of temptation and deception. At the end of the Millennium he will be loosed for a short season.

LOOSING OF SATAN AFTER THE MILLENNIUM.

After the thousand years are fulfilled, Satan will be loosed out of his prison and will attempt to deceive the nations.

> **Rev 20:7-10 Now when the thousand years have expired, Satan will be released from his prison.**
> **8   and will go out to deceive the nations which are in the four corners of the earth, Gog and Magog, to gather them together to battle, whose number is as the sand of the sea.**
> **9   They went up on the breadth of the earth and surrounded the camp of the saints and the beloved city. And fire came down from God out of heaven and devoured them.**
> **10   And the devil, who deceived them, was cast into the lake of fire and brimstone where the beast and the false prophet are. And they will be tormented day and night forever and ever.**

During the Millennium millions of natural people on earth will have had that period of time in which to accept Christ as Saviour and truly submit to God. Having retained their fallen nature, they will be subject in various ways to the influence of Satan when he is loosed. Satan will recruit millions of followers that will seek to help him overthrow the Kingdom of God, and he will lead them against the saints at Jerusalem.

The expression Gog and Magog [Rev 20:8] relates to the unbelievers who rebel at this time with Satan, and is not to be confused with the "Gog" and "Magog" mentioned in Ezek 38 and 39. As these rebel forces come against the Kingdom and seek to take the city, fire will descend from God and devour them. Satan, the great deceiver, will be cast, finally, into the lake of fire where the beast and the false prophet will have been confined since the Battle of Armageddon.

CHAPTER 20:
THE REALITY OF
LIFE AFTER DEATH.

Life after death is probably the single most important subject in the Bible apart from the cross of Calvary.

> Col 2:8 Beware lest anyone cheat you through philosophy and empty deceit, according to the tradition and opinions of men, according to the basic principles of the world, and not according to Christ.

The choice is yours because you can listen to what God says or else you can listen to human philosophy, man's opinions, religious tradition, scientific theories, religious cults and so many others who have their own opinions and thoughts on the subject of life after death **but if you do, you will be deceived!**

> 1 Tim 4:1 "Now the Spirit expressly says that in the last days some will depart from the faith, giving heed to deceiving spirits and doctrines of demons."

The Bible is the only true source of reference and the only true authority concerning what happens in life after death. In the Word of God, God Himself tells us of Heaven, Hell and the resting place of the dead. Do not listen to empty philosophies and hypothetical theories but turn to the God breathed Scriptures and find out what God says. I don't care who said it or what they are saying, if it doesn't agree with God's Word then cast it aside! You can't afford to be deceived by the devil and end up in hell!

What Jehovah's Witnesses say ...

"A dead person is unconscious, inactive and ceases to exist". "The doctrine of a burning hell for the wicked after death cannot be true."

What Spiritualism teaches ...

"Hell does not exist and neither does the devil - there is no such thing as the resurrection and the judgment."

What Christian Science says ...

"Death is an illusion and hell is a lie!"

What Armstrong of the Plain Truth says ...

"When a human being dies he is dead, unconscious and out of existence - hell is a myth!"

FALSE THEORIES AND MEN'S DOCTRINES ABOUT LIFE AFTER DEATH.

1.   Soul Sleep. When you die then you are dead like a dog, you sleep in the grave and you will know nothing until the resurrection takes place. The New Testament teaches that when we die physically we do not sleep in the grave but we continue to live on [spirit and soul] fully conscious.

> 2 Cor 5:8 "We are confident, yes, well pleased rather to be absent from the body and to be present with the Lord."

2.   Purgatory. THIS IS NOT IN THE BIBLE! Purgatory is taught as an in-between place [between heaven and hell] where you suffer and wait until the prayers of the saints can pray you into heaven stage by stage. According to Philippians 1:21-23 God's Word says "to die is gain" and not purgatory nor re-incarnation. In Luke 16:19-31 Jesus Himself, teaching about life after death, never once mentioned Purgatory!

3.   Re- Incarnation is the Eastern religious belief that, on the death of the body, the spirit and soul "transmigrates" or comes back to earth to live in another body, [a cat, a rat etc.] until you reach perfection and enter NIRVANA. The Bible is totally against this false Eastern philosophy.

Heb 9:27   And it is appointed for men to die once, but after this the judgment.

FEAR OF DEATH.

Heb 2:14,15   "Inasmuch then as the children have partaken of flesh and blood, He Himself likewise shared the same, that through death He might destroy him who had the power over death, that is, the devil,
15   and release those who through fear of death were all their lifetime subject to bondage."

Fear of Death is a terrible bondage. People, regardless of wealth, position or prestige have a very real fear of death . From politicians to rock stars and from sportsmen to movie stars, all can suffer this bondage of the fear of death. BUT Jesus **cancelled** the power of death. He took the sting of death.

THE GOSPEL FREES US FROM THE FEAR OF DEATH!

Jesus conquered the dominion of death and through His redemptive work brought life, eternal life to mankind.

> **John 5:24** "**Most assuredly, I say unto you, he who hears My words and believes in Him who sent Me has everlasting life, and shall not come into judgment, but has passed from death to life.**"

Death in the Bible always means separation, not ceasing to exist. Our views of death and our future destiny must be rooted in the Holy Scriptures. If we are to have the facts garrisoned with conviction and authority, we must go to the Word of God. Man invents his theories and assumptions but God speaks with precision on the subject of death and He gives us all the information He wants us to possess.

3 KINDS OF DEATH IN THE BIBLE.

1. <u>PHYSICAL DEATH</u> is the separation of the spirit and soul from the body. Death in the case of a Believer is called "sleep". This is in reference to the body, which will be awakened at the first resurrection.

2. <u>SPIRITUAL DEATH</u> is the condition of the natural man spiritually. He does not have the life of God dwelling in him. He is alienated from the Lord and separated from the life of God.

3. <u>ETERNAL DEATH</u>. The word DEATH is also employed in the Bible to describe ETERNAL separation from God. This is called the "SECOND DEATH" in the Scriptures.

If a person remains spiritually dead, rejecting Christ and

spurning God's grace, he will suffer Eternal Death - everlasting separation and banishment from the Holy presence of God - in the Lake of Fire. Professors of religion who have never been born again, church members who attended Sunday services, sang hymns and repeated creeds but never had a personal relationship with Jesus Christ, people who have come from respectable communities and enjoyed unblemished reputations but have never known the forgiveness of sins through Jesus' blood - all these and many more will stand there at the Great White Throne Judgment to hear the sentence of Eternal Death. They will be shut out forever from God's presence! Eternal banishment in the lake of fire!

THE BIBLE TEACHES CLEARLY ABOUT DEATH AND LIFE AFTER DEATH.

1.   At death we immediately go either to heaven or to hell and there is no intermediate place.

> **2 Cor 5:6,8   Therefore we are always confident, knowing that while we are at home in the body we are absent from the Lord.**
> **8   We are confident, yes, well pleased rather to be absent from the body and to be present with the Lord.**

2.   We are recognisable in the next life. We do not lose our personal identity but we will know each other. [**Please read Luke 16:19-31**].

3.   The real you, the spirit man inside your physical body is a duplicate and identical in shape, size, looks and form as your physical body. The spirit man has eyes, legs, tongue etc...according to **Luke 16:19-31**.

4.   God's Word teaches that after death we continue living on, fully conscious in the next life. [The rich man felt sensation and his memory was still working in hell]. The Bible does not teach that we are sleeping in the grave and that death is the end of life.

> **Phil 1:21,23** "For to me to live is Christ and to die is gain.
> **23** For I am hard pressed between the two, having a desire to depart and be with Christ, which is far better."

5.   Eventually the redeemed, righteous spirits will receive resurrection bodies [1 Thess 4:13-18]. Today when a Born Again Believer dies his righteous spirit and soul go immediately and directly to heaven to be with Jesus. The day is coming [Rapture] when his spirit and soul will be united with his body, this is when God will supernaturally gather up the ashes of each one and resurrect their body in a glorified state. In that glorified, resurrected body you will live forever.

N.B.   If the dead cease to exist or sleep in the grave as some teach then how would it be possible for Jesus to bring the spirits of the righteous dead with Him at the Rapture if they were not in heaven at that time?

6.   Today when a lost sinner dies his spirit and soul descends directly into the present hell in the underworld, fully conscious, awaiting trial at the Great White Throne Judgment. On the Judgment Day the unrighteous dead are temporarily released from hell and then united with their resurrection body to stand before God at the Great White Throne to be tried and sentenced.

Please read Revelation 20:11-15. Rev 21:8 reveals the bad company in hell.

7. God's Word DOES NOT teach that the spirits of the departed dead roam about in space or come back to the earth to visit and communicate with the living. The so-called spiritualist meetings that supposedly contact and communicate with departed spirits of our loved ones are FAMILIAR DEMONS, seducing spirits, to deceive us from the truth of God's Word.

So listen, Child of God, and reject the false theories about life after death: reject soul sleep, reject purgatory, reject incarnation and reject the idea of talking to the spirits of the departed dead.

8. The only way that you can escape hell and qualify for heaven is to be born again now in this life by personally receiving Jesus as Lord while you are still living in your body [earth suit]. Once you die and leave your earth suit [your body] then your ETERNAL DESTINY is forever sealed. This is NOT a game but extremely serious.

Because you are a spirit being you will live forever, either in heaven or in hell.
You are a spirit, you have a soul and you live in a body [1 Thess 5:23]. When you die physically and leave this earth the real you [spirit] will leave your earth suit or your body behind that is why it is absolutely essential to make Jesus your Lord and Saviour NOW, this side of the grave.

THE FACTS ABOUT LIFE AFTER DEATH GIVEN BY JESUS THE SON OF GOD.

READ LUKE 16:19-31

1. * The rich man suffered pain and torment in hell
- verse 23.

2.   * The rich man had eyes and could see in hell - verse 23.

3.   * The rich man could recognise Lazarus - proving that
     we do not lose our personal identity at death
                                                    - verse 23.

4.   * The spirit of Lazarus had a shape and form resembling
     that of his physical body because the rich man easily
     recognised him. Also Lazarus had a finger which
     must have been connected to a hand which was
     connected to an arm etc. etc. i.e. a body. - verse 24.

5.   * The rich man had a voice and cried out for mercy in
     hell   - verse 24.

6.   * The rich man had a tongue and experienced thirst,
     torment and great agony   - verse 24.

7.   * The rich man's soul was definitely in hell because he
     retained his memory and thinking faculties
                                                    - verse 25.

8.   * Lazarus was in Abraham's Bosom, a compartment of
     the underworld, a place of comfort and a place of
     waiting. The rich man was in hell; a place of
     excruciating torment   - verse 25.

9.   * No person was permitted to leave the underworld or
     cross the impassable gulf. This disproves the heresy
     of spiritualism and the ability to converse with the
     spirits of the departed dead   - verse 26.

10. * Lazarus was a beggar during his life on earth and
     now the rich man was a beggar in hell   - verse 27.

CHRIST'S RESURRECTION

THIRD HEAVEN

PARADISE

CHRIST THE FIRSTFRUITS
1 COR 15v20-23

ABRAHAM'S BOSOM WAS
EMPTIED AND THE
RIGHTEOUS WERE TRANSFERRED
TO PARADISE AT
CHRIST'S ASCENSION
ACTS 1v9-11
EPH 4v8-10

CALVARY

EARTH

GRAVE

EARTH

GRAVE

"THE UNDERWORLD"
SHEOL / HADES

PRESENT HELL

LOST SINNERS

GREAT
GULF

ABRAHAM'S
BOSOM

OLD TESTAMENT
SAINTS

(NOW EMPTY)

THE FIVE UNDERWORLD DEPARTMENTS

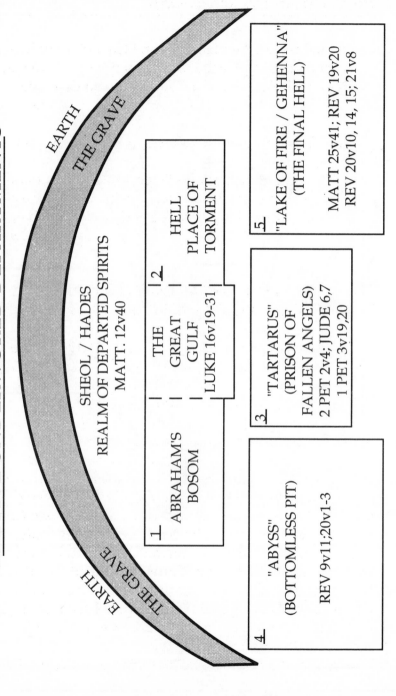

11. * Hell is a REAL place, not an idea, not a myth, not a figment of a preacher's imagination! Hell is a reality - a real place of eternal suffering and damnation
- verse 28.

   * LUKE 16 proves that the grave is NOT the end!

12. * The time for people to listen to the Gospel and be saved is NOW - it is too late after death. Hell is a place of no return, no fire escape and no second chance
- verses 29-31.

THE FIVE DEPARTMENTS IN THE UNDERWORLD OF DEPARTED SPIRITS.

1. ABRAHAM'S BOSOM: [Luke 16:19-31]. Before Christ's resurrection this was the abode of the righteous souls and spirits after leaving their bodies at physical death. All the righteous went to this place. They were not born again. They were saved by faith in the blood sacrifices, [saved on credit] under the Old Testament system. They were waiting for the Christ, the promised Saviour to redeem them and take them to heaven! The devil had the power of death and of the underworld before Christ conquered him [Col 2:14-17, Heb 2:14,15, & Rev 1:18]. That it is located in the heart and lower parts of the earth is clear from Matt 12:40 and Eph 4:7-10. Christ conquered death, hell and the grave during His crucifixion and during the three days that He was in the underworld. He captured all the righteous souls that were in Abraham's Bosom and took them to heaven when He ascended on high [Eph 4:7-10]. He now has the keys of death and hell [Rev 1:18].
But ever since Christ liberated the righteous from Abraham's

Bosom, all the righteous spirits that leave their bodies go to heaven immediately [2 Cor 5:8, Phil 1:21,23]. Abraham's Bosom is now empty, unless the present hell has been enlarged to take in what was formerly Abraham's Bosom. [Many Bible teachers believe this and use Isa 5:14.]

2. HELL: [Luke 16:19-31]. This was the TORMENT DEPARTMENT in the unseen world and still is and will yet be the abode of all the wicked souls and spirits of men, from Adam to the end of the Millennium. Then, at this time, all the wicked will be liberated out of this prison, will be given immortal bodies and be judged before being cast into the Lake of Fire forever [Rev 20:11-15 ; 21:8].

The Greek word "Hades" in the above verses literally means, "The Unseen World", or the **World of Departed Spirits**. It is the equivalent of the Hebrew word, **"Sheol"** and is never used to denote the grave, Abyss, Tartarus or the Eternal Lake of Fire where the wicked souls will be tormented forever and ever. Wicked souls and spirits are now in a conscious state of torment in hell! [Luke 16:19-31]. This temporary place of torment, before the Judgment and the eternal hell, might be compared to the city jail where prisoners are kept until their trial. The only difference between the punishments in the present and future prisons is the degree of torment that is meted out to them at the Judgment, according to the deeds done in the body.

So then, Child of God, understand the fact that human spirits went into TWO DIFFERENT PLACES in the underworld before Christ conquered death, hell and the grave. There was a great gulf between the two compartments [Luke 16:26].

3.   TARTARUS: [2 Peter 2:4, Jude 6,7, 1 Peter 3:19,20 and compare Gen 6:1-7 & 11-13]

This prison is the special one for the fallen angels that sinned before Noah's flood. No human beings or demons ever go into this department that we have any record of in Scripture.

This group of fallen angels who came to the earth and had sexual relationships with the daughters of men [Gen 6:2], producing an offspring of giants in the earth was part of Satan's plan to pervert the Human race and so stop Christ, the Promised Seed, coming!

This sinful, unnatural relationship and abnormal race that was produced was a major reason for Noah's flood.

1 Pet 3:18,19 At some point during Christ's three days and nights in the underworld, after He had conquered Satan, Christ went into Tartarus and proclaimed to the fallen angels in prison that their plan to corrupt the human race had failed and that He had come as the Promised Seed, making Salvation available for mankind!

4.   THE BOTTOMLESS PIT / OR ABYSS: This is the fourth department in the underworld. It is the abode or prison of demons. No human being ever goes to the Abyss.

In the New Testament, the Greek word is ABUSSOS, and means abyss, an immeasurable depth. It is a VERY DEEP CHASM IN THE LOWER PARTS OF THE EARTH. It is translated "Deep", [Luke 8:26-31] and "Bottomless Pit" [Rev 9:1-3, 20:1-3]. This is the place where Satan will be imprisoned during the Millennial Reign of Christ.

5. LAKE OF FIRE: This department is the ETERNAL HELL and perdition of wicked men, demons, fallen angels and all rebellious creatures who have ever rebelled against God. It is called "THE GEHENNA OF FIRE" and is always translated "HELL"
[Matt 5:22,29,30, Mark 9:43-45,47, Luke 12:5 and James 3:6]. This department is also called "THE SECOND DEATH"which is the "LAKE OF FIRE" [Rev 20:6,14]. This final hell is prepared for the devil and his angels [Matt 25:41-46] and for all other rebels and is eternal in duration [Rev 20:10-15, Matt 25:36]. We have no record of anyone being in the Lake of Fire at present. The Beast and the False Prophet will be the first to be cast into it. This will take place before the Millenium [Rev 19:20]. They will still be there 1,000 years later when the devil and the other rebels will be cast into it [Rev 20:10-15]. If they are there for 1,000 years in torment and have not been annihilated, why should any other man have hopes of being annihilated within a few moments of getting there?

That there will be degrees of punishment in Hell, as far as remorse and **the torment of conscience**, are concerned is clear from Matt 10:15, 11:22, 12:41, 23:14, Mark 6:11, 12:40, Luke 10:14, 11:31,32. These degrees of punishment will be because of the kind of sins committed by one that were not committed by another. No man will be punished or could have remorse over something that he did not do. The same is true in the case of the saints. One will be given a greater reward than another, according to the deeds committed in the body. Heaven, as far as **a place** is concerned, will be alike to all, but there will be different rewards for the righteous!

THE BLESSEDNESS OF HEAVEN

Heaven is a place of holiness
Revelation 21v27

It is a place of beauty
Psalm 50v2

It is a place of unity
Ephesians 1v10

It is a place of perfection
1 Corinthians 13v10

It is a place of joy
Psalm 16v11

Heaven is a place where there will be no tears
Revelation 21v4

There will be no sickness
Revelation 22v2

There will be no pain
Revelation 21v4

There will be no death
Revelation 21v4

There will be no thirst or hunger
Revelation 7v16

There will be no more sin
Revelation 21v27

There will be no night
Revelation 21v25;22v5

There will be no need for the sun or the moon
Revelation 21v23

The river of life is there to ensure everlasting life
Revelation 22v1

The tree of life is there to ensure abundant life
Revelation 22v19

BIBLE FACTS ABOUT HEAVEN

* Heaven is only for those who have been born again —
JOHN 3v3

* Jesus Christ Himself is the architect and supervisor of the
construction of the believer's mansion in heaven —
JOHN 14v3

* The name of the city Jesus is preparing for us is the New Jerusalem —
REVELATION 21v2

* It is described as a glorious city, likened to pure gold and clear glass —
REVELATION 21v11,18

* The NEW Jerusalem is 12 000 furlongs equal in length, width and
height, which is1 500 miles long, wide and high —
REVELATION 21v16

* The city rests upon 12 layers of foundational stones, with each layer
being inlaid with a different precious gem —
REVELATION 21v19,20

* The wall around the city is made of pure jasper —
REVELATION 21v18

* The height of the wall is 215 feet —
REVELATION 21v17

* The wall has 12 gates, 3 on each of the 4 sides and
each gate is made of solid pearl —
REVELATION 21v12,21

* The palaces inside the NEW Jerusalem will be made of ivory —
PSALM 45v6-8

* The throne of God will occupy the central palace —
REVELATION 22v1

* The city will shine with and be enlightened by God's glory —
REVELATION 21v11:22v5

* The city will be the bridegrooms gift to the bride, Christ's church —
REVELATION 21v2,10

*The eternal location of the NEW Jerusalem will be earth itself —
REVELATION 21v2,3

CHAPTER 21:
THE GREAT WHITE
THRONE JUDGMENT.

Rev 20:11-15   Then I saw a great white throne and Him who sat on it, from whose face the earth and the heaven fled away. And there was found no place for them.

12   And I saw the dead, small and great, standing before God, and the books were opened. And another book was opened, which is the Book of Life. And the dead were judged according to their works, by the things which were written in the books.

13   The sea gave up the dead who were in it, and Death and Hades delivered up the dead who were in them. And they were judged each one according to his works.

14   Then Death and Hades were cast into the lake of fire. This is the second death.

15   And anyone not found written in the Book of Life was cast into the lake of fire.

This is the final judgment in Scripture and is the greatest trial in human history - even the holocaust will pale in this eternal damnation of sinful humanity. As we look at this last judgment we want to clearly establish the following points.

1.   **When** will it take place?

2.   **Where** will it take place?

3.   **Who** will be there to be judged and sentenced?

4.   **Why** will they be there?

5.   **What** will be the outcome of the great white throne judgment?

6.   **How** can we miss this judgment?

THE SUBJECTS JUDGED

The text identifies the judged ones, saying, "The dead, the small and great, stand before God." No trump will sound for them, as for the sleeping saints called more than 1,007 years earlier. The eternal power of God will assemble them. The graves of all the wicked dead of all the centuries will be opened. From Cain down to those who follow Satan at the end of the Millennium - all will stand before God. Hell will give up its victims and spirit, soul and body will unite for the Great Trial. All classes of people will be there.

There they stand before the merciless gaze of Him who sits upon the throne. On that day every unsaved person of all ages will stand before Almighty God - the Cains, the Herods, the Pharoahs, the Hitlers, the Mussolinis, Volitaire, the drunkards, the prostitutes, the child molesters, the murderers, the thieves, the wife beaters, the evil dictators, the wicked kings, ungodly business tycoons, the harlots, bartenders, the blasphemers, the merchants of death [drug pushers], the Gurus and those deceived by the false cults and doctrines of demons [the Hare Krishnas, the Jehovah's Witnesses, Mormons etc]. King Saul will be there, Judas will be there, religious preachers and their congregations will be there, respectable sinners will be there PLUS every single Christ-Rejecting sinner who has ever lived and died without being born again.

People out of every nation will stand before God on that day; Americans, Arabs, Portuguese, Costa Ricans, Germans, Chinese, Russians, Australians, Canadians, Zulus, the French, the British etc. etc.

They have spurned His offer of grace; now an accounting for sins must be made. No saved person will be before that throne; not a single believer will be among that vast unnumbered company. All the righteous dead will have risen at the first resurrection, for this is most certainly a judgment of the spiritually dead. "I saw the dead both great and small". Believers are never spoken of in this manner. They are partakers of everlasting life, and of them the Lord Jesus Christ has said, "whosoever liveth and believeth in Me shall never die" [John 11:26]. Those who stand before the Great White Throne Judgment have been raised from the place of the dead, but not from the state of death. They are released out of hell for a brief time to stand before God at the Great White Throne and receive an even greater eternal punishment.

> John 5:28,29 "Do not marvel at this; for the hour is now coming in which all who are in the graves will hear His voice
> 29 and come forth - those who have done good, to the resurrection of life, and those who have done evil, to the resurrection of damnation".

Just as saints at the first resurrection receive new bodies capable of enjoying all the unlimited beauties of eternal life, so the wicked dead will have vessels, "fitted to destruction", that they might experience the unceasing torments of eternal damnation.

The angels "that sinned" and "are now bound" in Tartarus

will also be loosed from their long confinement in chains and be judged at this judgment [2 Pet 2:4, Jude 6,7].

THE TIME OF THIS FINAL JUDGMENT

This last judgment, that of the wicked dead, will take place after the 1,000 years of Christ's reign on this earth. Satan, loosed after being bound for the Millennium, will lead a brief final revolt against God. His followers will be utterly destroyed by fire from heaven and he will be cast into the lake of fire. Time will then be over, and the eternal ages will be ready to begin.

THE PLACE OF THIS FINAL JUDGMENT

The judgment is to be before the Great White Throne of God, which will still be in heaven, for it is not to come down to the earth until after the renovation of the earth by fire after the New Heaven and the New Earth are completed [Rev 21:1-5]. This seems to be further proved by 2 Pet 3:7 where it states that the renovation of the earth takes place during the final judgment. It seems to be pictured also in Rev 20:11 at the same time as the final judgment.

THE BASIS OF THIS FINAL JUDGMENT

Rev 20:12 ... and the books were opened; and another book was opened, which is the Book of Life. And the dead were judged out of those things which were written in the books, according to their works.

THE JUDGMENT OF THE UNSAVED DEAD

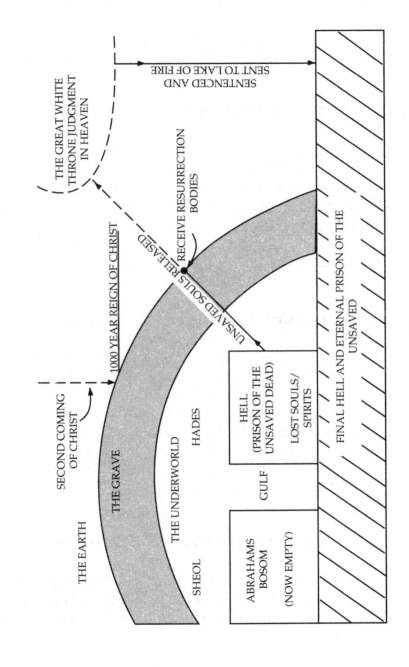

BIBLE FACTS ABOUT HELL

(1)   Hell is a place originally prepared for Satan and
his fallen angels
Matthew 25v41

(2)   Hell is a place of unquenchable fire
Mark 9v43

(3)   Hell is a place of memory and remorse
Luke 16v19-31

(4)   Hell is a place of eternal damnation,
suffering and torment
Luke 16v19-31

(5)   Hell is a place of eternal misery and pain
Revelation 14v10,11

(6)   Hell is a place of eternal separation and no return
Revelation 20v15

(7)   Hell is a place of undiluted divine wrath
Revelation 14v10

(8)   Hell is a place of unsatisfied lustful cravings,
frustration and anger
Matthew 13v42

(9)   Hell is a place of evil company
Revelation 21v8

(10)   Hell is the eternal prison house of the damned and is
located in the centre of the earth
Matthew 12v40

On that day not one individual will be set free - at this judgment there can be no pardon and no stay of execution.

Every secret sin and every wicked crime will be uncovered and exposed on that day. You see God keeps excellent records and He has on file a detailed account of every single sin, every injustice, every wicked deed and every ungodly crime. On that day every sin will be called to account, will be exposed, judged and the punishment decreed.

Think about the billions of unsaved people who will stand before God crying out in agony and great anguish as they see in full detail the beauty and blessing of heaven which they have eternally missed and the agony of the eternal flames awaiting them.

The only reason why they are at the Great White Throne is because they spurned the Gospel, blasphemed God and rejected Christ.

The one "work" of man that determines his eternal destiny is his rejection of Jesus Christ. This unwillingness to believe leads to "works" proceeding from the unsaved heart which... treasures up ... wrath against the day of wrath and revelation of the righteous judgment of God, Who will render to every man according to his deeds [Rom 2:5,6].

At that judgment will be not only the open books revealing the record of a person's life, but also the "Book of Life" will be opened. It will stand as the indisputable record that those who appear at the Great White Throne are not numbered amongst the redeemed, and the finality of this judgment testified to by the fact that they are not enrolled in the Book of Life.

If you compare Exodus 32:33, Deut 25:19, Psalm 9:5 and
Psalm 69:28, then you must come to the conclusion that
every person has had his name written into the Book of Life
- and the sin of rejecting Christ causes their name to be
blotted out of the Book of Life!

Not one name of an unsaved person will be found in that
book. These are judged as wicked. What they had been in
heart and in motive, they also had been in life. The record of
the "book" and the records of "the books" tally with one
another.

THE RESULT OF THIS FINAL JUDGMENT

In the resurrection of the unjust, the bodies come from the
grave and the souls from hell. The pronouncement of
judgment at the Great White Throne is called the "second
death". In contrast with the first death, soul and body are no
longer separated, because lost soul and resurrected body
stand before the throne. But there is a separation - the
eternal separation from God. The contents of death and of
hell will be cast into the lake of fire. In Rev 20:10 we read that
at the close of the Millennial Age and following the devil's
revolt, he is cast into the lake of fire, where the Beast and the
False Prophet are. The same book also says,

> ... **These both were cast alive into the lake of fire burning with**
> **brimstone [Rev 19:20].**

Now, after 1,000 years, the devil is committed to the same
place of torment. This certainly crumbles to smithereens the
false theory of annihilation. Read these dreadful words
concerning those who stand at this Great White Throne

Judgment, "And whoever was not found written in the Book of Life was cast into the lake of fire" [Rev 20:15]. The following chapter of Revelation says,

> **Rev 21:8 But the fearful, and unbelieving, and the abominable, and the murderers, and the fornicators, and the sorcerers, and idolaters, and all liars shall have their part in the lake which burns with fire and brimstone, which is the second death.**

You say, "Is this a place or is it a condition?" Everything in the context indicates it to be a place. These are resurrected people who will populate the lake of fire forever and forever in eternal agony.

Numbered in that vast crowd will be those who laughed at Noah, the one's who scorned the blood of Egypt's Lamb, the people who stoned the prophets, the mob who despised and crucified the Lord Jesus. But that is not all.

Every person who has rejected Christ will face that judgment. The books will be opened, and they will see in terrible array all the sins that they ever committed. Their names will not be found in the Lamb's Book of Life. They will be cast into the lake of fire, which is called the second death, and that will be "forever and ever".

All human beings in hell and in death along with the angels in Tartarus and the demons in the Abyss and every rebel against God will be cast into the lake of fire to be punished forever and forever [Rev 20:10-15, 21:8, Matt 25:41,46].

The degrees of punishment will be the result of this judgment, as degrees of rewards will be the result of the judgment of the saints at the judgment seat of Christ [Matt 7:2, 10:15, 11:22-24, Luke 11:31,32]. Hell, as far as the torment of fire is concerned, will be alike for all the lost, as much as heaven, as far as bliss and comfort are concerned, will be alike for all the redeemed. The degrees of punishment will come through the torment of the conscience and the inward self over the deeds committed, which will eat more deeply into the innermost being as the ages come and go into the eternal future.

The judgment passed upon each individual will be eternal. The same terms that are used in describing the eternity of Heaven are used in describing the eternity of hell, so if one is eternal the other one must be.

Billions will end up in the lake of fire doomed and damned **FOREVER**

-       Because they were deceived by the devil.

-       Because of a religious social Gospel they listened to and believed in.

-       Because they loved sin and darkness and rejected the Saviour.

  John 3:17,19 "For God did not send His Son into the world to condemn the world, but that the world through Him might be saved.
  19 And this is the condemnation, that the light has come into the world, and men loved darkness rather than light, because their deeds were evil."

  Heb 2:3[a] How shall we escape if we neglect so great a salvation...

Friend, right now if you are NOT born again you can be and you can miss the Great White Throne Judgment by personally making Jesus Christ your Lord.

> **Rom 10:9,10** **If you confess with your mouth the Lord Jesus Christ and believe in your heart that God has raised Him from the dead, you will be saved.**
> **10 For with the heart one believes to righteousness and with the mouth confession is made unto salvation.**
>
> **Rom 10:13** **For "whoever calls upon the name of the Lord shall be saved."**

Why don't you call upon the Lord to save you right now!

CHAPTER 22:
REACHING YOUR
UNSAVED LOVED ONES.

As you come to the final chapter of this book I am sure by this time that God's Word on End Time Prophecy and the influence of the Holy Spirit in your life has motivated you in the following ways ...

1. To love and serve the Lord Jesus Christ as never before.

2. To eliminate any sin or spiritual lukewarmness out of your life.

3. To be a faithful, committed member of a local church that exalts Jesus and God's Word.

4. To live your life each day in expectation of the Rapture.

5. To go all out as a soulwinner and actively fulfill the Great Commission of Mark 16.

KEY TRUTH: SOULWINNING IS EVERY BELIEVER'S RESPONSIBILITY.

Prov 11:30 ... And he who wins souls is wise.

Ezek 3:18 "When I say to the wicked, 'You shall surely die', and you give him no warning, nor speak to warn the wicked from his wicked way, to save his life, that same wicked man shall die in his

iniquity; but his blood I will require at your hand."

James 5:20   Let him know that he who turns a sinner from the error of his way will save a soul from death and cover a multitude of sins.

Child of God, in these last days you should have a burden for the lost and especially for the salvation of your family and unsaved loved ones. Knowing what you know about the nearness of the Rapture and the horrendous events of the Tribulation you cannot afford to neglect to reach your family before it is too late.

HOW TO BELIEVE GOD
FOR YOUR UNSAVED FAMILY.

Matt 21:22 "And all things, whatever you ask in prayer, believing, you will receive".

Many of the scriptures that you use for your needs to be met in your every day walk in this life can be applied to the salvation of your family. The secret is believing the Word of God and standing in the gap until their conversion is sure. Establish this one thing in your mind right now that God is not your problem.

You are not to beg God for the salvation of your loved ones. He has promised them to you. Some people spend years crying and pleading with God and see very few results. This is the result of traditions of men who do not know the first thing about our God who will perform His Word.

1.   **Realise your Unsaved Family is being held Captive by Satan.**

2 Cor 4:3,4 But even if our gospel is veiled, it is veiled to those who are perishing,

4 whose minds the god of this age has blinded, who do not believe, lest the light of the gospel of the glory of Christ who is the image of God, should shine on them.

Satan or the devil is called, "the god of this world" [world referring to those who are not born again]. You are either in the Kingdom of light with God as your Father, or you are in the kingdom of darkness with Satan as your father, god and master. There is no in-between. You are either a child of God or a child of the devil [Eph 2:1-3]. According to these verses, Satan blinds the mind of the unbeliever, making it virtually impossible for him to see the truth of God's Word. He will do all he can to keep a sinner from being born again.

The natural man, or unsaved person, lives by his senses and reason, for this is the only way he knows.

1 Cor 2:14 But the natural man does not receive the things of the Spirit of God, for they are foolishness to him; nor can he know them, because they are spiritually discerned.

The spiritual man, on the other hand, lives by faith in the Word of God. He is led by the Holy Spirit who lives in his spirit.

2.   You can break Satan's Power over their Lives.

We have found that the minds of our loved ones are being blinded from the truth of God's Word, but what can we do about it?

Matt 18:18 "Assuredly, I say to you, whatever you bind on earth will be bound in heaven, and whatever you loose on earth will be loosed in heaven."

> **Luke 10:19** "Behold, I give you the authority to trample on serpents and scorpions, and over all the power of the enemy, and nothing shall by any means hurt you."

Jesus said that we, as believers, have power over the enemy. The word power in the Greek means authority. Praise God! We have authority over all the power of Satan in the lives of our loved ones. We do not have authority over people's wills, but we do have authority over the devil's evil influence on them.

Whatever we bind - or in other words, refuse to allow on earth - God in heaven will refuse to allow. Also, this verse says that whatever we loose, or allow on earth, God in heaven will also allow it.

According to these passages, in the name of Jesus, we can bind the devil's works in the lives of our husbands, wives, sons, daughters and loose the Spirit of God to minister to their hearts.

How is this accomplished? By opening your mouth and saying with authority and boldness,

"Satan in the name of Jesus Christ, I bind you from interfering with the Word of God reaching my loved ones so that they can hear the Word, believe it in their hearts, and make confession unto salvation. I break your power over them in Jesus' name and command you to loose your grip on them!"

We release our authority over the devil by speaking words of faith! As a born again child of God you have a legal right and authority to stand in the gap for the salvation of your family and release them from the kingdom of darkness.

Acts 26:18 "to open their eyes and turn them from darkness to light, and from the power of Satan to God, that they may receive forgiveness of sins and an inheritance among those who are sanctified by faith in Me."

We need to break the power of the devil over our unsaved loved ones, because the devil has their minds blinded. In the name of Jesus you take your authority over the devil and demon forces -

YOU break the satanic influence,

YOU break every curse over that family [e.g. occult, spiritualism, false religion, bondage of tradition etc].

YOU break the power of natural inheritance [e.g. chronic sickness, financial bondage, misfortune etc].

HOW TO PRAY THE PRAYER OF BINDING AND LOOSING.

Matt 18:18 [Amp]. "Truly, I tell you, whatever you forbid and declare to be improper and unlawful on earth must be what is already forbidden in heaven, and whatever you permit and declare proper and lawful on earth must be already permitted in heaven".

Matt 12:29 "Or else how can one enter a strong man's house and plunder his goods, unless he first binds up the strong man? And then he will plunder his house".

In the name of the Lord Jesus Christ, I break the power of the devil over [insert persons name] and I claim his deliverance. That means deliverance from the devil and full salvation in Jesus Name Amen. [Write their names in a prayer list in the front of your Bible.]

You have the power of attorney to use the mighty name of Jesus to come against the enemy that has blinded the minds of your loved ones, and is hindering them from accepting the Lord Jesus Christ as Saviour and Lord.

You can break Satan's power and influence in Jesus name!

You can bind the power of the enemy by using the NAME OF JESUS!

You must SEE your position and power in Christ as a child of God.

SEE the power of your prayer life.

SEE your authority as a Born Again Believer.

God has not forgotten any of your children or your family!

It is every Christians privilege and responsibility to do something positive about seeing their family saved and coming into the Kingdom of God.

3.   BE SPECIFIC **Name and Claim the Salvation of each Unsaved Family Member.**

Once you have commanded the devil to take his hands off their lives and have bound him from interfering with their coming to God, you must claim, by faith, the promise of God concerning their salvation.

> Acts 16:31   "Believe on the Lord Jesus Christ, and you will be saved, you and your household."

When you have found what God has said about the matter, begin to put your faith into action by speaking the Word only and acting like the Word is so ... even if the circumstances don't change immediately. Begin to do what **Romans 4:17** says by "calling those things which be not as though they were". This is what faith is all about.

APPLY THE LAW OF FAITH AND THE LAW OF CONFESSION.

Say with your mouth: Father, Your Word declares that if I believe on the Lord Jesus Christ, I shall be saved and my family will be saved. I believe on You, Jesus, and I am born again of Your Spirit. Therefore my household shall also be saved. I thank you for it in Jesus name Amen!

After claiming your loved one's salvation according to the Word of God, begin to thank the Lord for answering your prayer of faith.

4.   **Pray that the Lord of the Harvest would send Labourers to them so that they can hear the Word.**

   Luke 10:2 Then He said to them, "The harvest is truly great, but the labourers are few; therefore pray the Lord of the harvest to send out labourers into His harvest".

Even though you have broken the power of the enemy over your family in Jesus name and are standing in faith on the Word of God for their salvation, they will never be born again unless they hear the Word of God [Rom 10:14,17]. How can men or women have faith in what Jesus has done for them if no one shows them the Word of God? How are people to receive Jesus as Lord and Saviour unless they are first told how? People have to hear the message of Jesus Christ.

Many times it takes someone outside the family to bring the message to them. That is why Jesus tells us in Luke 10:2, the harvest is truly great but the labourers are few; pray ye therefore the Lord of the harvest, that He would send forth labourers into His harvest.

Jesus is telling us to pray that God would cause born again men and women of God to cross the paths of our loved ones lives and to have an opportunity to share this all-important message with them. By your prayers you can send labourers or witnesses who will carry the Word of God, and speak it to your loved ones. You may not know the identity of the labourers, or you could even be one of them yourself. If you are the labourer the Lord of the harvest wishes to use, God will speak to your heart and send you with His Word. It is up to Him.

So act on the principle of binding and loosing: of binding the power of the enemy and praying the Lord of the harvest into action.

Remember effective prayer means taking into God's presence His own Words.

Our Father God has great compassion for the family. He does not want to see one member saved and another lost. He is a FAMILY LOVING GOD.

5.   **At All times you Must Walk in Love with your Loved Ones and let them See Jesus in You.**

Now this is a crucial point: God has never told us to push or drive the sinner to make a decision for Christ. People are to be loved into the Kingdom - NOT forced. The Bible says if Christ is lifted up He will draw all men unto Him. Jesus doesn't force - He draws.

Gal 5:6 says that faith works by love. This applies particularly to our faith in the area of believing for our loved ones. We can believe God and confess Acts 16:31, Luke 10:2 and the other scriptures but if we aren't walking in love with those whom we are believing for, our faith will be nullified.

When you are born again, you received into your spirit the very nature of God, which is love [Rom 5:5]. You have the love of God, or the God kind of love in you! You don't have to pray for it or beg God for it - it's already in you! This kind of love is an unconditional love. In other words, it loves regardless of how it is treated - good or bad.

Praise God, we can love as the Word tells us to because that love is in us. What we must do is release that love and get it out where others can see it and benefit from it.

Think love thoughts. Speak love words. Do love things. Even though your family may do you wrong, let that love dominate you at all times. It's not easy at first; but the more you practice it, the easier it becomes. Remember:**Love never fails** [1 Cor 13:8] **love always wins out!**

6.   **Intercede with your Understanding and then with your Spirit.**

In Eph 1:16-19 there is a prayer that Paul prayed under the inspiration of the Holy Spirit. As Christians who are believing for our loved ones, we can pray this prayer every day, thanking the Lord that their eyes are being opened to the truth of God's Word concerning salvation.

Another way we can pray for them effectively is to intercede in the Spirit [in other tongues]. Many times we come to the place where we just don't know what to pray in a situation. This is where interceding in the Spirit comes in.

According to Romans 8:26,27 when we pray in an unknown tongue for the needs of other people, we are praying the perfect will of God into the situation. Acts 2:4 says that the Spirit is giving the utterance. As we intercede in the Spirit, we are pulling down the strongholds of Satan in their lives [2 Cor 10:3,4].
Take time to pray in the Spirit for those you are believing for. You will see results.

7. **Don't give up! Stand on God's Word exercising Patience and Perseverance [Heb 10:35,36].**

While you are standing in faith for your loved ones salvation, you will have to exercise PATIENCE and PERSEVERANCE!

Patience according to W.E. Vine, is "the quality that does not surrender to circumstances or succumb under trial. It is the opposite of despondency and is associated with hope".

Perseverance, in Webster's Dictionary, means "to persist in anything undertaken; to maintain a purpose in spite of difficulty or obstacles".

Many times people "miss it" by giving up too soon.

Eph 6:13 says, having done all, to stand. Having done all you know the Word of God says for you to do, stand! Some take longer than others to respond to the conviction of the Holy Spirit on their hearts.

The enemy will come to you and say, "Now let's be realistic. Look at the situation, you don't really believe that they will ever be saved, do you? Why don't you just give up hope and admit that they will never come to the Lord?"

If Satan can keep you in the realm of reason and keep your eyes on the circumstances, get ready for defeat. If he can get you to start saying, "I guess I'm just wasting my time. They will never come to the Lord in a million years," then you have lost. Remember, you have what you say [Mark 11:23].

If you keep the devil in the arena of faith, you will whip him every time. When he comes to you with those discouraging thoughts, don't think on them; cast them down in Jesus name according to 2 Cor 10:5.

True faith in the Word of God never backs down in adverse circumstances. When you stand on the eternal Word of God for the salvation of your loved ones and put all your trust in Him, failure is impossible.

KEY SCRIPTURES WHEN STANDING IN THE GAP FOR YOUR LOVED ONES.

Luke 19:10 "for the Son of Man has come to seek and save that which was lost."

Acts 16:31 So they said, "Believe on the Lord Jesus Christ, and you will be saved, you and your household". [Family]

Acts 11:14 "Who will tell you the words by which you and all your household will be saved".

Matt 18:18,19 "Assuredly, I say to you, whatever you bind on earth will be bound in heaven, and whatever you loose on earth will be loosed in heaven.
19 Again I say to you that if two of you agree on earth concerning anything that they ask, it will be done for them by My Father who is in heaven."

Psalm 2:8 "Ask of me and I shall give thee the heathen for thine inheritance, and the uttermost parts of the earth for thy possession."

Prov 11:21 "The seed of the righteous will be delivered and saved!"

Matt 9:37,38 Then He said to His disciples, "The harvest truly is plentiful, but the labourers are few.
38 Therefore pray the Lord of the harvest to send out labourers into His harvest".

Matt 21:22 "And all things, whatever you ask in prayer, believing, you will receive."

Job 22:30 [Amp] "He will even deliver the one [for whom you intercede] who is not innocent; yes, he will be delivered through the cleanness of your hands".

Isa 54:13 All your children shall be taught by the Lord, And great shall be the peace of your children.

Isa 49:25 "For I will contend with him who contends with you, and I will save your children".

Acts 2:39 "This promise is unto you, and to your children".

1 Tim 2:4 "Who desires all men to be saved and to come to the knowledge of the truth."

2 Pet 3:9 "The Lord is not willing that any should perish but that all should come to repentance".

Matt 18:14 "Even so it is not the will of your Father who is in heaven that one of these little ones should perish".

Prov 11:30 [Amp] "The fruit of the [uncompromisingly] righteous is a tree of life, and he who is wise captures human lives for God [as a fisher of men] - he gathers and receives them for eternity".

2 Cor 10:4,5 For the weapons of our warfare are not carnal but mighty in God for the pulling down of strongholds,
5   casting down arguments and every high thing that exalts itself against the knowledge of God, bringing every thought into captivity to the obedience of Christ.

Psalm 126:6 He who continually goes forth weeping, Bearing seed for sowing, Shall doubtless come again with rejoicing, Bringing his sheaves with him.

Gal 6:9 And let us not grow weary while doing good, for in due season we shall reap if we do not lose heart.

2 Chron 15:7 "But you, be strong and do not let your hands be weak, for your work shall be rewarded!"

KEY SCRIPTURES FOR BACKSLIDERS.

Isa 57:18 "I have seen the ways of the backslider and <u>I will heal him</u> and restore him!"

Isa 44:3 For I will pour water on him who is thirsty, And floods on the dry ground; I will pour out My Spirit on your descendants, <u>And My blessing on your offspring;</u>

Jer 31:16,17 Thus says the Lord: "Refrain your voice from weeping, And your eyes from tears; For your work shall <u>be rewarded</u>, says the Lord, And they <u>shall come back from the land of the enemy</u>.

TODAY RECEIVE JESUS CHRIST AS SAVIOUR AND LORD OF YOUR LIFE.

Romans 10:9,10,13 "That if you confess with your mouth the Lord Jesus and believe in your heart that God has raised Him from the dead, you will be saved, "For with the heart one believes unto righteousness, and with the mouth confession is made unto salvation". "For whoever calls upon the name of the Lord shall be saved"."

To receive Jesus Christ as Lord and Saviour of your life, sincerely pray this prayer from your heart ...

Heavenly Father, I thank you for sending Your Son Jesus Christ to die for me on the cross. Lord Jesus I believe that You died for me and that you shed Your blood for my salvation. Lord Jesus I believe that You are the Son of the Living God and that You rose again on the third day. Right now Lord Jesus come into my life as my Saviour and be Lord over my life. According to **Romans 10:9,10** I now confess Jesus Christ is Lord of my life - I renounce the devil and all his works in my life - from this moment on the devil has no place in my life and no power over me in Jesus' name! Now I am a child of God and a righteous New Creation in Christ! Amen!

Write to me today and let me know about your decision for Christ and we will send you information to help you grow spiritually.

PASTOR NORMAN K. ROBERTSON
RHEMA MINISTRIES S.A.
P.O. BOX 433
RANDBURG 2125 SOUTH AFRICA.

If you would like to engage Pastor Norman Robertson for a special seminar, convention or Bible Conference in your area, write to

PASTOR NORMAN ROBERTSON
RHEMA MINISTRIES S.A.
P.O. BOX 433
RANDBURG 2125
SOUTH AFRICA.

PRAYER REQUEST.

Let us join our faith with yours for your prayer needs.

Fill out below and send to :

Pastor Norman K. Robertson
P.O. Box 433
Randburg 2125 SOUTH AFRICA.

My prayer request is ...

_____

_____

_____

_____

_____

_____

_____

NAME_____

ADDRESS_____

CITY_____

POSTAL CODE_____

I'd like to order _____ copies of this book.

Please send me details of your latest teaching tapes._____

Norman, your ministry has really helped me so according
to GALATIANS 6:6 I want to bless your ministry with the
enclosed offering._____